N A R A
ENCOUNTERS

From [Nara's] Kōfuku-ji it is a short walk to the Kasuga Shrine. The path leading up to the shrine is bordered by towering cryptomerias, and by an amazing procession of stone lanterns, reputedly ten thousand in all.

Donald Keene

N A R A
ENCOUNTERS

*Edited by Keiko I. McDonald
and J. Thomas Rimer*

New York WEATHERHILL Tokyo

© 1997 by Weatherhill, Inc. All translations by the editors except where noted. The cooperation of all photographers and publishers who have contributed to *Nara Encounters* is gratefully acknowledged; specific credits are cited in the "Notes on the Images and Authors." We also gratefully acknowledge the generous support of the Nara city administration in the making of this book.

First edition, 1997

Published by Weatherhill, Inc.
568 Broadway, Suite 705, New York, N.Y. 10012
Protected by copyright under the terms of the International
Copyright Union; all rights reserved.

Printed in Hong Kong

Library of Congress Cataloging in Publication Data
Nara encounters / edited by Keiko McDonald and J. Thomas
Rimer.—1st ed.
p. cm.
ISBN 0–8348–0387–9 (soft : alk. paper)
1. Nara-shi (Japan)—Description and travel. I. McDonald, Keiko
I. II. Rimer, J. Thomas.
DS897 .N35N297 1997
952' . 184—dc21   97–2452 CIP

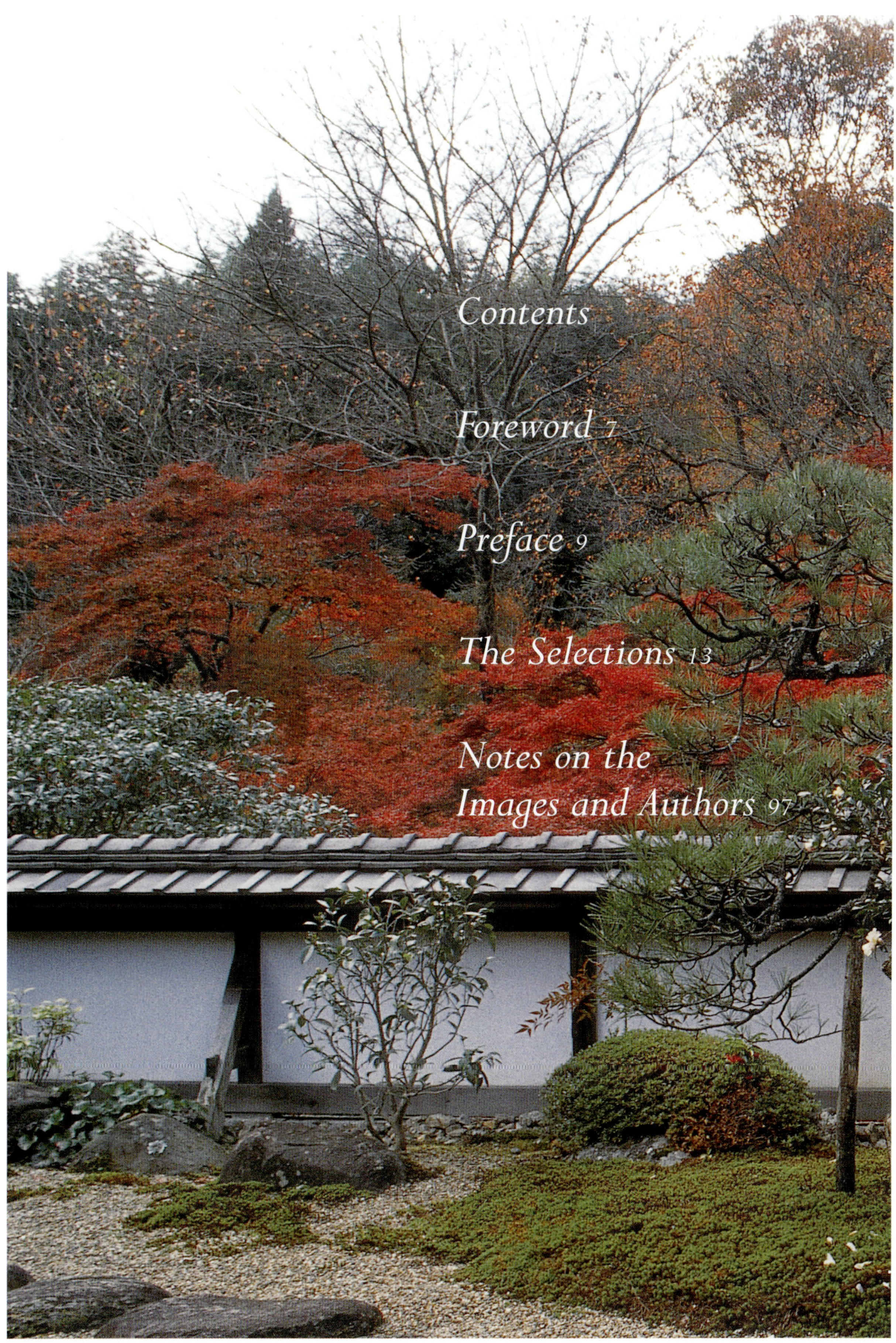

Contents

Foreword 7

Preface 9

The Selections 13

Notes on the
Images and Authors 97

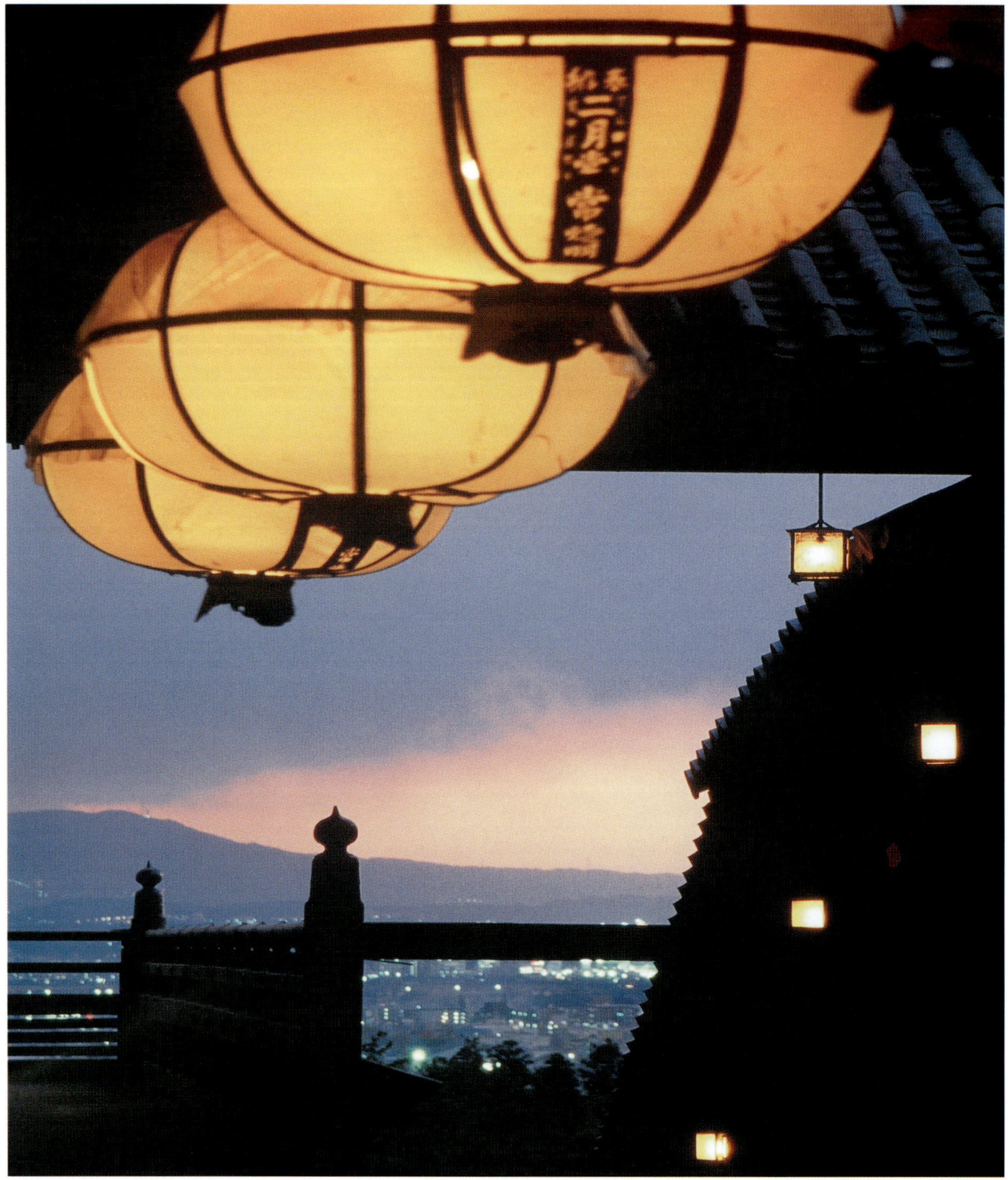

I passed scarlet gateways whose great purple roofs of thatch are a wonderful foil for the blossoming trees; more temples, hundreds of lanterns, more temples, gateways and lanterns, till my mind has a confused sense of the mass of temples, trees, colour, and pleasant forms. Now we were rattling down the streets of Nara…

SIR ALFRED EAST

Foreword

The city of Nara is indeed proud of its many beautiful sights. To the east of the city is Nara Park, two and a half miles long and almost half again as wide. Herds of deer wander the lawns there.

There too, ancient shrines and temples rise above the tops of the trees. Among the most famous are the Kōfukuji Temple and the Tōdaiji Temple, both classic examples of the dynamic Buddhist art of the Tempyō era (710–784).

West of this former capital are other treasures from that era. Saidaiji Temple, Yakushiji and Tōshōdaiji are just three of the many Buddhist monuments whose soaring pagodas and statues speak for the grandeur of this old imperial city.

Thanks to its beautiful natural setting and to the splendors of its cultural heritage, our city draws visitors from all around the globe. Their numbers increase every year, thanks to Nara's proximity to the newly constructed Kansai International Airport.

I sincerely hope that *Nara Encounters* will inspire you to visit our city and make its sights and events part of your own life.

Yasunori Ohkawa
Mayor of Nara

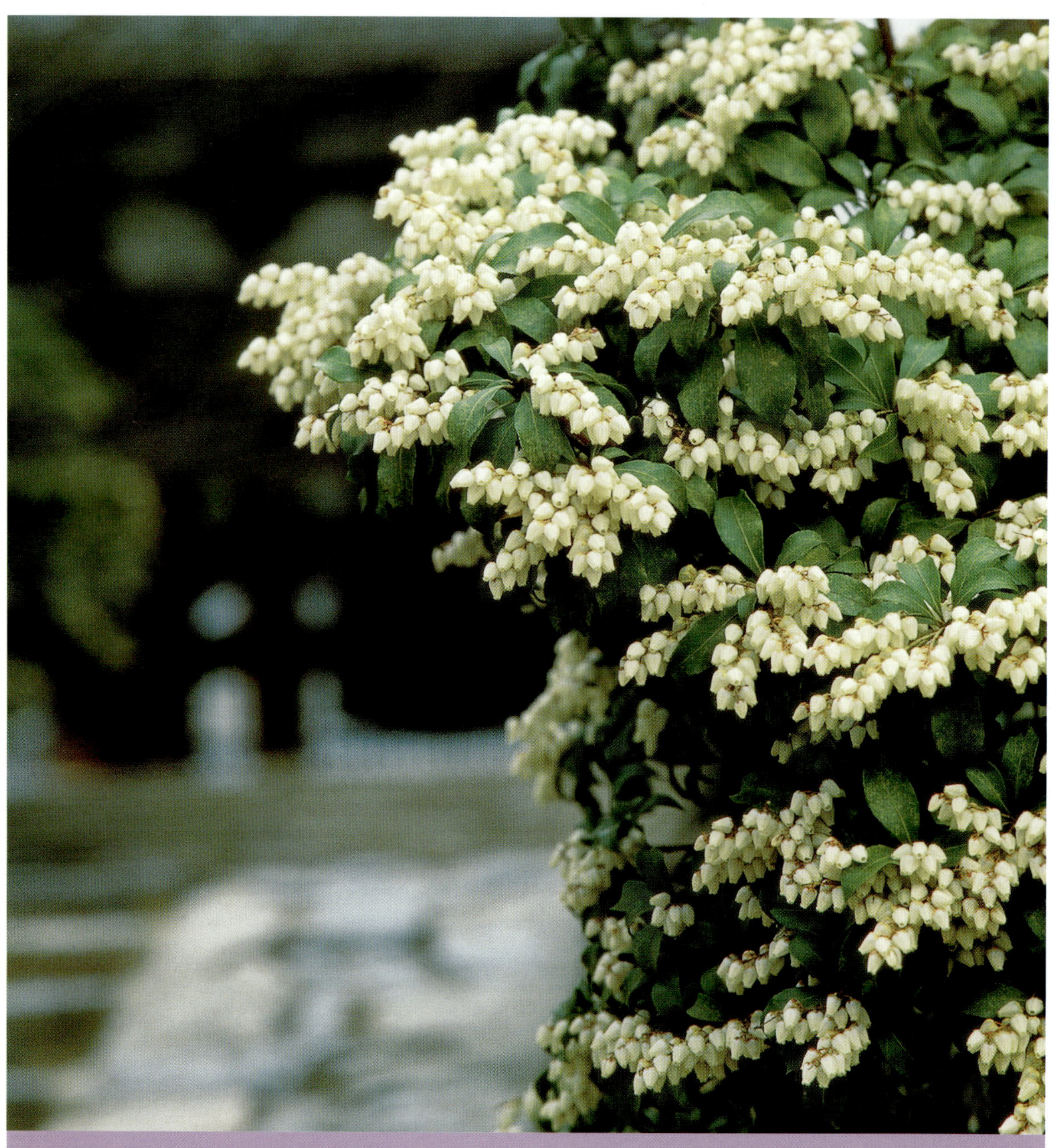

A ruined gate
Covered in bloom
Asebi flowers.

Shūōshi

Preface

Countless are the mountains in Yamato,

But perfect is the heavenly hill of Kagu;

When I climb it and survey my realm,

Over the wide plain the smoke-wreaths rise and rise,

Over the wide lake the gulls are on the wing;

And beautiful land it is, the Land of Yamato![1]

As early as the seventh century, the Emperor Jomei celebrated his divine sovereignty over his domain: the peaceful, fertile plain of Yamato. It was an ideal territory in which to construct the cities and palaces for a succession of Emperors, and in 710 Nara was established in the northern part of the plain as the first permanent capital of Japan. The city was named Heijōkyō (roughly "Citadel of Peace") and its layout was patterned after Ch'ang An, the capital of China during the Sui and T'ang Dynasties (589–907). In its original design, Nara formed a rectangle about three miles long and three-quarters of a mile wide, with streets laid out in a grid pattern. The impressive Suzaku (Red Sparrow) Boulevard, some 277 feet wide, ran from the palace entrance all the way to the southern gate of the capital.

The Nara period (710–718) was to become one of the most dynamic in the history of Japan. Three male and three female sovereigns came to the throne in this time of complex political, social, and cultural change. There was a lively cultural exchange with Ch'ang An, which remained the magnet for all of East Asian civilization from the seventh to the ninth centuries. Official envoys from Nara were frequently sent to China, and Buddhist monks and artists of every kind were brought back from the continent to enrich the culture of Japan.

The founders of Nara enthusiastically adopted the Chinese bureaucratic and legal systems. Buddhism, also imported from Korea and China, prospered, as evidenced in the magnificence of the temples and statues created. Nara reached the apogee of its grandeur during the twenty-four year reign of the Emperor Shōmu (725–749). Ono Oyu, a noted poet of the *Man'yōshū,* summarized it well:

> The capital at Nara
> Beautiful in blue earth
> Flourishes now
> Like the brilliant fragrance
> Of the flowers in bloom.[2]

This ruler's dynamic endeavors were epitomized by the construction of the great Tōdaiji temple complex, which he designated in 741 as the headquarters for all of the provincial Buddhist temples in the nation. The official dedication ceremony of the colossal fifty-four foot bronze statue of the Buddha took place eleven years later. In attendance was Emperor Shōmu himself, all the nobility, and many dignitaries and visitors from abroad, some coming from as far as India.

A flourishing literature expressed the robust spirit of the young nation, now brought under the control of a centralized authority. The *Kojiki* (Record of Ancient Matters), the earliest book of historical and literary texts in the Japanese language, was compiled by imperial order in about 712. An imperially commissioned anthology of verse also appeared toward the middle of the century. The *Man'yōshū* (Collection of Ten Thousand Leaves), containing some 4500 poems, stands as the oldest and some would say the greatest in a long line of court poetry anthologies modeled upon it. Many of the poems are especially noteworthy for the strong sense of place which they express, usually areas identified with Yamato. *Sangaku* ("miscellaneous music") was another creation of this period and was performed on ceremonial occasions at the great temples and monasteries. This music would later serve to contribute to the musical elements in the great medieval *nō* dramas.

In 784, less than a century after Nara's founding, the administrative capital was shifted to nearby Nagaoka. Ten years later it was moved again, this time to Kyoto, which remained the imperial capital until the beginning of the Meiji restoration in 1868. Even so, the ancient capital of Nara retained its great allure, both culturally and politically. The Kasuga shrine, for example, which was founded in 710 as the tutelary shrine of the powerful Fujiwara family, continued to serve as a center of worship and as a place to display the cultural patronage of this family, which during the Heian period became the nation's most powerful clan.

Musicians attached to the major temples in Nara endeavored to preserve *gagaku* ("classic court music"), adopted by the court from musical forms that had taken root in Japan when introduced from the continent some two centuries earlier. The *nō* drama, which reached its first maturity around 1400 through the work of Kan'ami and his celebrated son Zeami, owed much to Nara as well, since the various *nō* troupes found important audiences in the old capital. Zeami's son-in-law Zenchiku made Nara the headquarters for his own Komparu troupe. During the medieval period, Nara was particularly famous for the "torchlight" *nō* performances, so called because they were given after dark under burning torches set up in the compounds of temples and shrines.

Over the centuries, Nara, like Kyoto, suffered its share of disasters, both from war and from nature. In the great medieval epic *The Tale of the Heike,* there is a particularly vivid chapter devoted to a description of the burning of Nara in 1180. According to this and other accounts, some forty thousand horsemen wreaked havoc on the city, led by the vengeful Taira Kiyomori, head of the Heike clan. "Like an autumn moon," the text reads, "the eighty-four thousand signs of Buddhahood vanished."[3]

After this disaster, a succession of Japanese rulers saw to it that Nara was restored, and the old city was to remain a sanctuary for pilgrims, both religious and artistic, for many centuries. In the seventeenth century, Matsuo Bashō, the greatest of the traditional *haiku* poets, celebrated the timeless beauty of the capital:

> Nara the seven-fold
> Seven sacred buildings
> Many-petaled cherry blossoms.[4]

Even now, this Citadel of Peace continues to attract visitors from all over Japan. The city has provided an abundant source of creative inspiration for countless generations of writers, from the early poets of the *Man'yōshū* to such important modern novelists as Shiga Naoya, Mishima Yukio, and Inoue Yasushi. It is not surprising, therefore, that hundreds of literary works have been set in Nara. By the latter part of the nineteenth century, Western visitors were also coming to Japan and recording their impressions. Many of them, too, fell under Nara's spell, and their appreciative and often moving comments appear throughout this book.

Nara, like all the world, has changed a great deal since World War II. In some ways, it is rapidly becoming a kind of modern satellite of Osaka, the second largest city of Japan, which lies close by. Nara is an active academic center and boasts one of the two oldest women's colleges in the country. Nevertheless, it still retains the atmosphere of an ancient center of culture, showing affinities with similar cities around the world, such as Beijing or Versailles.

Like all old and beautiful places, Nara must struggle to preserve its essence in the face of rapid and often heedless change. And indeed, Nara has fared remarkably well, certainly better than any similar Japanese city. Thanks to the far-sighted (and sometimes hard-headed) planning undertaken by the city government, the so-called "Nara Town" now preserves a number of homes representing several centuries of urban history. The traditional arts and crafts of Nara also continue to flourish as important parts of the local economy. The most famous of these include the making of masks and the manufacture of calligraphy brushes and India ink.

This book is an attempt to convey to readers Nara's sense of pride of place. The city itself makes such beautiful photographs possible, and the images can speak for themselves. We have done our best, when possible, to seek out writings that match the photographs in celebrating the charms of this ancient city, and it has been easy enough to find the words of writers, Japanese and foreign alike, who were eager to attempt to record their own sense of Nara's particular allure. In a general sense, we hope that the book may serve as a kind of guide to the city itself, and, more importantly, to its special place in the imagination of those who have written about it. That gentle aim in and of itself partakes of the aesthetics of the court anthologies of poetry, which so often celebrated the beauties of this ancient capital. Yet it would be well to remember, that Nara, like any ancient city privileged to be thriving today, is entirely modern and is so faced with a complex and perhaps paradoxical challenge. The city must preserve its antiquity and yet accommodate the myriad and ever-changing needs and aims of ordinary life on the eve of the twenty-first century.

Our brief "Notes on Images and Authors" invite readers to seek out a wealth of related literary and historical works, most available in English translation. At the least, we hope that these evocative photographs and accompanying texts will persuade those who examine the book that Japan's ancient Citadel of Peace is a place they may wish to visit and explore for themselves.

KEIKO I. MCDONALD

J. THOMAS RIMER

---

[1] This translation can be found in *The Man'yōshū*, edited by the Nippon Gakujutsu Shinkōkai (Columbia University Press).

[2] Ian Hideo Levy, trans., *The Ten Thousand Leaves* (Princeton University Press).

[3] Helen McCullough, trans., *The Tale of the Heike* (Stanford University Press).

[4] The translation by Sir George Sansom can be found in his *History of Japan to 1334* (Stanford University Press).

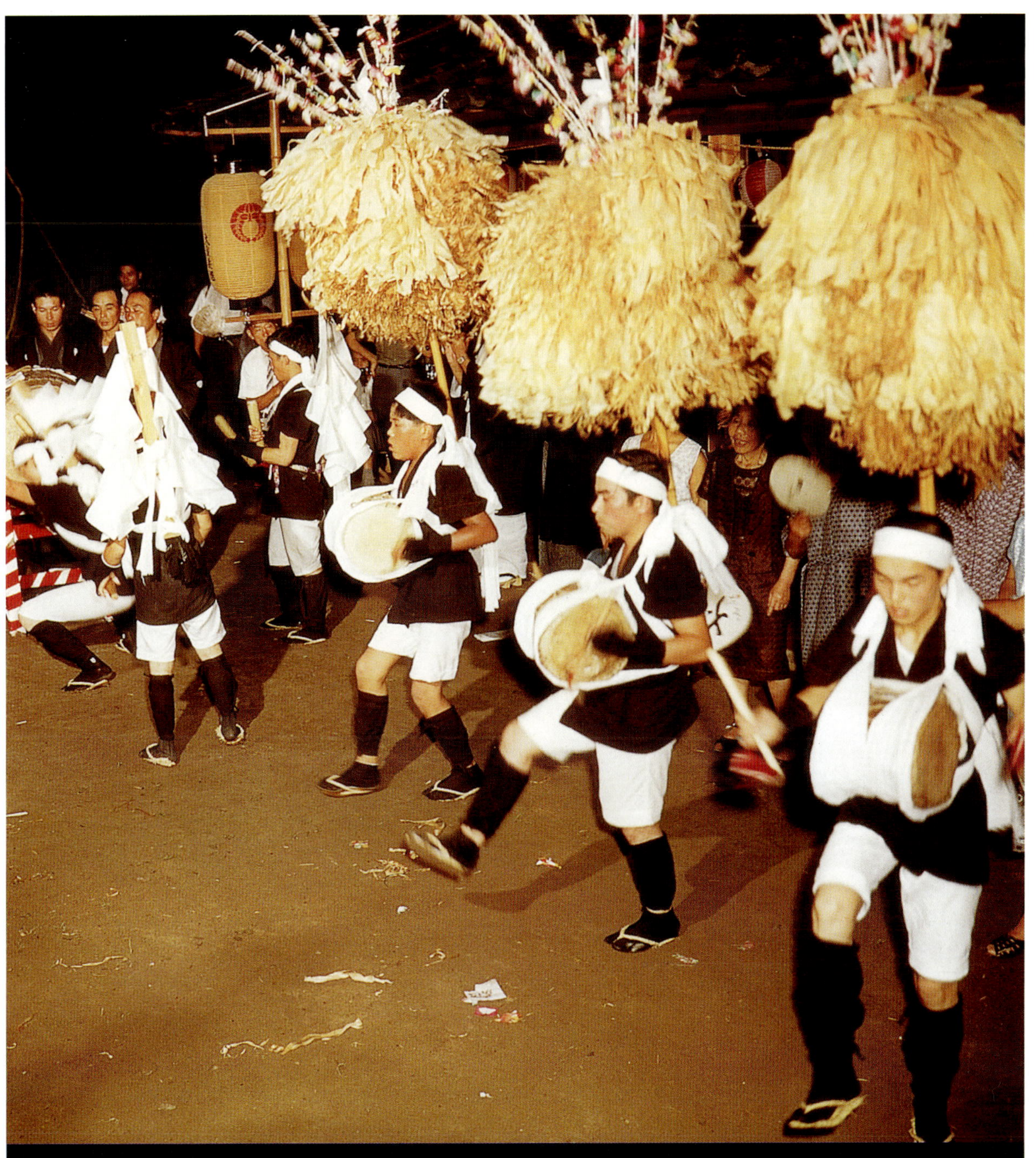

Men and women
And their shadows
Dancing.

SANTŌKA

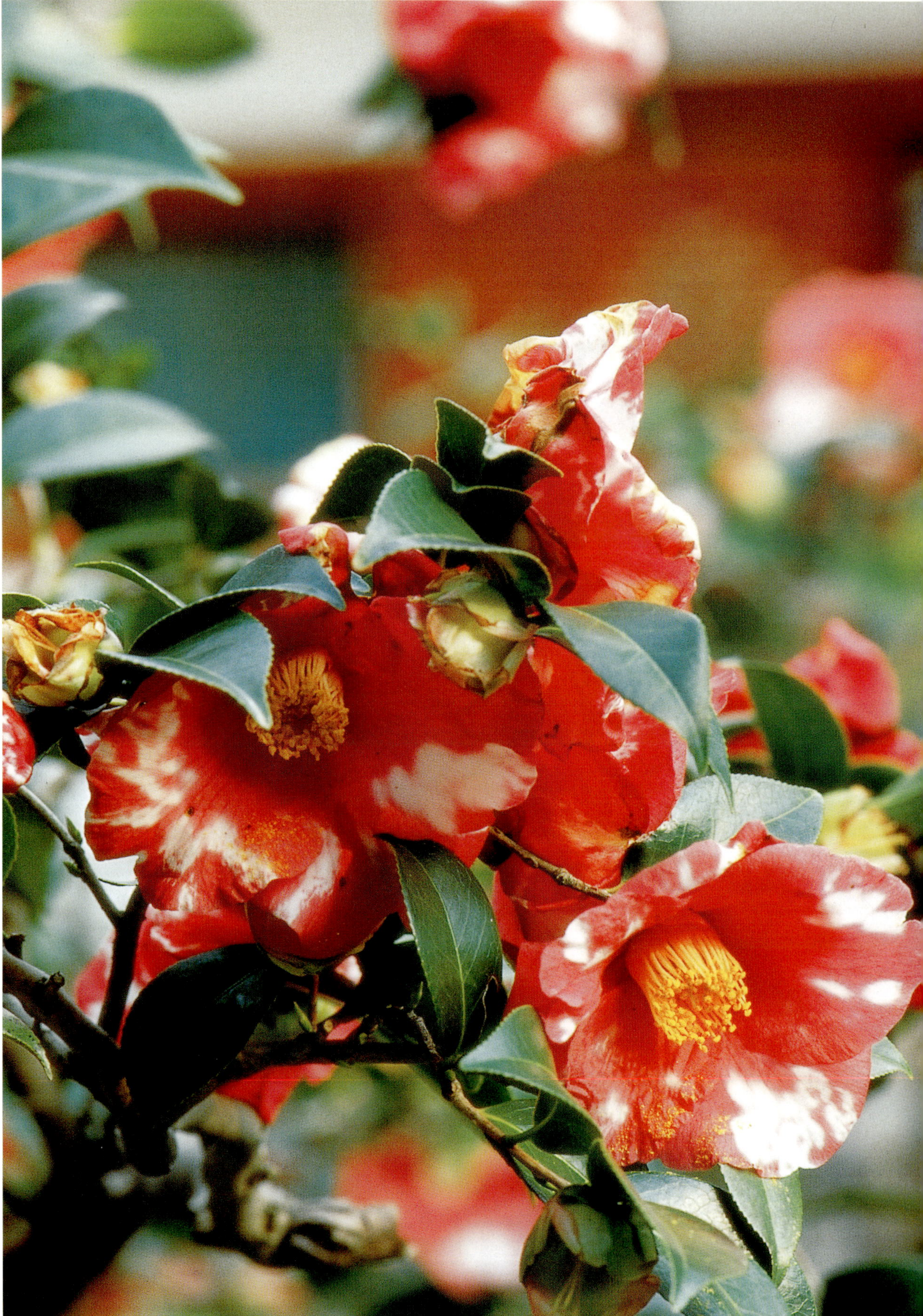

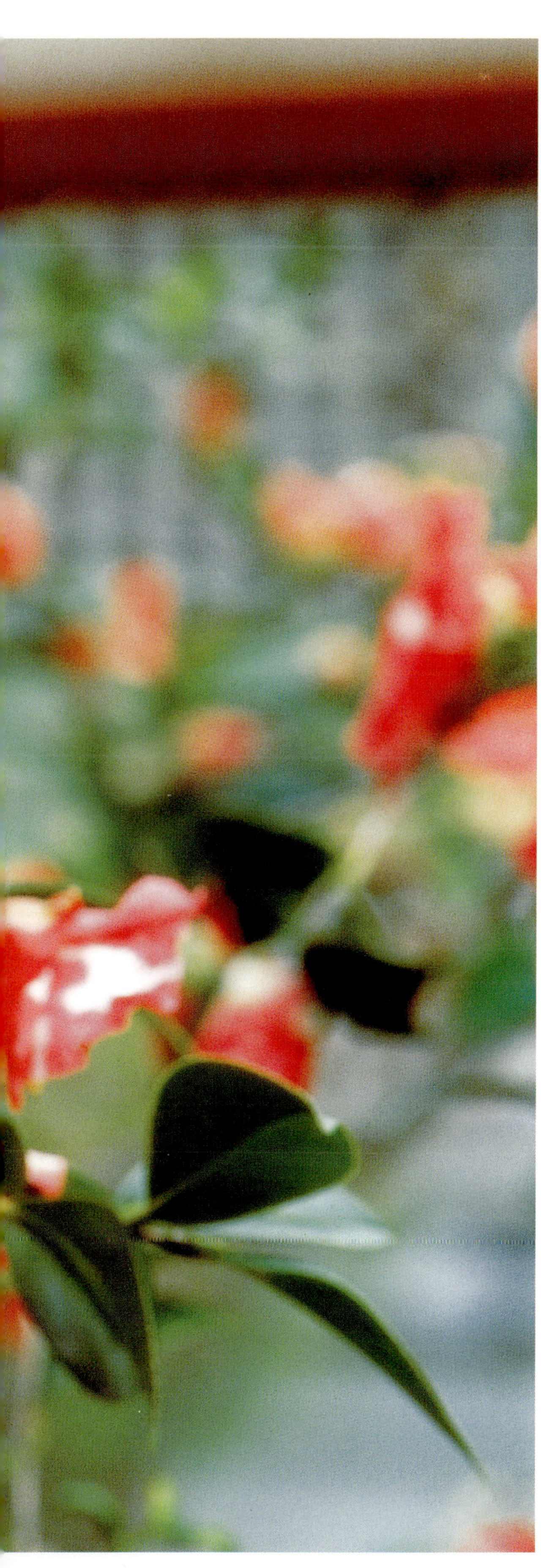

In this high place
   Of Yamoto,
In the gently elevated
   Meeting place,
By the Hall of the First Fruits
   There is growing
A wide-leaved
   Sacred camellia tree.
Like its leaves,
   Wide and calm,
Like its flowers
   Shining brilliantly
Are you, O high-shining
   Sun-prince!
Partake, O my lord,
   Of the abundant wine!

FROM THE RECORD OF
ANCIENT MATTERS

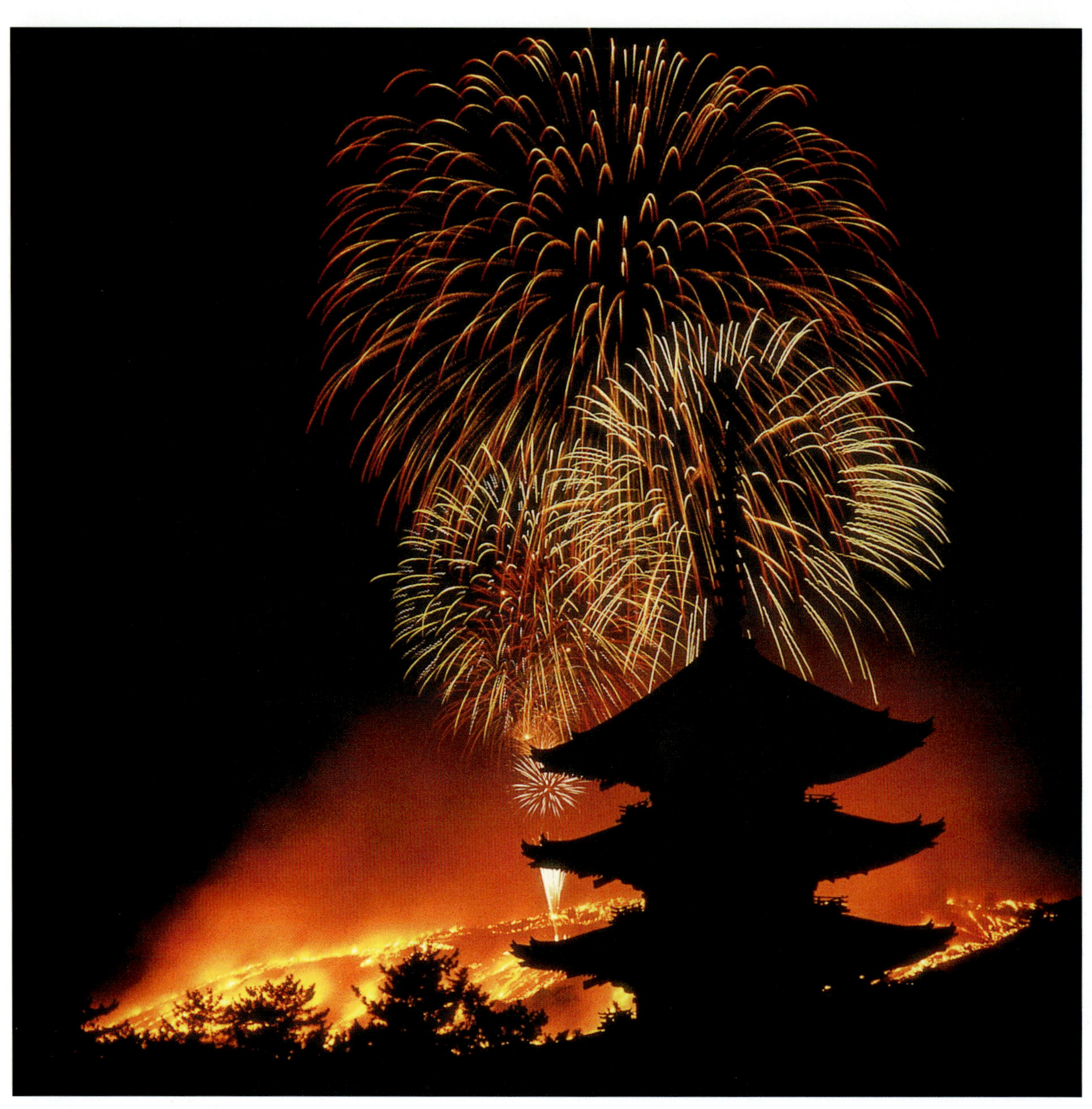

On Mikasa Mountain

Like the crown

On a lofty altar,

The birds cease crying

Only to start again—

Such is my longing for her.

YAMABE NO AKAHITO

"*T*he monks of the southern capital became enemies of the court first by siding with Prince Takakura when he went to the Onjōji, and then by going out to meet him, which was even worse. We must attack both the Kōfukuji and Miidera," the authorities in the capital said…

The Kōfukuji was the hereditary temple of the Fujiwara clan, founded by Tankaikō's vow. It was grievous beyond measure that it should all have been turned to smoke in an instant—the Sakyamuni image in the Eastern Golden Hall, brought to Japan during the first days of Buddhism; the Kanzeon image in the Western Golden Hall, which had sprung spontaneously from the earth; the corridors on all sides, beautiful as rows of gems; the two-storied Nikaidō, resplendent in vermilion and cinnabar; the two pagodas, their nine rings glittering in the sky.

FROM THE TALE OF THE HEIKE

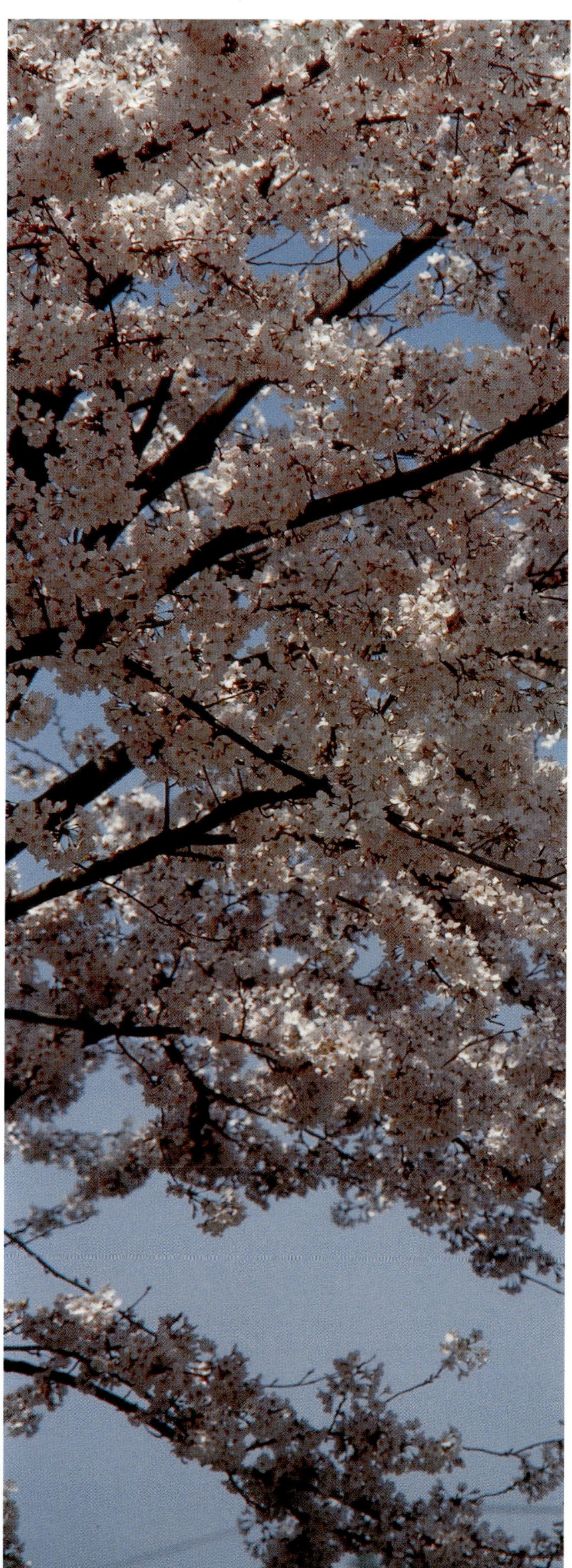

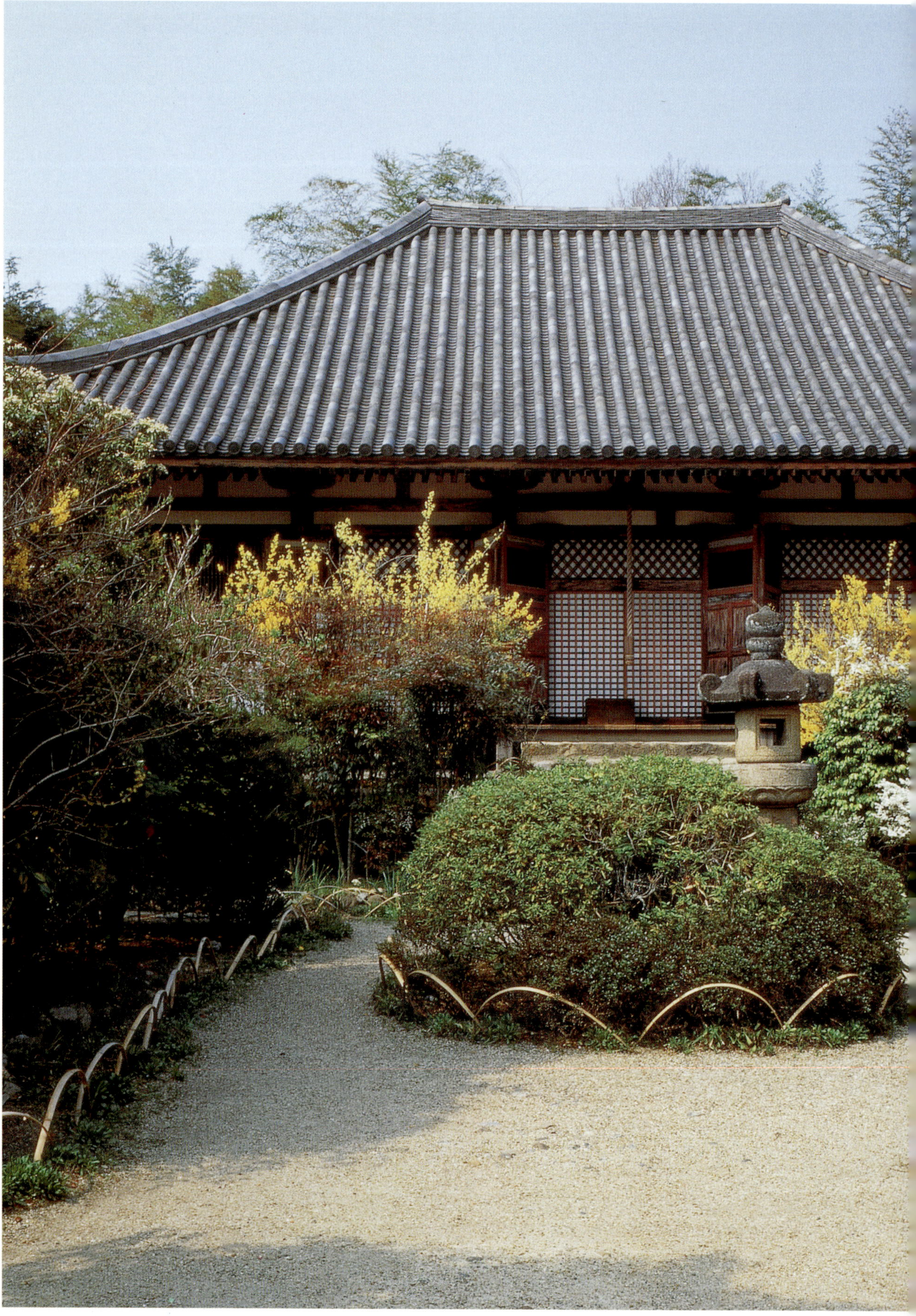

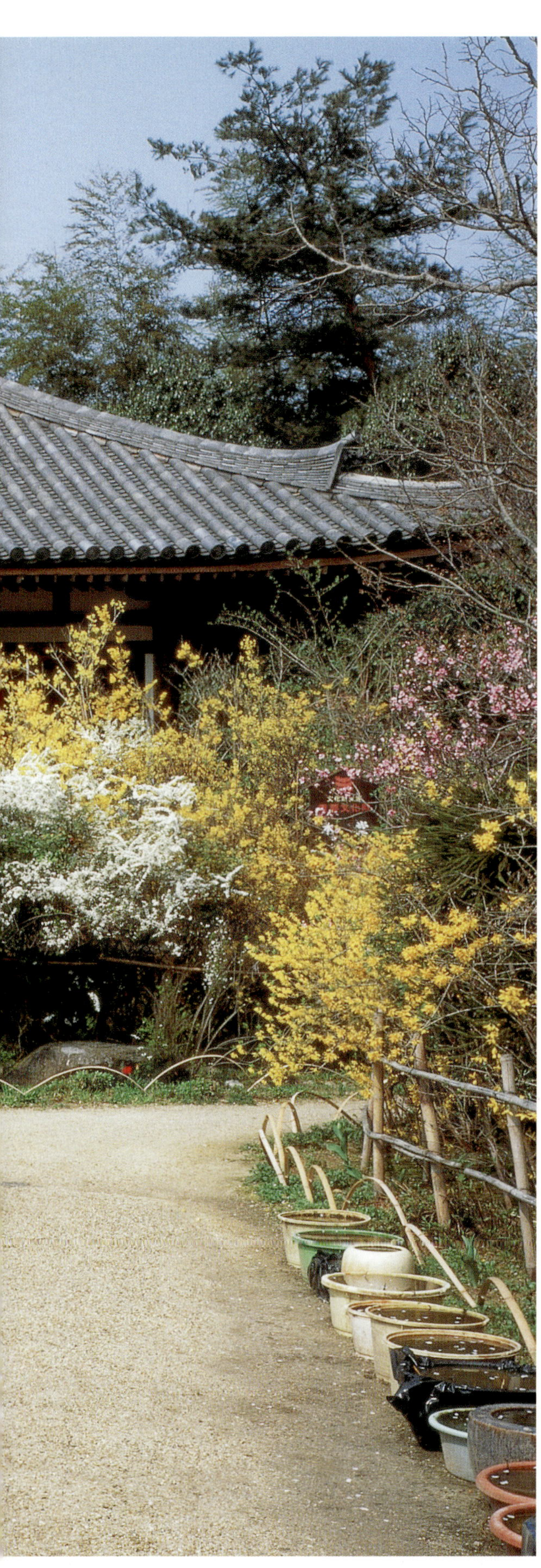

Never do the ripples cease

In the shallows of the Saho river

Where the plover cries,

Nor does my longing for you.

LADY ŌTOMO

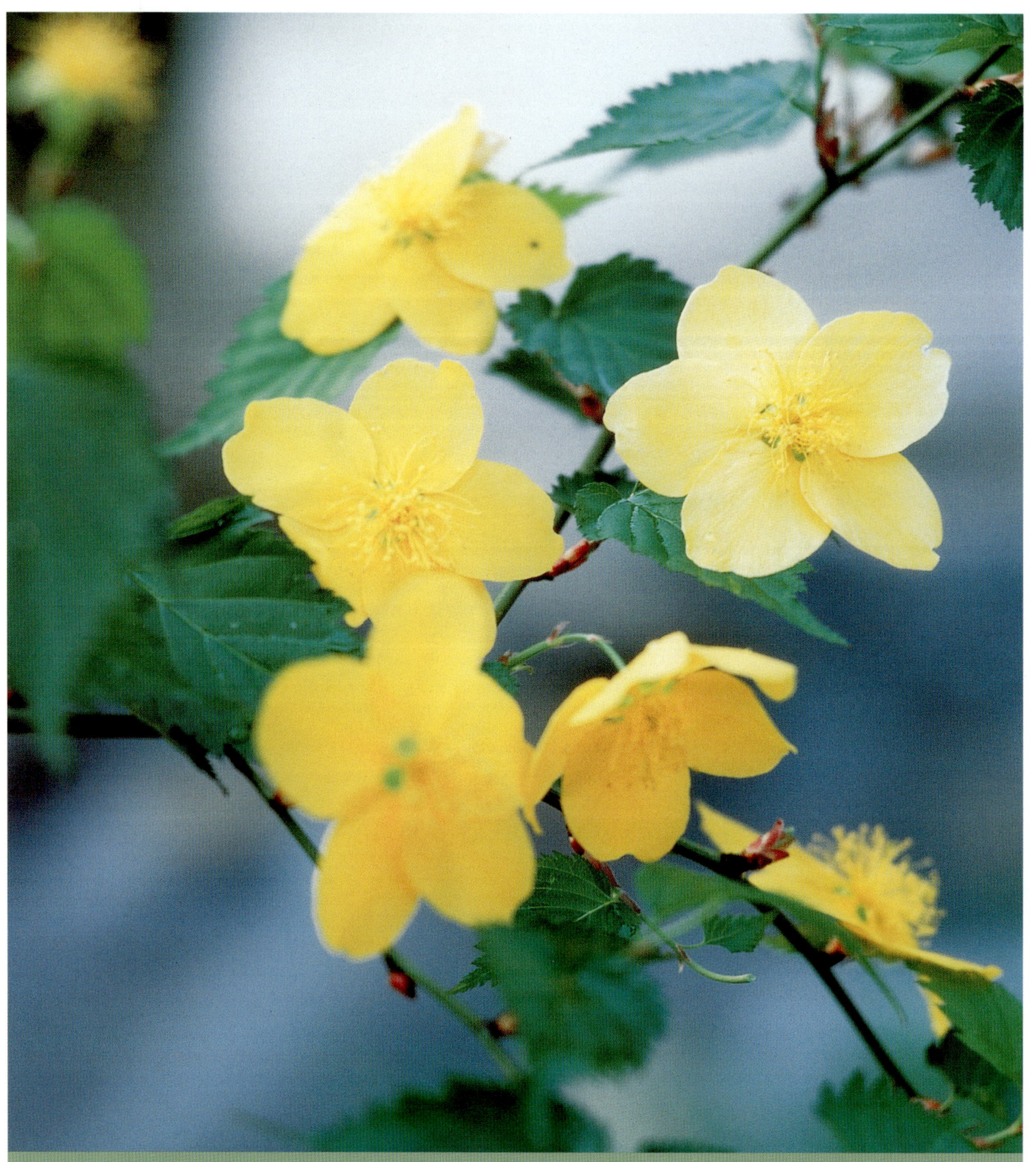

Catching the reflection
Of the mountain roses,
The spring is yellow!

Ransetsu

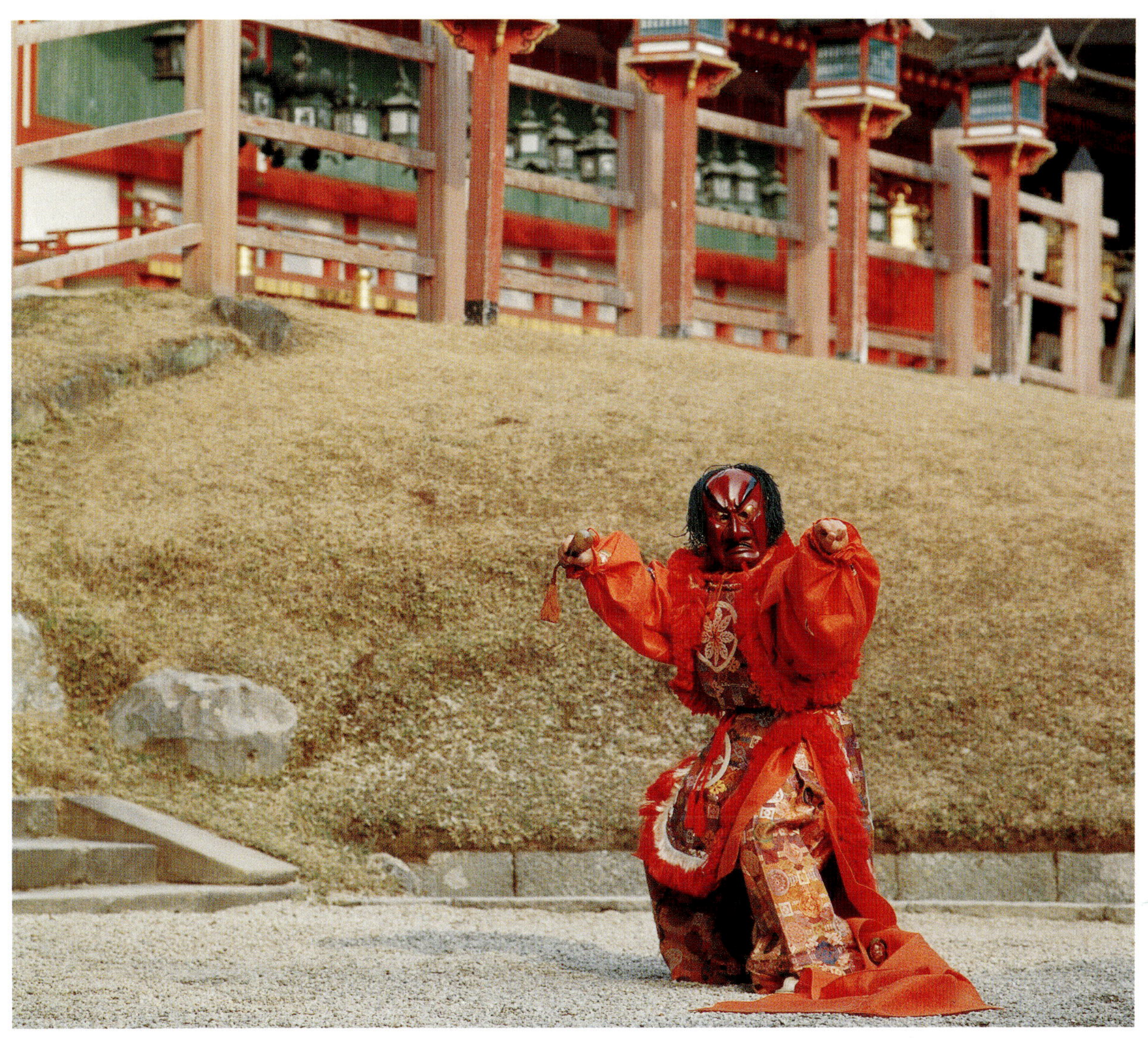

*T*hen the dances begin. As the dancers move they extend their arms stiffly and symmetrically with the fingers held taut. They bend their legs in deep pliés. Sometimes they wear huge frightening masks with gaping maws. Meanwhile the dissonances and weird melodies of the music collide and the pulsing beats of fives and nines or fours and twelves, punctuated by the drums, vibrate delicately and uncertainly in the Westerner's ears. Somehow the antiquity of the dance and music is immediately evident. In fact, the entire performance is so remote from one's previous artistic experience either in Asia or the West that it comes as no surprise to learn that *bugaku* first appeared in Japan some thirteen hundred years ago, not long after the fall of the Roman Empire.

FAUBION BOWERS

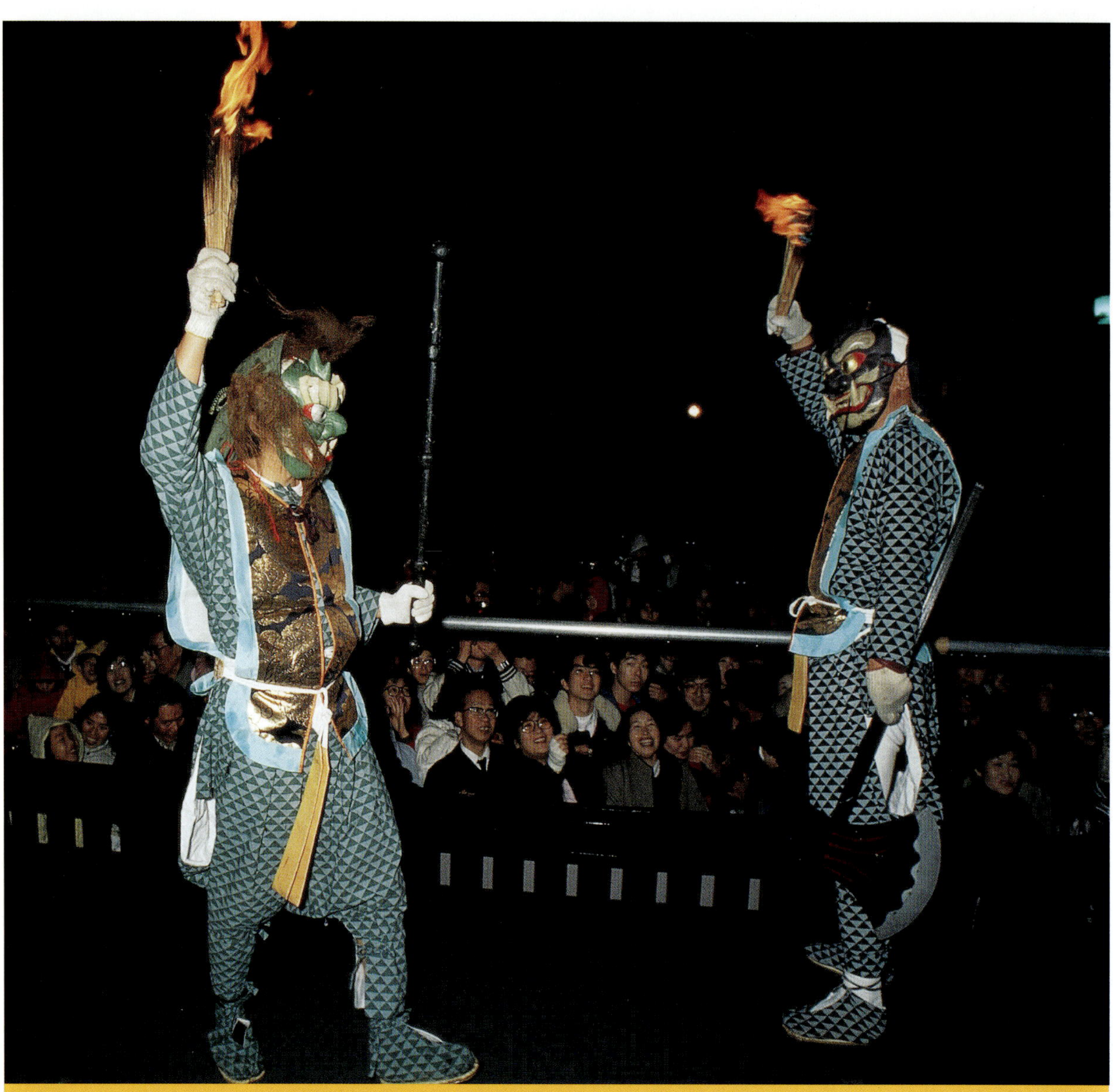

Fuku wa uchi! (Fortune in!)
Fuku wa uchi! (Fortune in!)
Oni wa soto! (Devils Out!)

TRADITIONAL SAYING

Naokichi said there was a place to fish on the way to Kōriya-
ma and insisted that we go there. The stream he mentioned
seemed to be near Daianji, the temple associated with a number
of theatrical performances.

SHIGA NAOYA

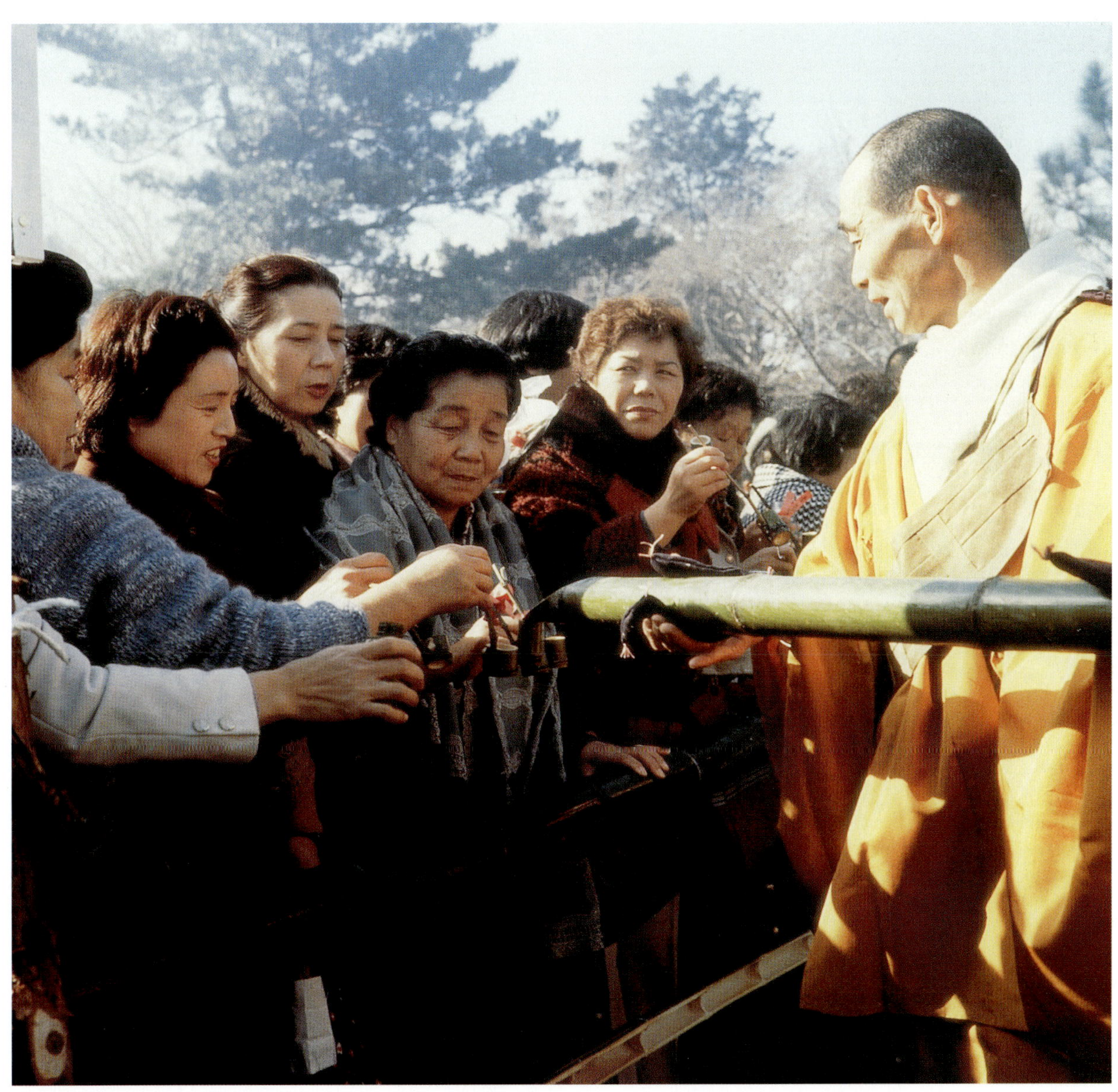

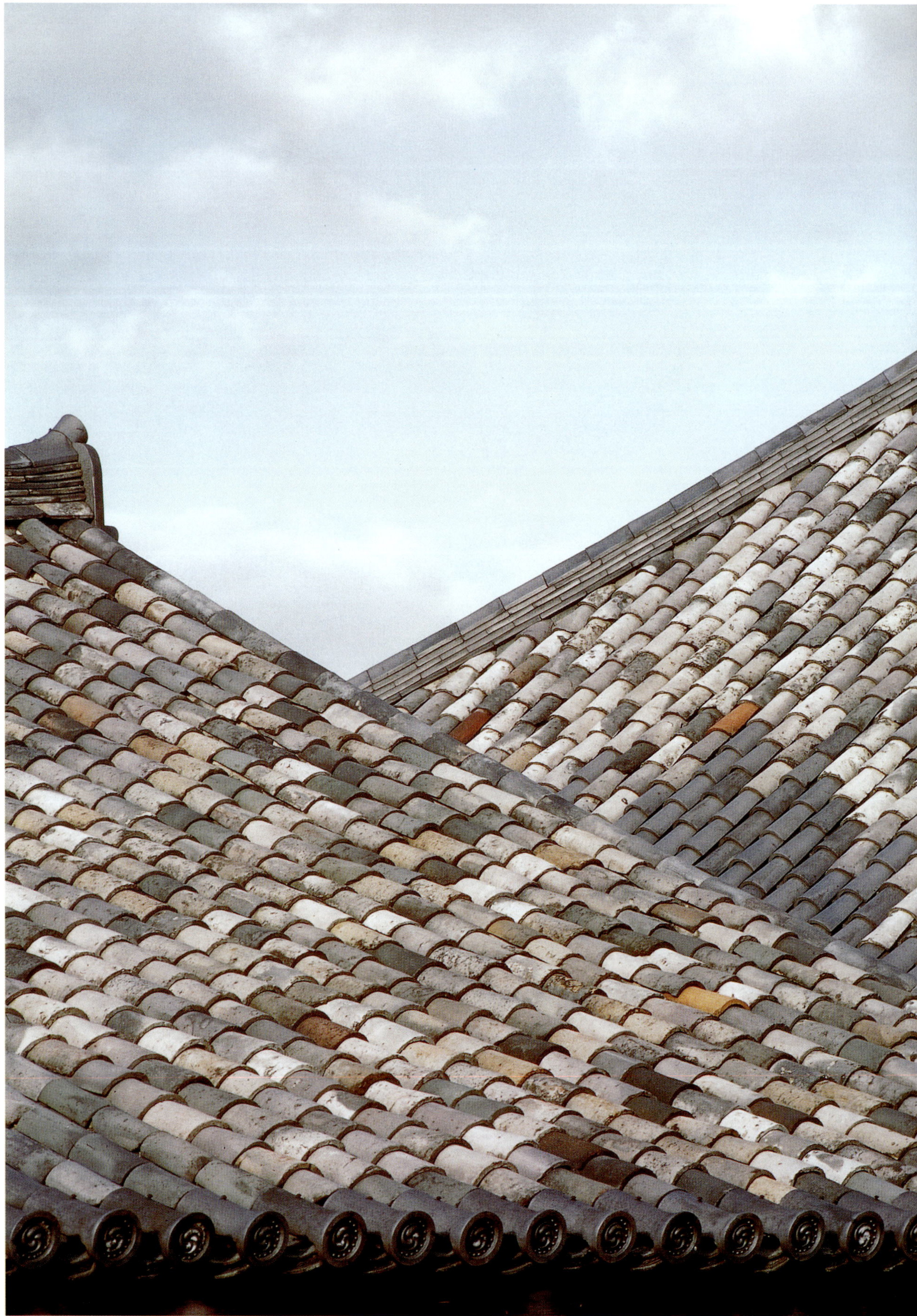

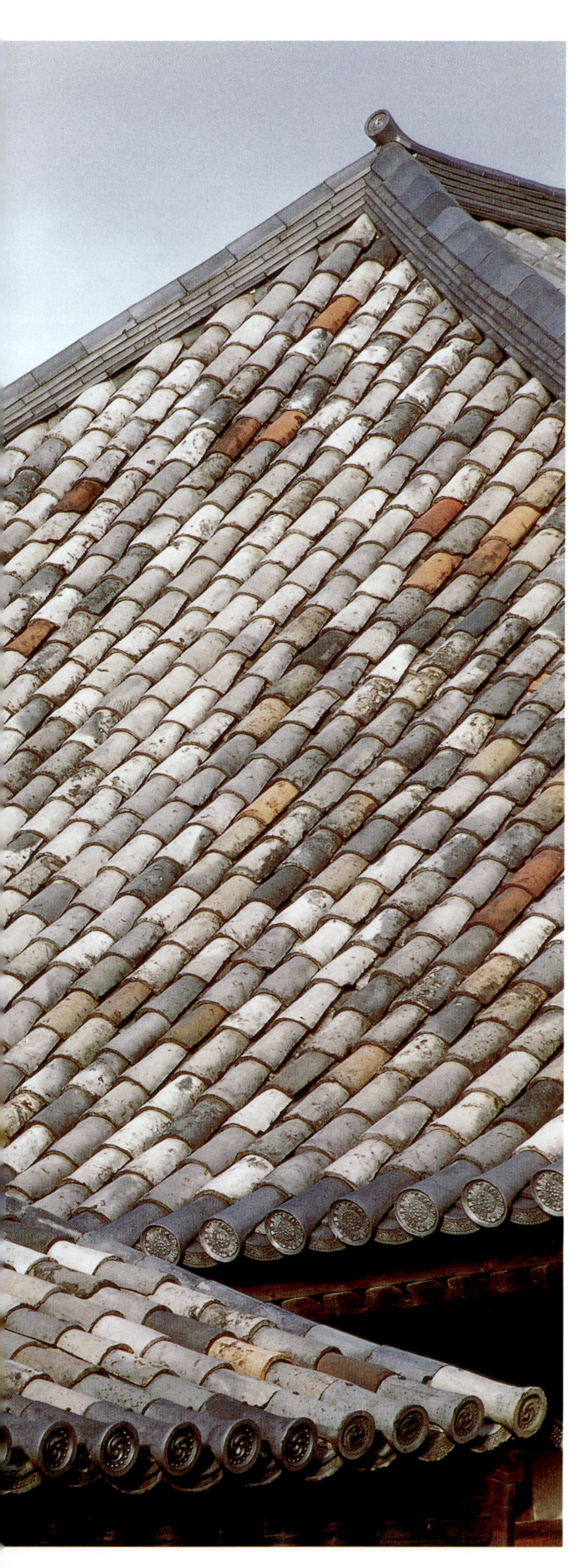

Shina followed Tadashirō in silence. She was neither sullen nor angry. She was silent because she did not know what to say.

As usual in the rainy season, the sky was leaden. It began to drizzle again. Yokota's house was located near the Pleasure Pavilion at Gangōji Temple.

SATŌ AIKO

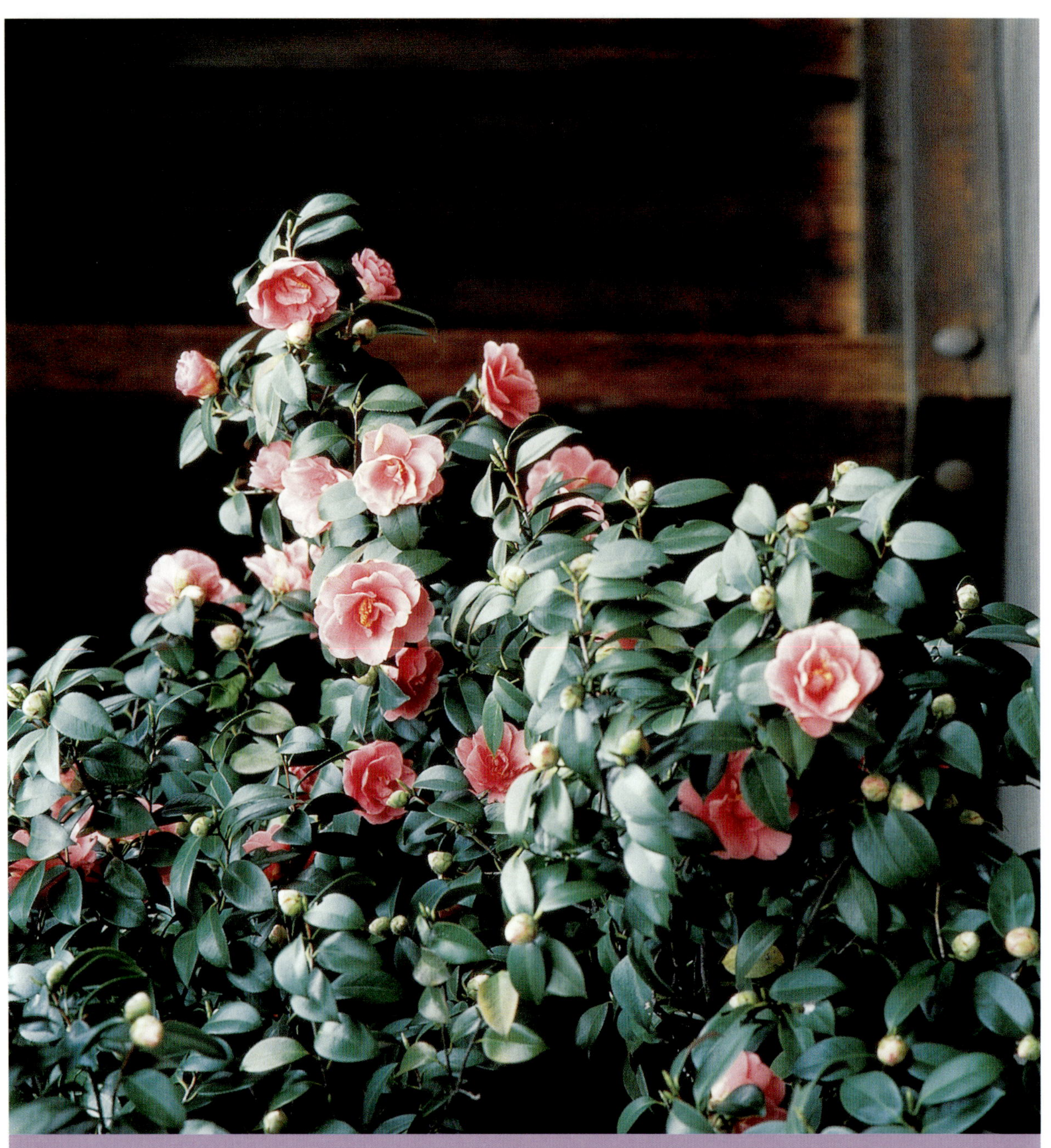

The camellia flower,
About to fall,
Was caught in its own leaves.

SHŌHA

*W*hen you leave the road leading into the village, turn a little to your right. There you will find a small dilapidated temple called the Kairyūōji. I entered the old gate with its four pillars and felt relieved to be standing in the shade. It was close to harvest time. Heads of rice could be seen waving all across the Yamato plain. The sight of it dazzled my eyes. I looked at the gate, which seemed ready to collapse at any moment. Then I realized that this plain, with all its blessings of warm sunlight, held the ruins of the old capital.

Hori Tatsuo

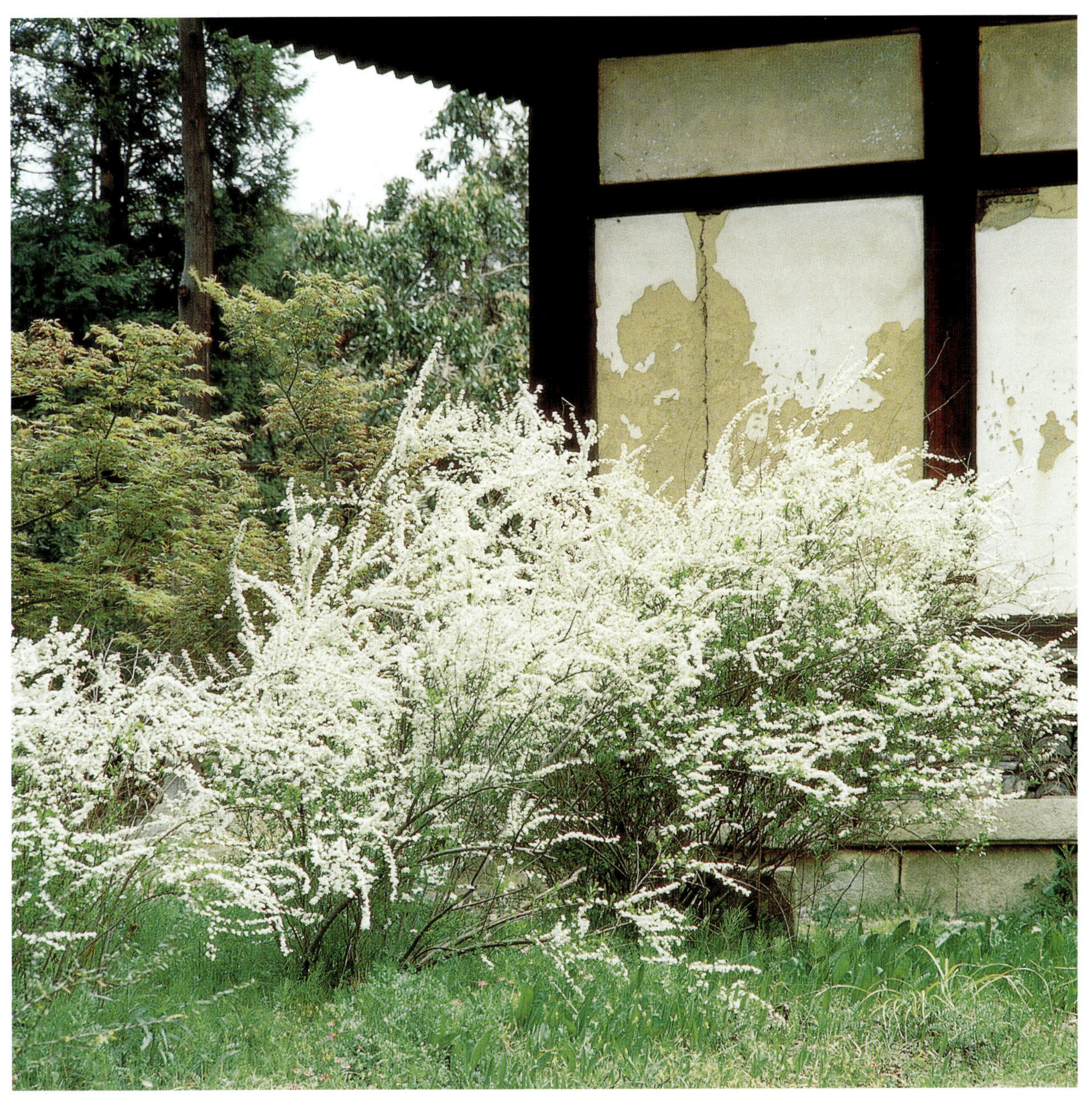

The Yagyū Valley lies at the foot of Mount Kasagi, northeast of Nara. In the early seventeenth century it was the sight of a prosperous little community…yet not populous or bustling enough to be called a town. It might naturally have been called Kasagi Village, but instead its inhabitants referred to their home as the Kambe Demesne, a name inherited from the bygone age of the great privately owned manorial estates.

EIJI YOSHIKAWA

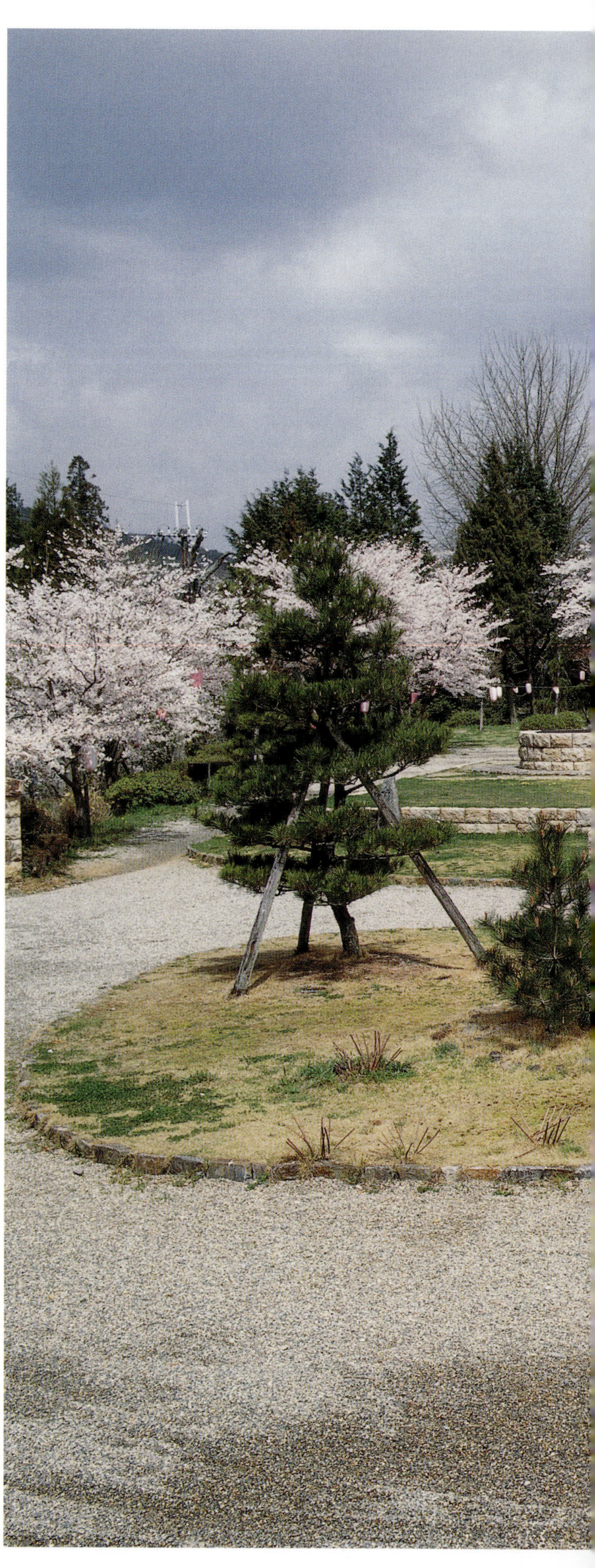

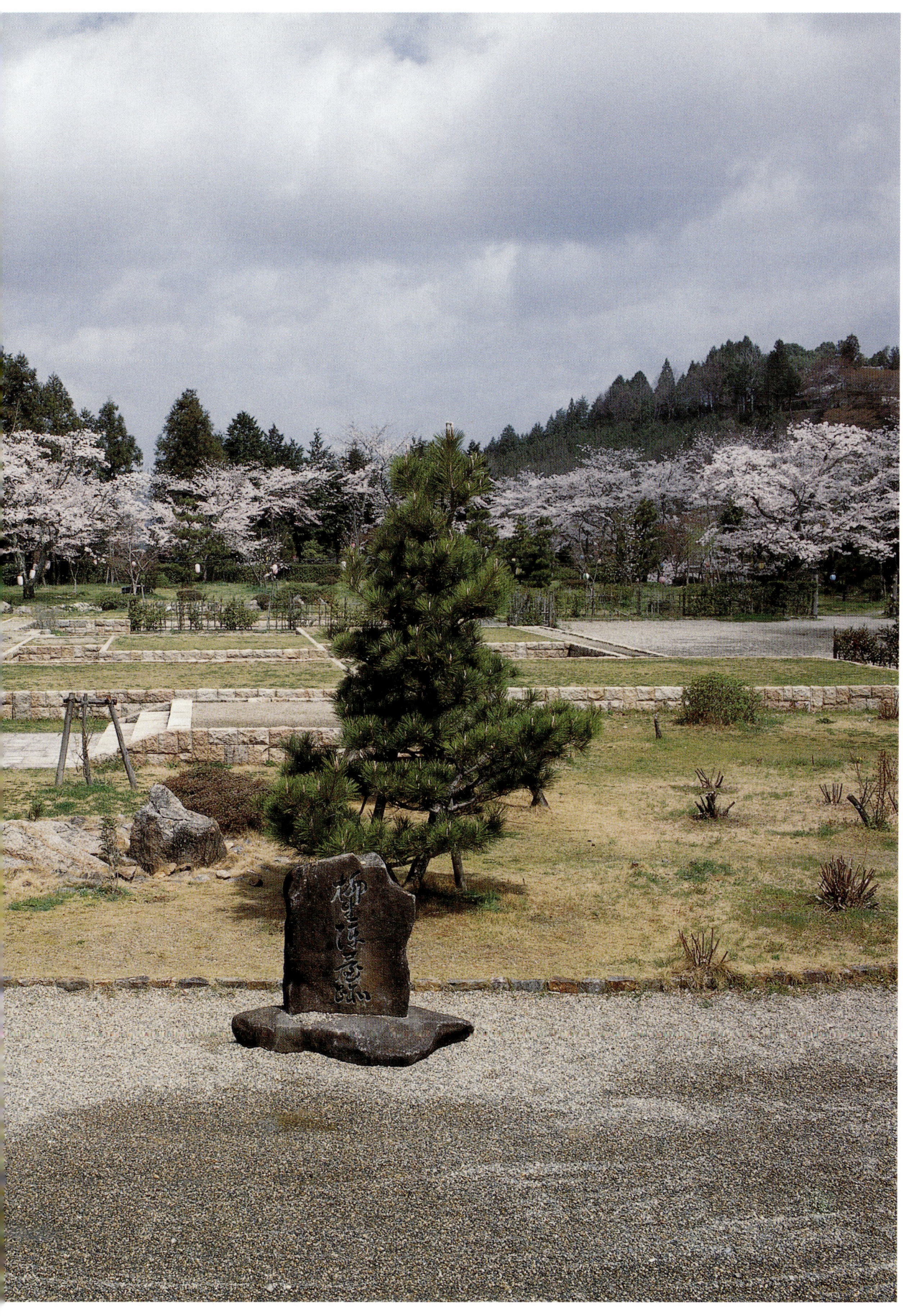

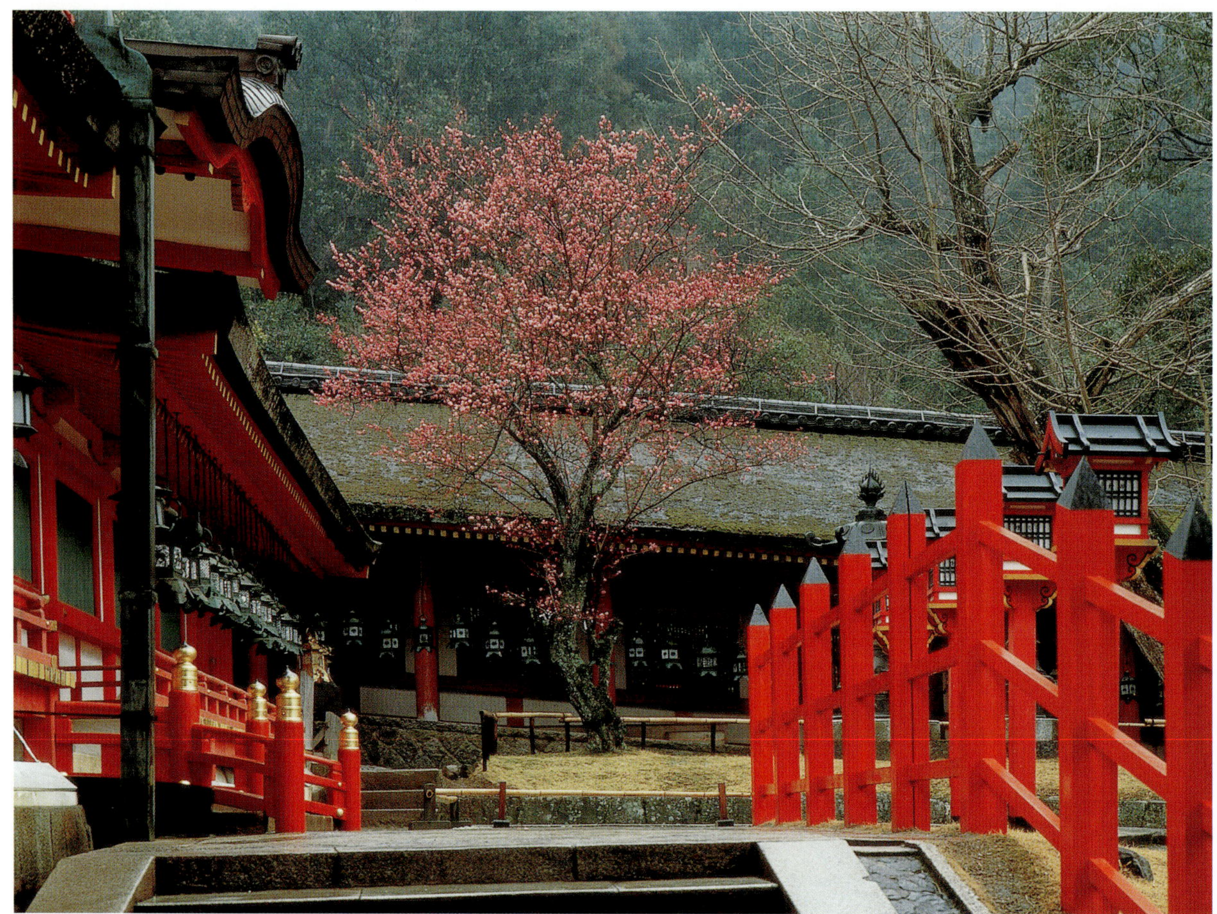

*W*e are in a long covered passage or corridor, painted vermillion, if I remember right, and leading uphill. This, too, was hung with lanterns; and at the back, in and between the galleries, are those enormous cryptomeria trees. The shrine itself is quite a small building; and at this moment a priest comes down towards us with a quick, youthful step, wearing a cloak of watery green silk, like a surplice of green-blue silk over a white gown or kimono… He wears one of those hats of black gauze which we have only seen before in the figures upon sliding screens.

SACHEVERELL SITWELL

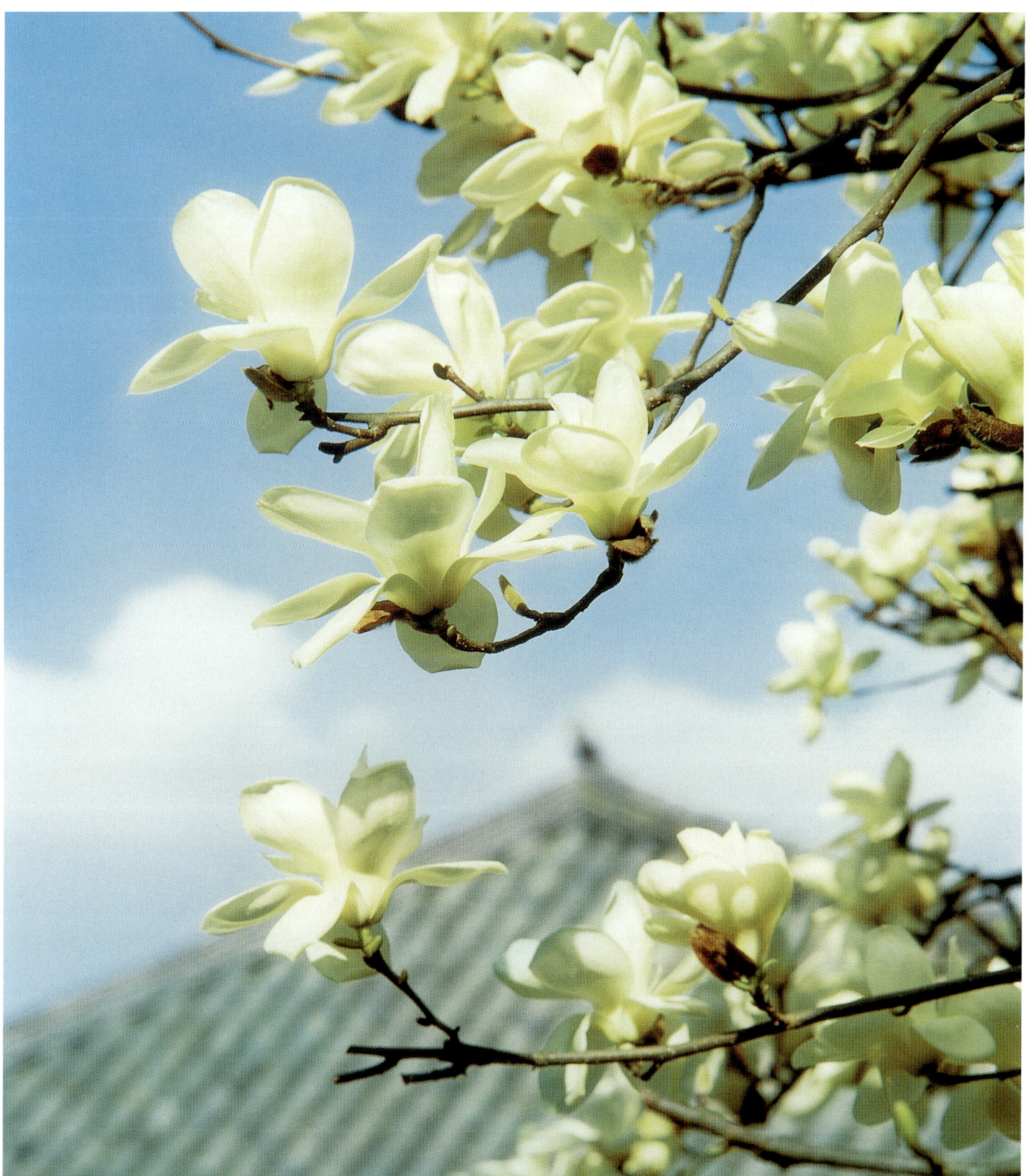

Akishino Temple was only a five-minute ride from Saidaiji Station. It was small. Pampas grass grew by the wayside, thick and white with a silvery sheen. The temple in its thicket of trees was very quiet.

Tachihara Masaaki

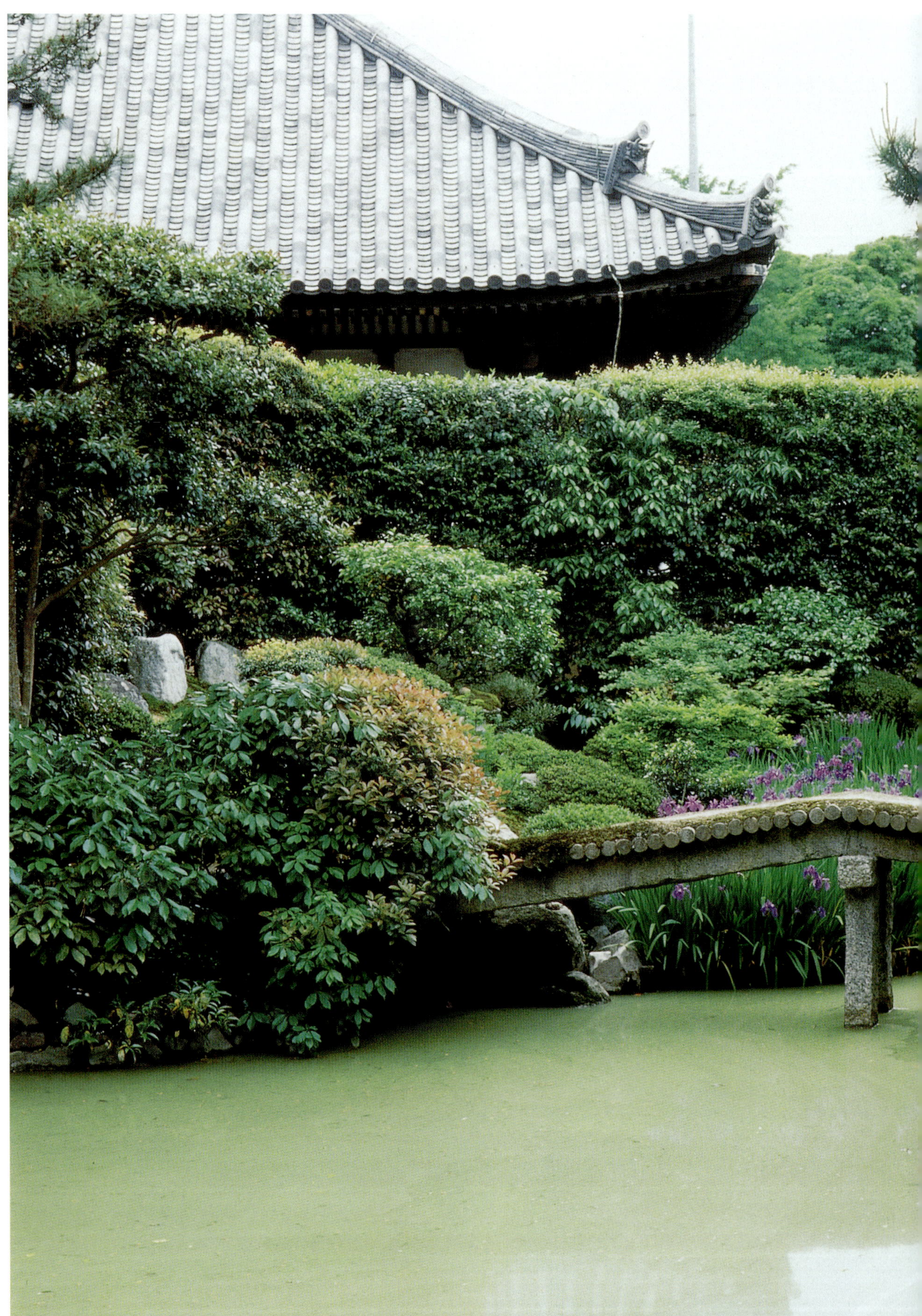

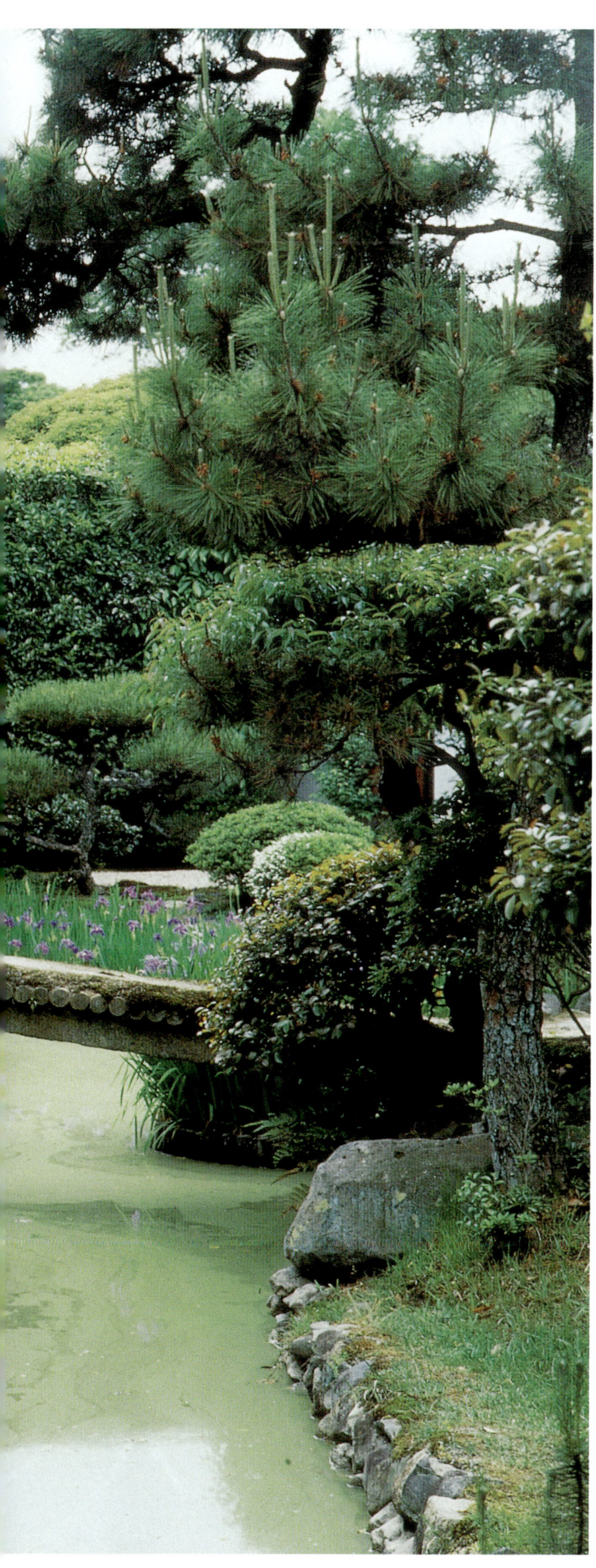

*I*n the plain below Nara there are other monasteries and a nunnery… Hokkeji, where there is always an Imperial princess for an abbess. In this temple is a wooden sculpture of Kannon, made according to tradition by an Indian sculptor who came to the nunnery and was so captivated by the beauty and saintliness of the Empress who lived there as a nun that he wanted to carve her image, but could come no nearer to accomplishing this than by copying her reflection in the lotus pool.

SACHEVERELL SITWELL

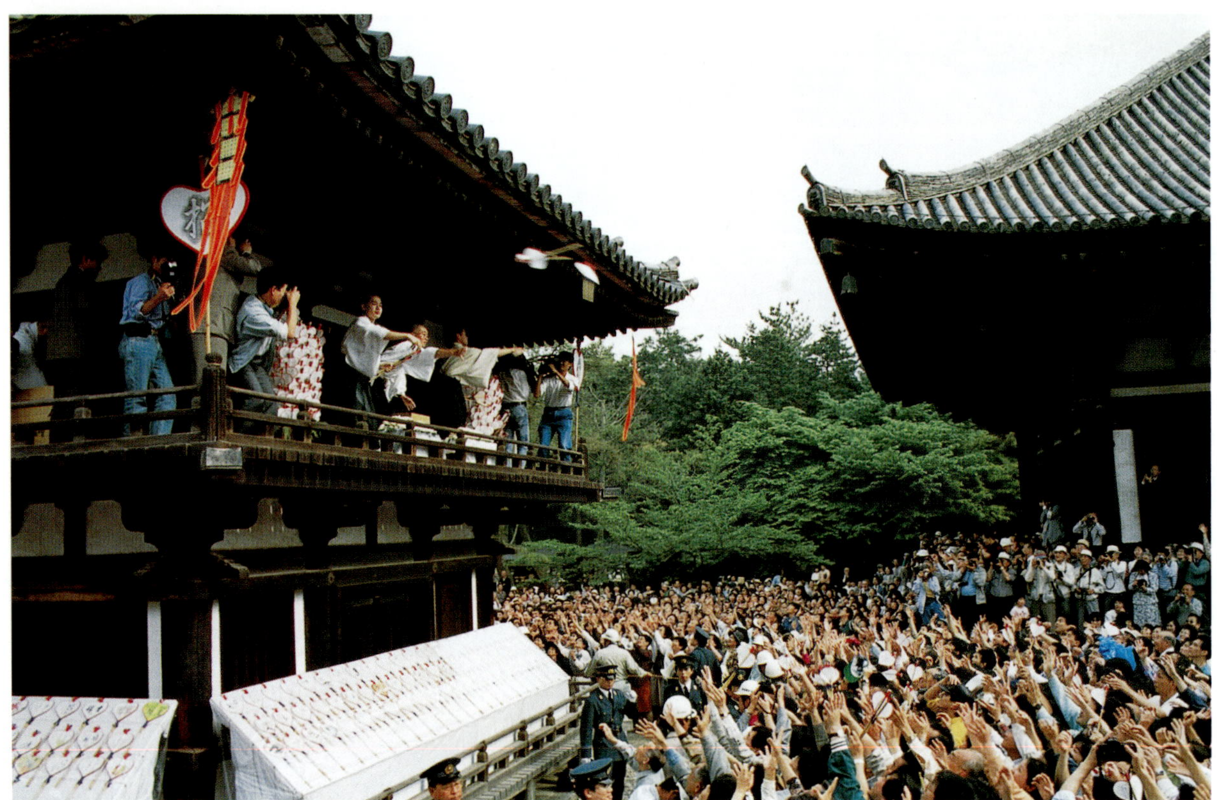

Incidental mention of fans occurs in the oldest official annals of the country. Thus, under the date of A.D. 763, we read of Imperial permission being granted to a courtier to bring his staff and fan into the palace precincts, on the score of age and infirmity. Apparently fans were then tabooed by strict etiquette, which is remarkable, as they afterwards became an indispensable adjunct of Court dress for both sexes.

BASIL HALL CHAMBERLAIN

Yamato Plain—
A fairy appears
From Mount Wakakusa,
Gently laying
A robe over me,
As I fall into a doze.

YOSANO AKIKO

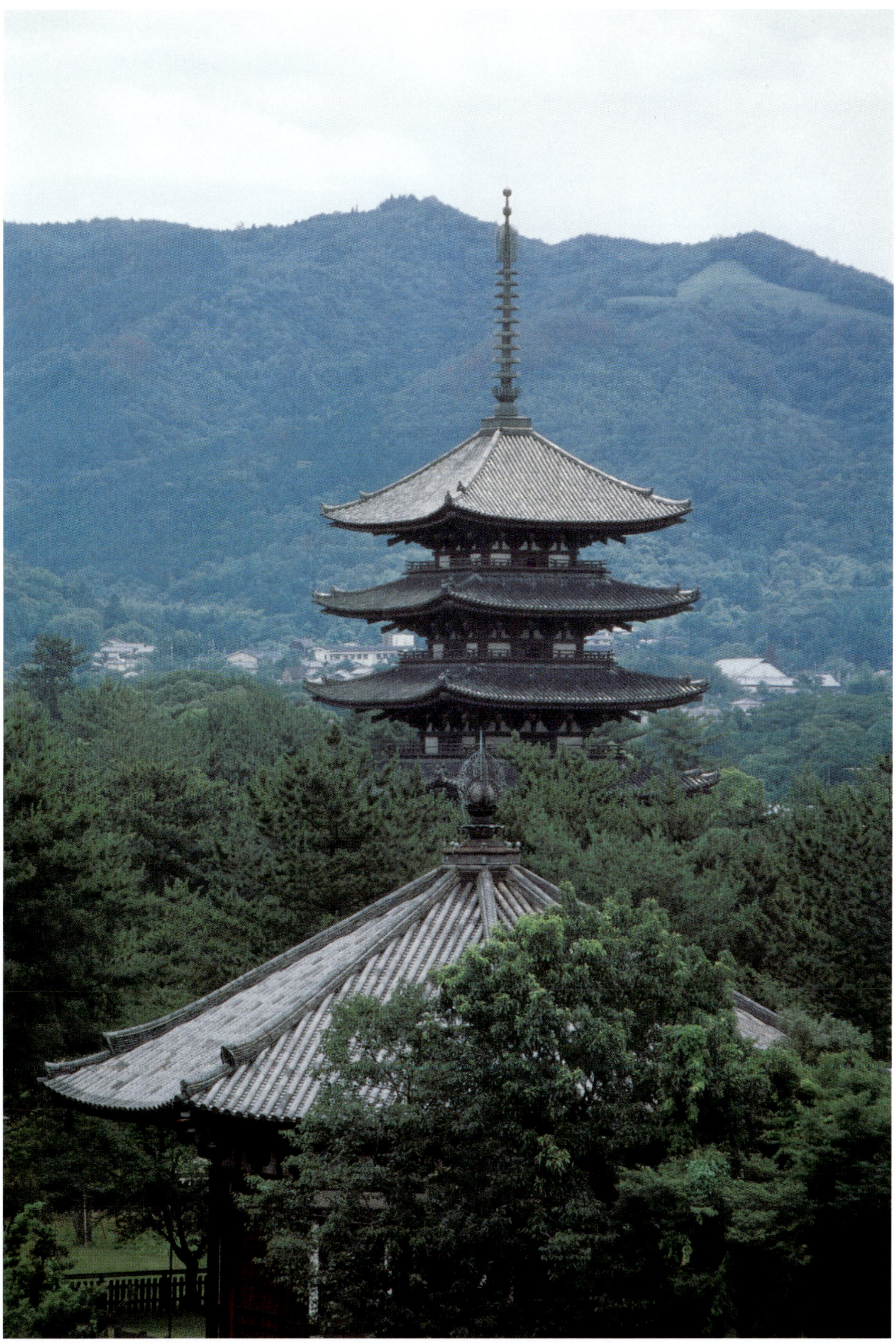

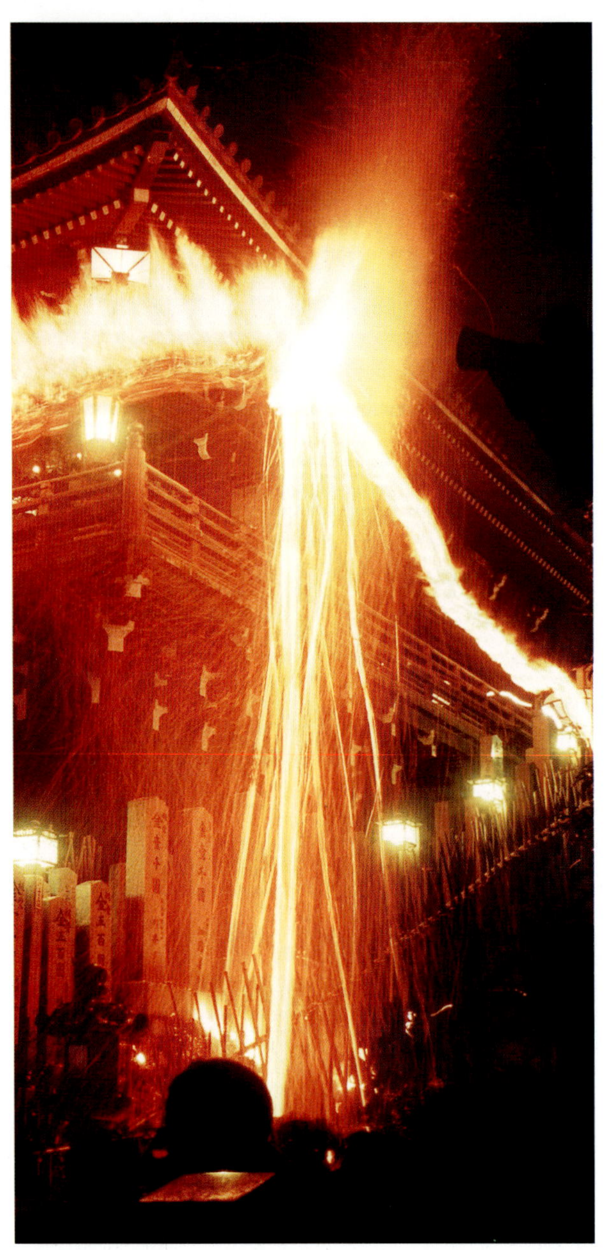

*T*he rites at the Nigatsu Hall begin each year on the first of March, but they do not reach their climax until the night of the twelfth with the burning of the crate-like torches, followed by the dipping of the sacred water and the secret Tartar rituals performed early on the morning of the thirteenth. The ceremonies on the night of the twelfth attract the largest crowds…

The moment for lighting the huge pine-torches was at hand, and the party, guided by a priest, made its way in the darkness through the milling crowd under the platform of Nigatsu Hall… Now the "Sevenfold Messages" were beginning. The chief votary, holding aloft a blazing brand, ran up and down the stone steps again and again, a bold figure in his girded-up robes. The stentorian voice proclaiming each of the "messages"—the offering of incense, the business of the ritual, the attendance at the worship, and the rest—combined with the dripping of the flames from the torches to complete the aura of solemnity. To these spectators who knew nothing of the ancient traditions of esoteric Buddhism or Dual Shinto, the somehow significant presence of the chief votary, his distracted bearing, his intent movements, all seemed like portents of a great calamity about to begin.

Then, when the votary was gone and the torchlight no longer illuminated the stone steps, the utter desolation suggested that something would surely occur at any moment on the emptiness of the steps. Kazu was not especially devout and was seldom moved by anything she could not see with her own eyes, but as she stood there, clutching the bamboo railing, and looked up the stairs rising chilly and faintly white in the darkness, her eyes following them to the temple and platform above, she felt as if soon her heart would also mount the stone steps and share in some momentous happening in an invisible world.

MISHIMA YUKIO

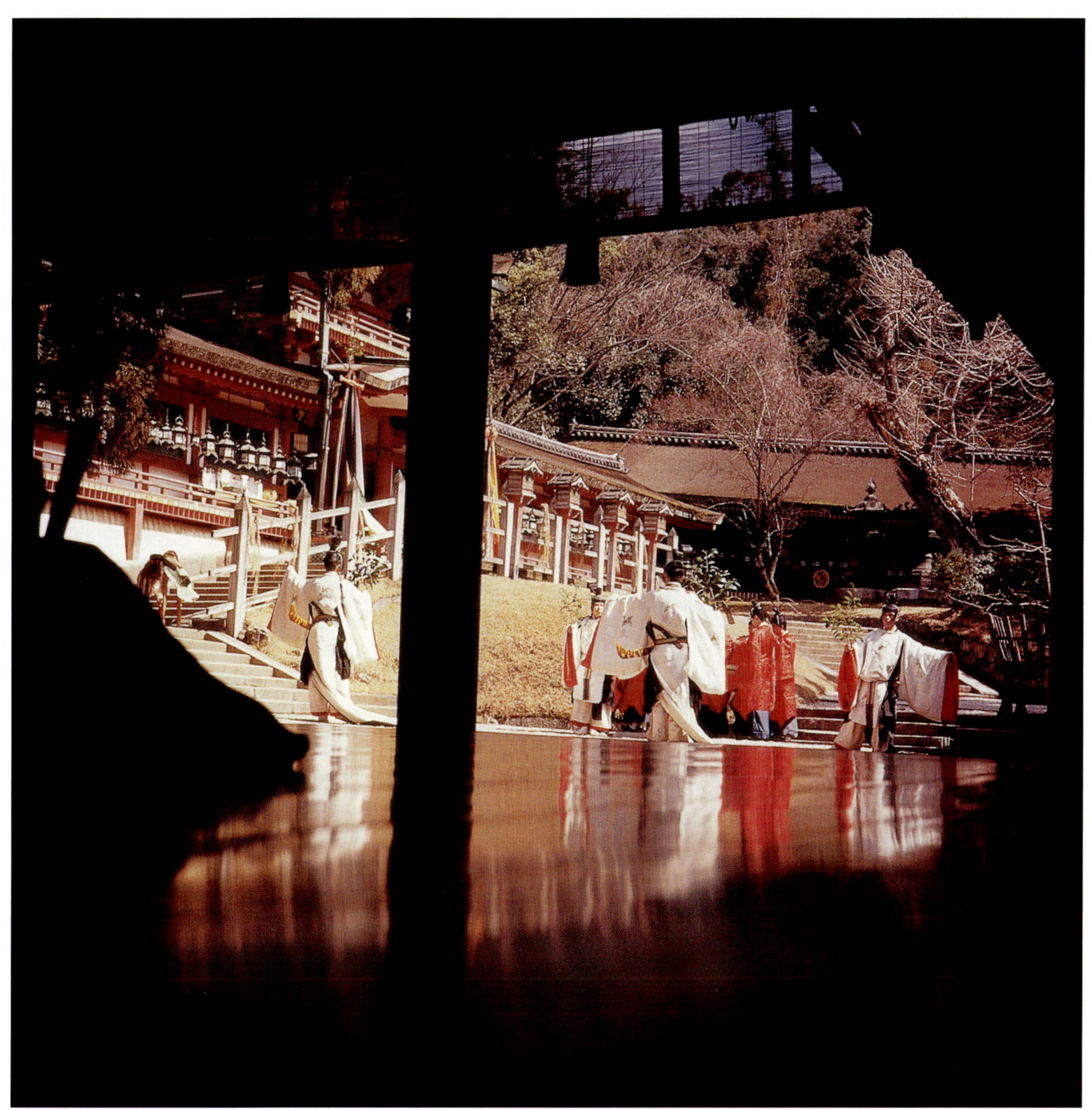

Oh how the shrine

    showers blessings: all Four Sanctuaries

    showers blessings: all Four Sanctuaries,

    heirs to divinity bequeathed of old,

    from the Age of the Gods show, clear and pure,

    the divine intention mingling with the dust.

Yes, even the wind,

    playing through the pines of Mikasa Grove

    rustles no boughs; ah, a peaceful scene

    rustles no boughs; ah, a peaceful scene!

KOMPARU ZENCHIKU

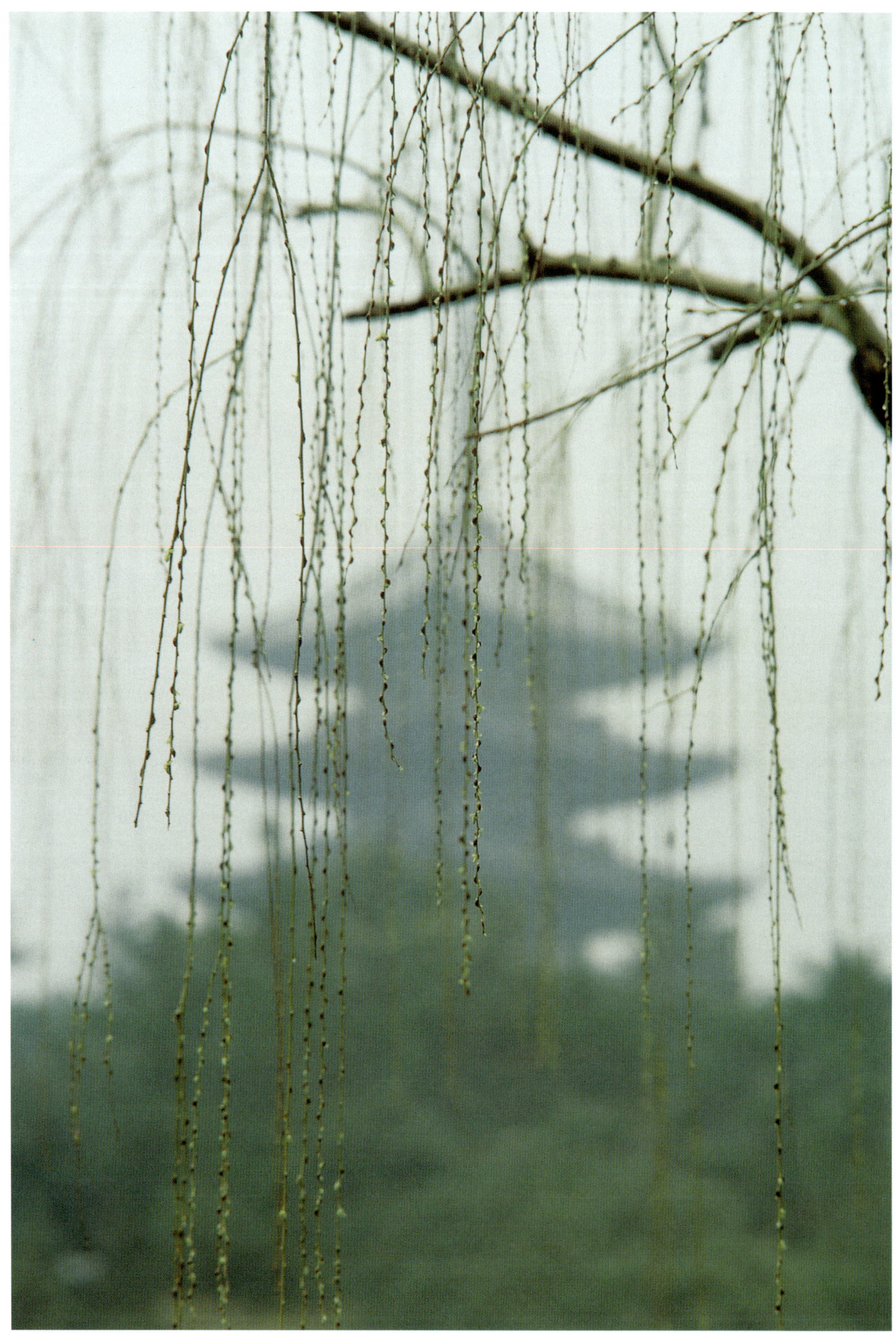

Oh, how green

The threads of the willow

Over the flowing water!

ONITSURA

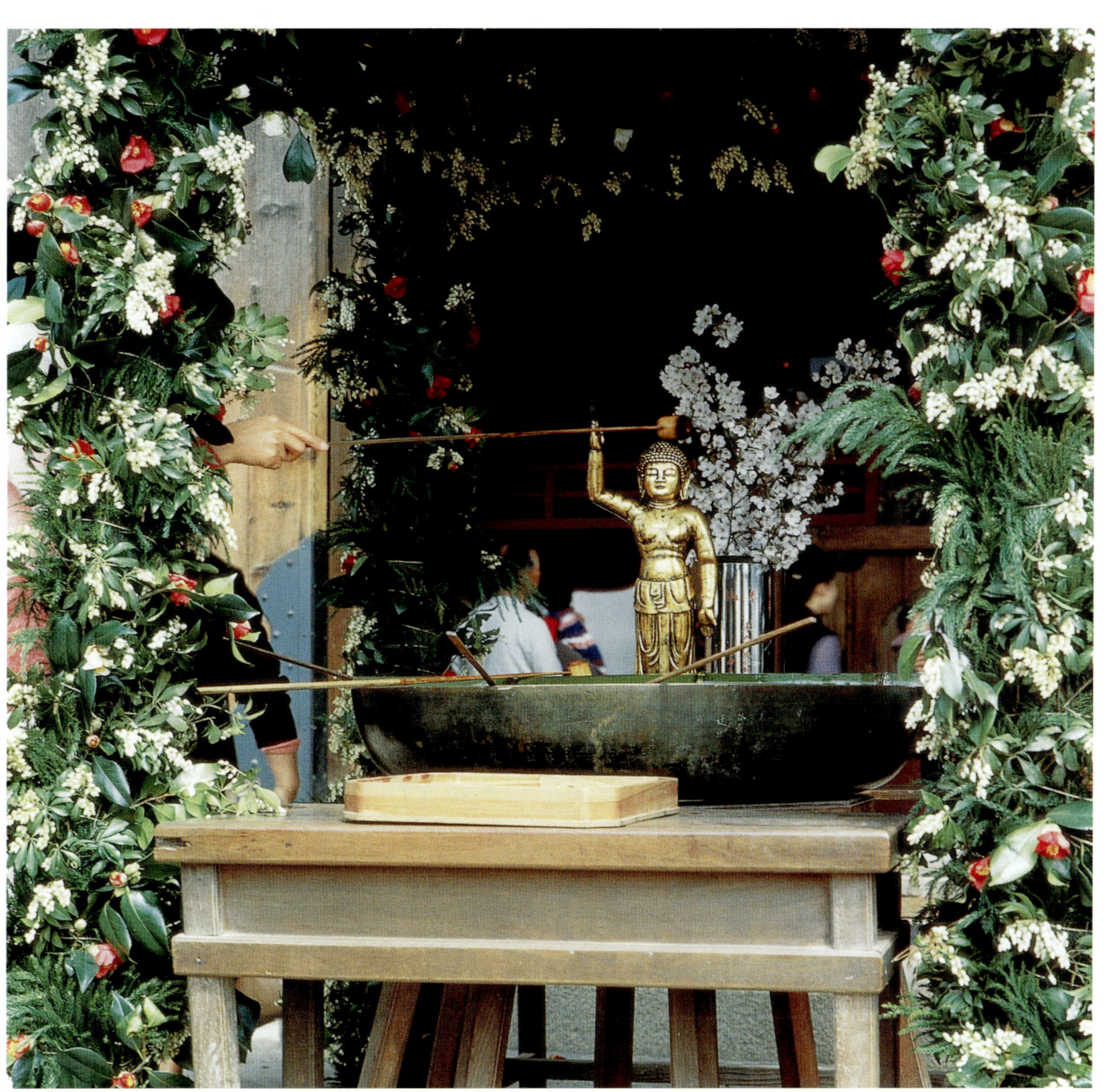

Picking the nameless flower

I offer it to the Buddha.

SANTŌKA

39

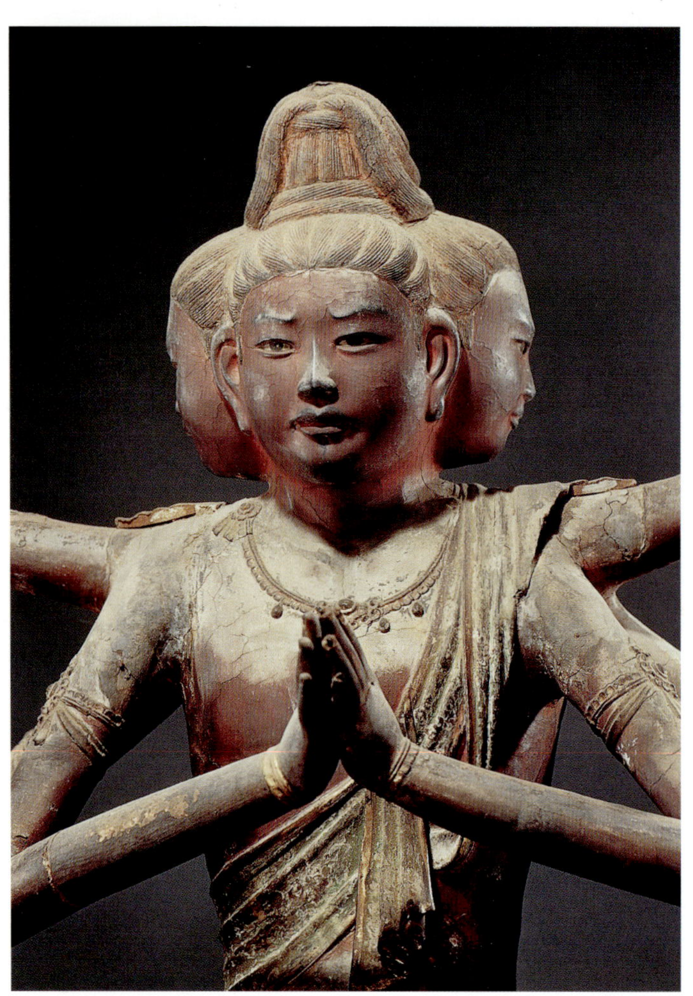

*T*he favorite medium during the Nara period was dry lacquer, a technique which originated in China and which became so popular that it almost completely replaced plain wood. One kind of dry-lacquer statue had a solid core, either of wood or clay, but there was another kind, called hollow dry-lacquer, in which the core was removed and replaced by a wood skeleton, the result being a much lighter work which could easily be carried around in processions or removed from temples in case of fire…

Among the earliest and finest of the hollow dry-lacquer statues are the "Hachibutsu," or "Eight Guardian Devas," which are believed to have been made in 734… The loveliest of them is the famous Ashura, a mythological Hindu demon king who, after his conversion, was supposed to have become one of the eight guardians of Buddha. Being an Indian deity, he is represented in a style and with an iconography very different from that found in other Japanese Buddhist figures. The most noticeable change is the bright red color of his faces and arms and legs and the dark red of his hair. Equally foreign to the Japanese artistic tradition are his multiple arms and heads, which are also typically Indian and became increasingly common in the Japanese Buddhist art of this and subsequent periods. Generally speaking, the multiplication symbolized the supernatural power of the deity, but it also was supposed to represent the many different aspects of the god. In the Ashura image, for example, each face symbolizes a different quality, just as the various hands of the statue are held in different gestures.

HUGO MUNSTERBERG

Would that I might keep the wisteria

As they are!

The flowers appear as though

They might bloom forever.

EMPEROR GODAIGO

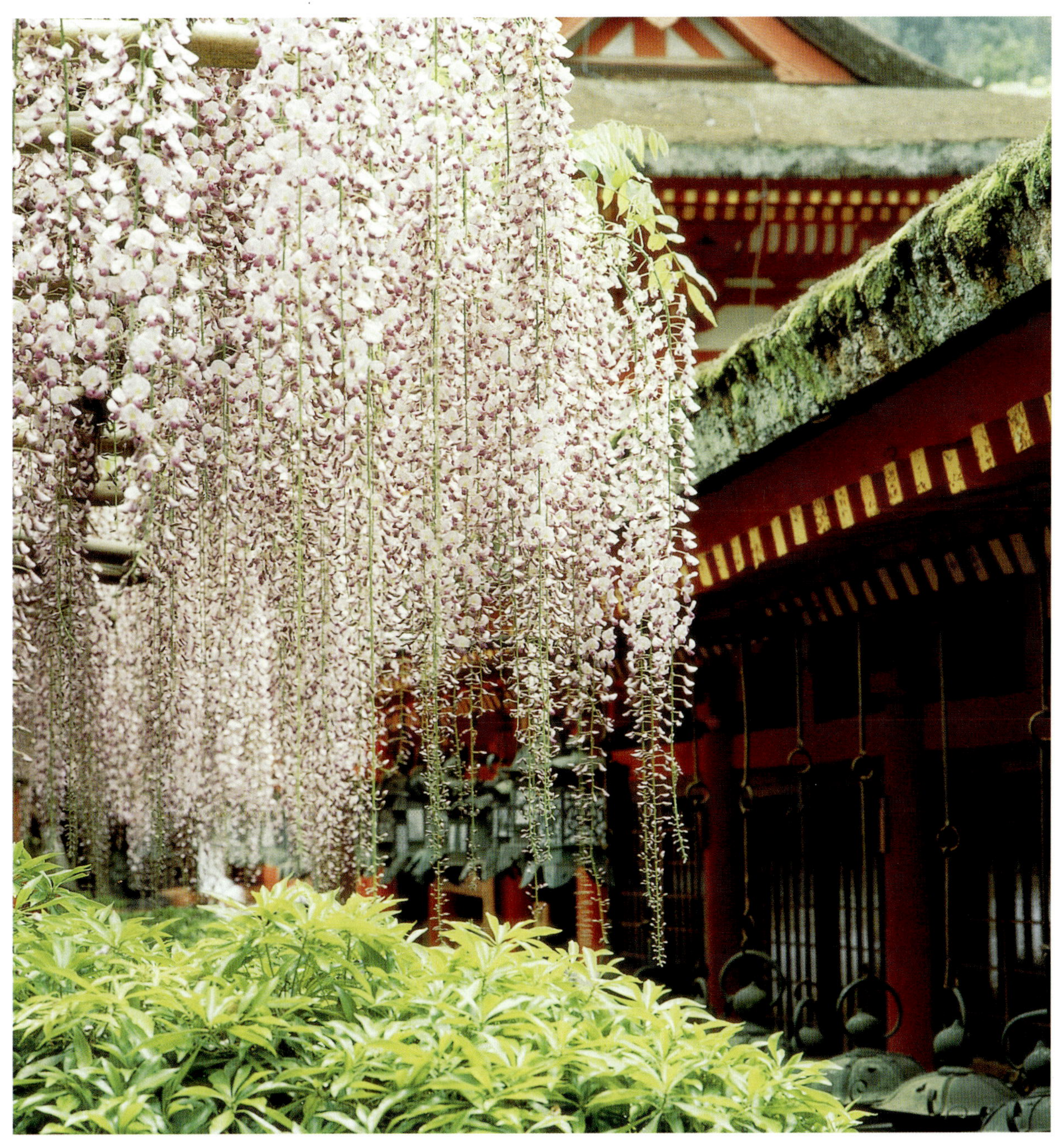

The ringing of the rock

On which the holy footprints are cut

Reaches to heaven

And even earth resounds:

For father and mother,

For all men.

THE FIRST BUDDHA'S FOOTPRINT POEM

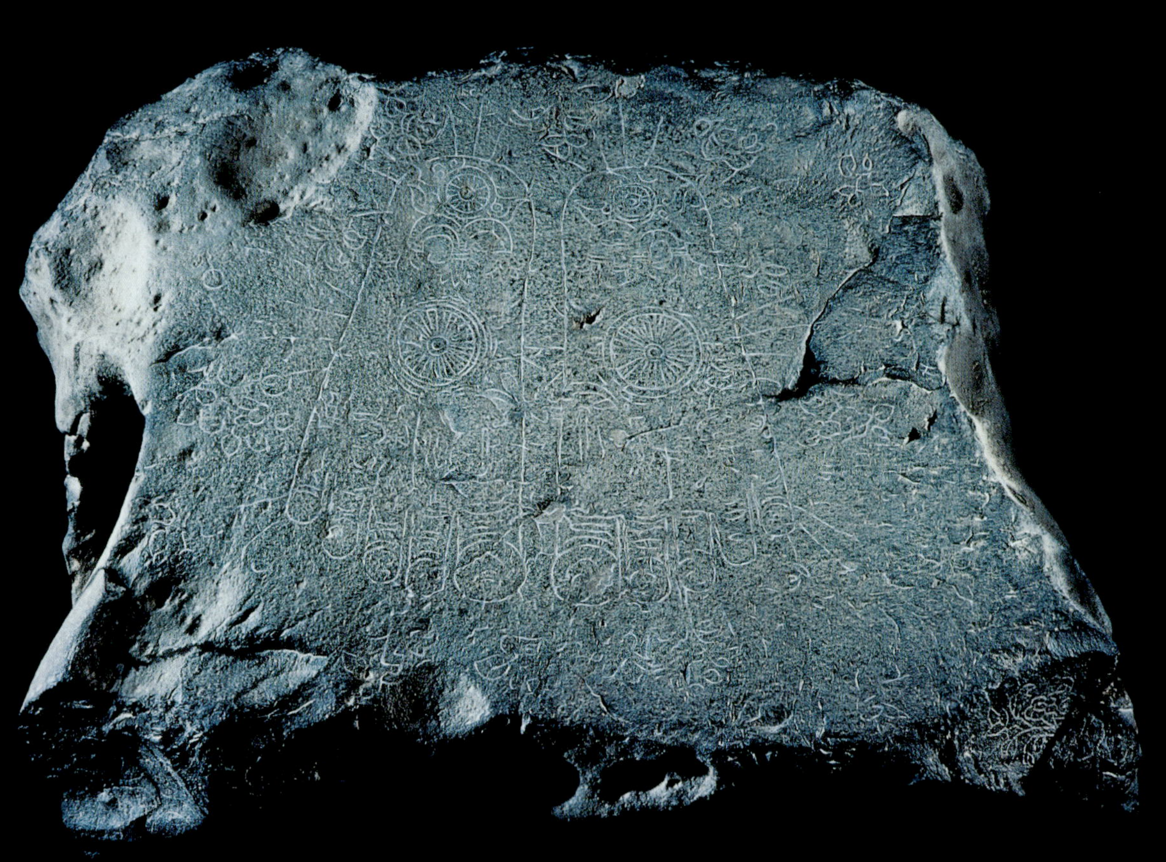

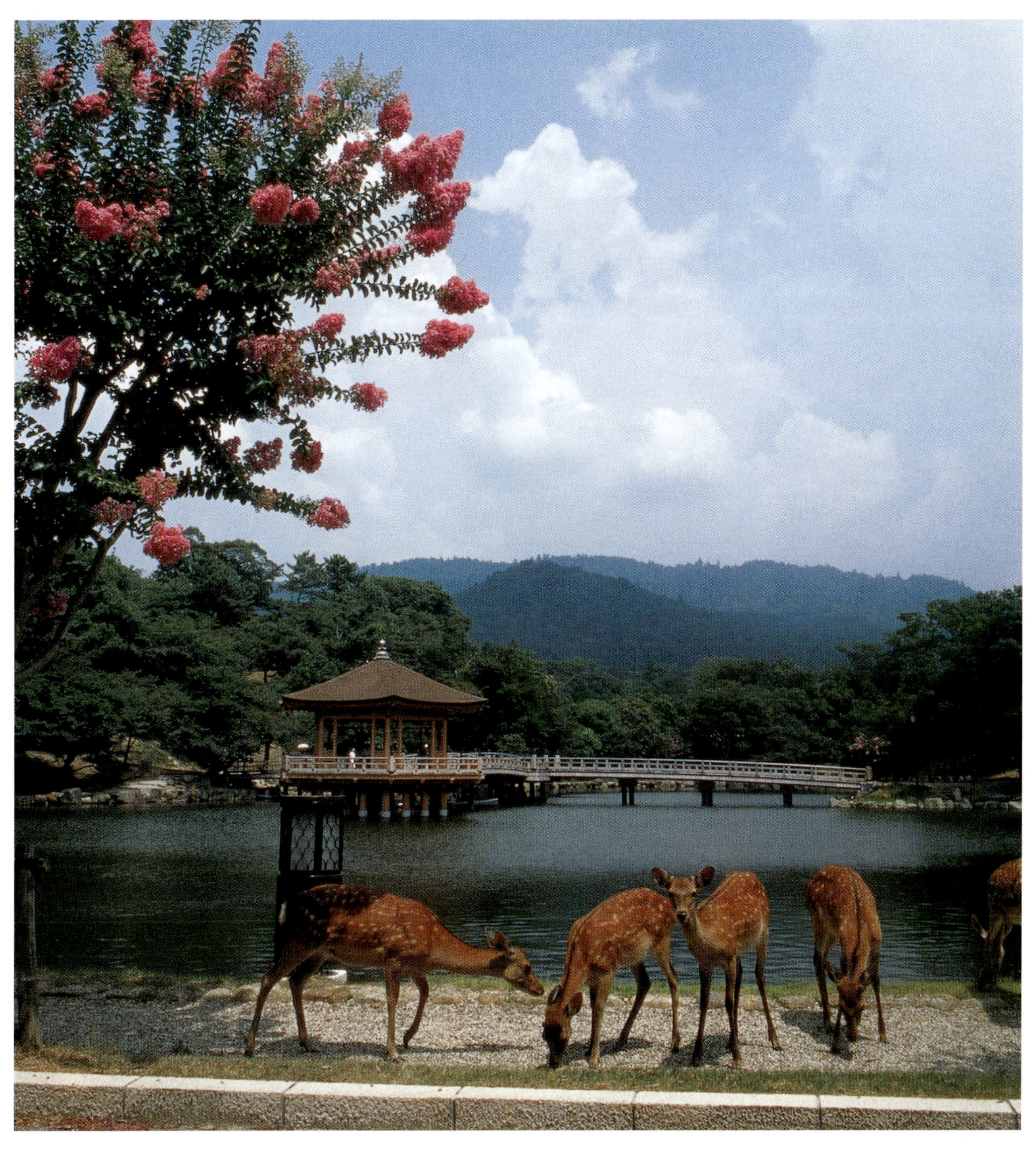

No leaf stirs:

How awesome,

The summer grove!

Masaoka Shiki

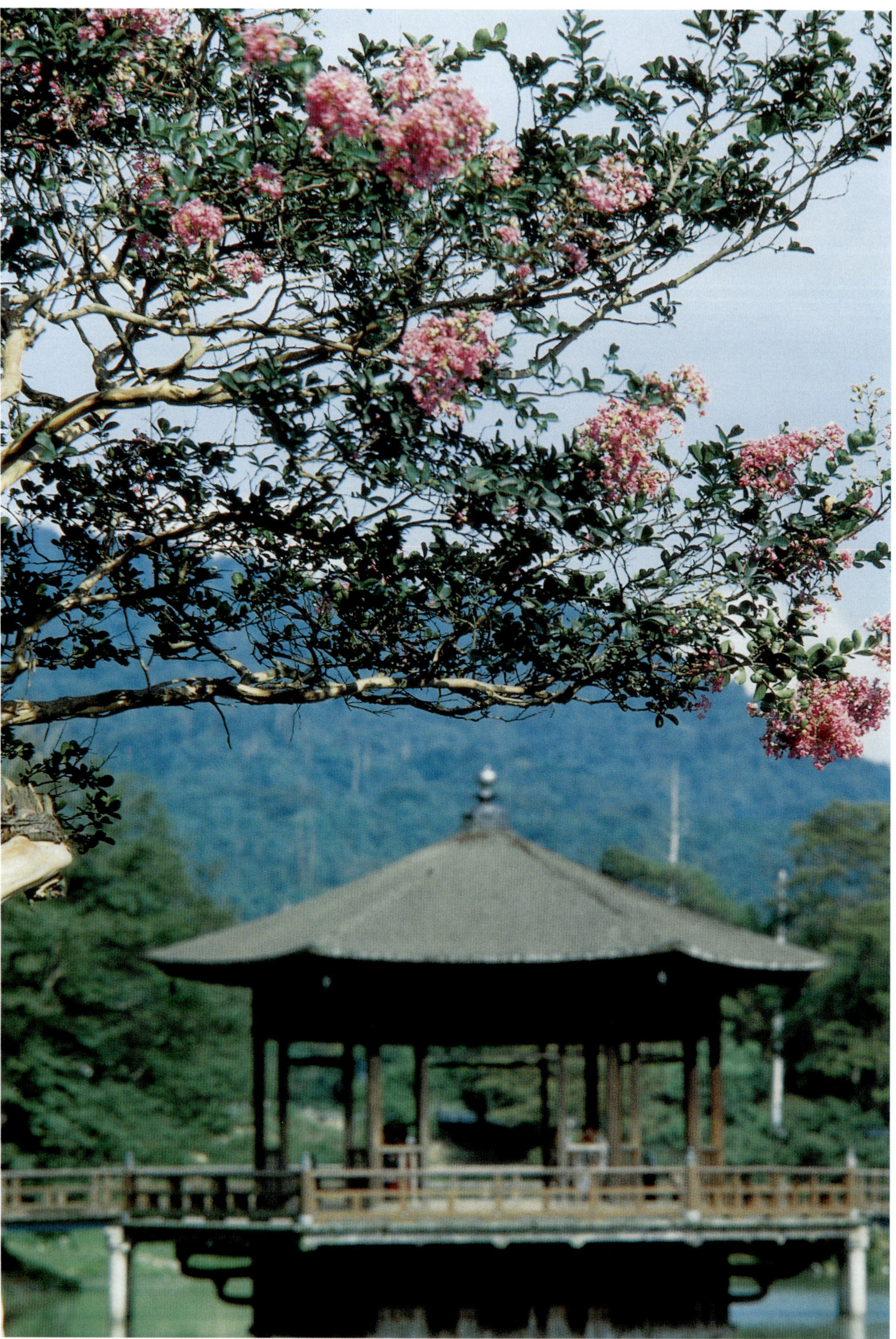

*S*agi Pond was ringed with glowing red azaleas. Boats were floating in the summer sun reflecting off the water. I rested at the Ukimidō [Floating Pavilion], soothed by the wind blowing over the pond.

If only I might remain a bit longer

In this maze of a world,

Lifting up

The torch of Buddha's wisdom!

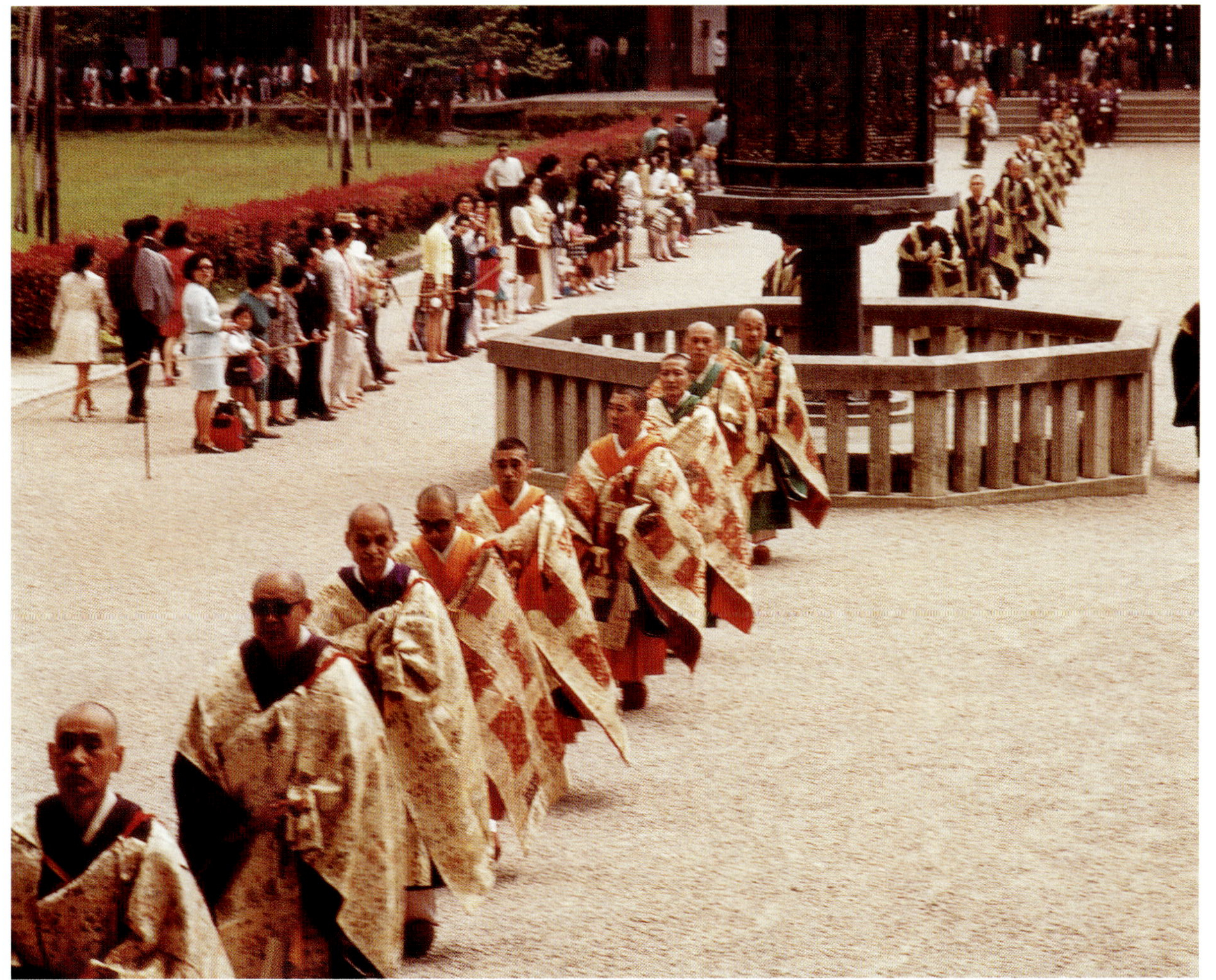

*I*n the third month of the first year of Eikyō [1429], torchlight performances of *nō* were carried out at the Kōfukuji temple. On the fifth day of the month, the Komparu and Kanze troupes were asked by the priests in charge of the festivities to perform in competition. On this occasion, lots were drawn to see who would perform the opening play. The Kanze troupe won, and [my brother] Motomasa performed…

Zeami Motokiyo

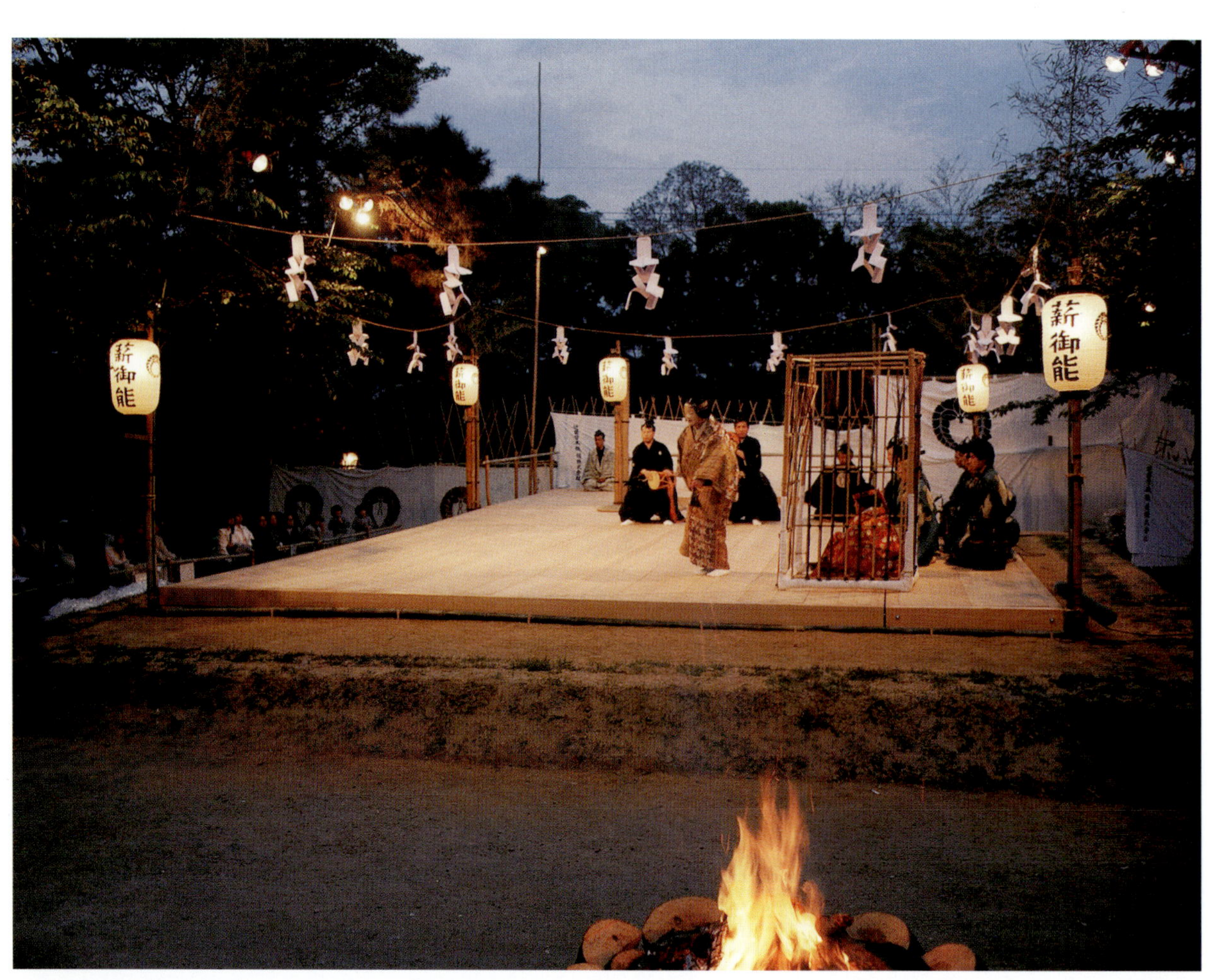

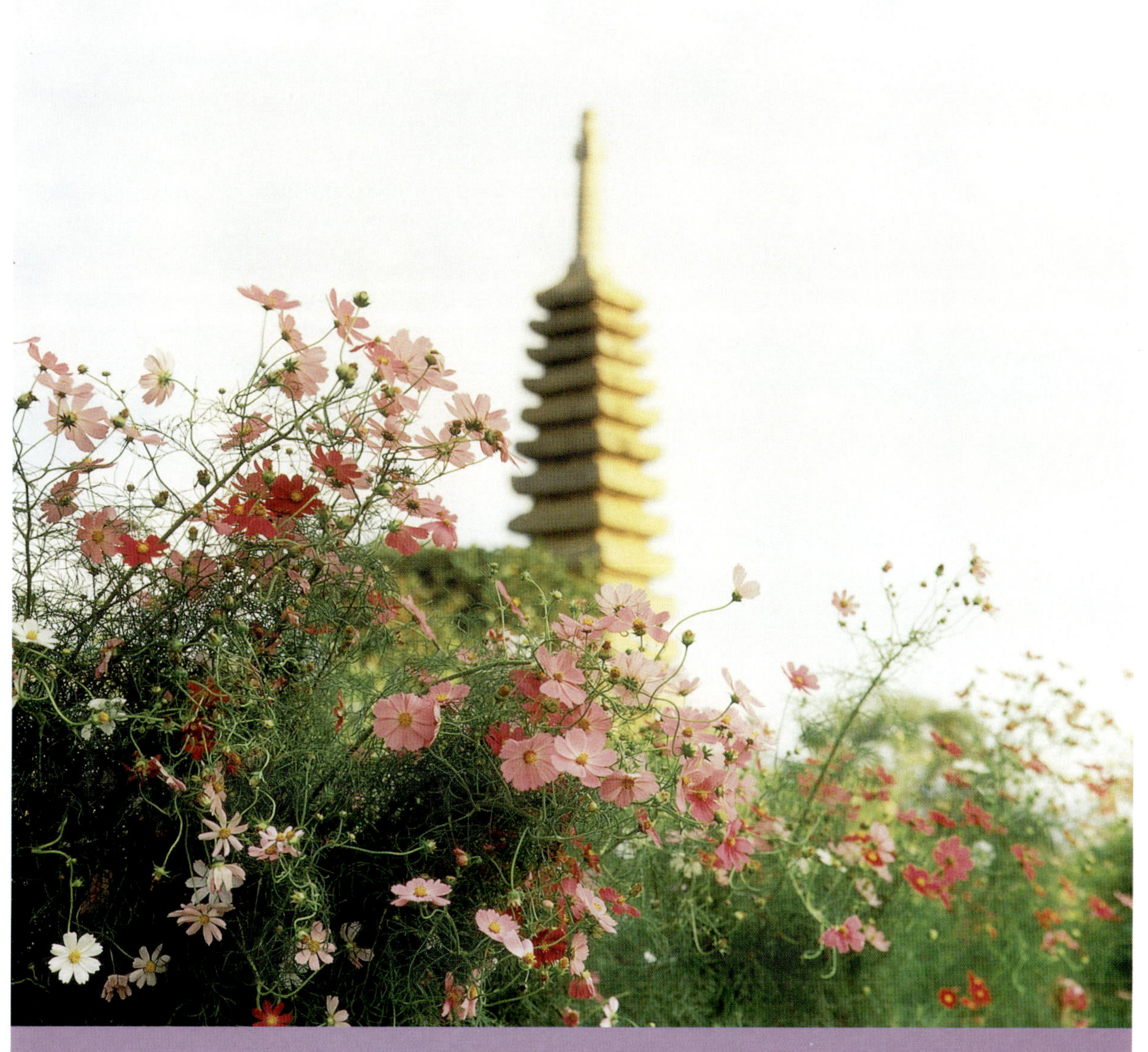

Nara, the ancient capital,
Is now deserted by the
Throngs of old;
Only the blossoms still visit,
Their loveliness still
Unchanged.

EMPEROR HEIZEI

In the deep mountain recesses

I could grasp

The meaning of existence

In the blowing wind.

FUJIWARA NO YOSHITSUNE

*I*n the kingdom of Miyako there is a densely populated city called Nara which has many large and rich temples; I spent some days there and saw three outstanding things of note. One of them is a great metal idol as big as the tower of the gate of Evora, which, as it is in Portugal, I may use as a comparison. I am not mistaken in this because a pigeon perching on top of the idol's head looks like a very small bird to anybody gazing up from below. I do not know how many paces long is the idol's hand, but its face would be about four spans broad. Two other statues, almost as big, are found on either side of the idol; there also stand two other statues, wooden and extremely large, which are so fearful that when I went up to them I was lost in admiration at the sight of such huge demons. This temple is a great centre of pilgrimage.

GASPAR VILELA

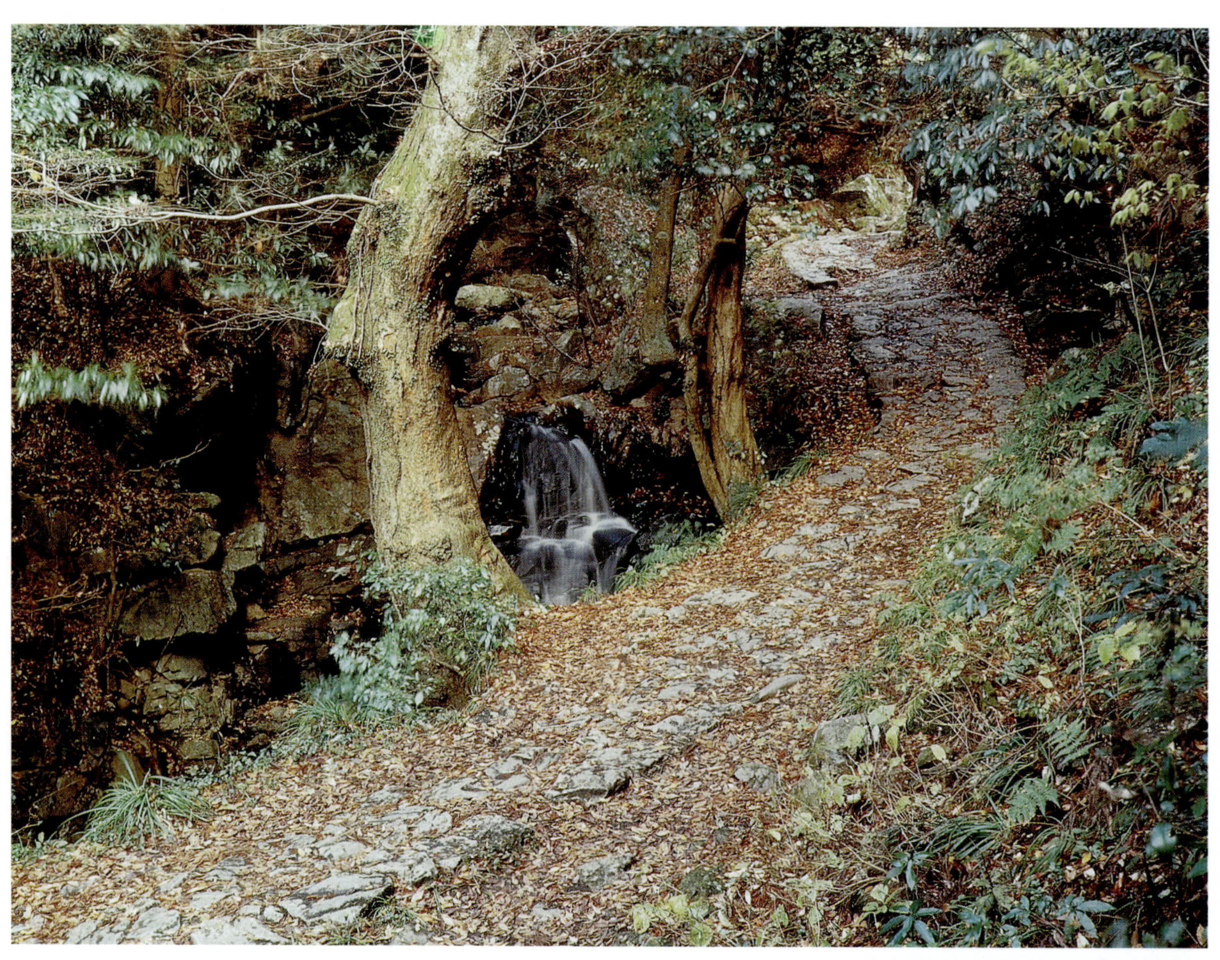

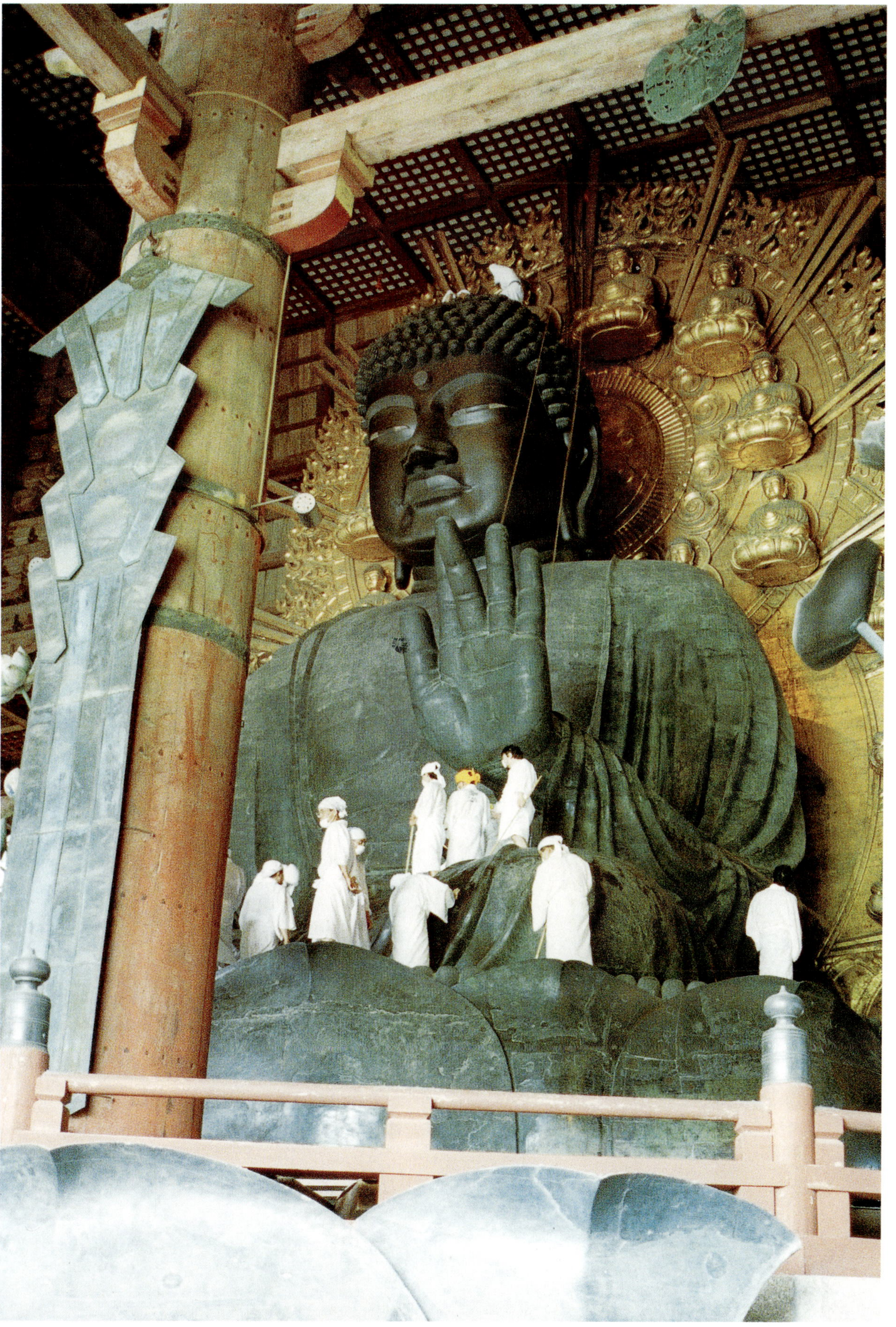

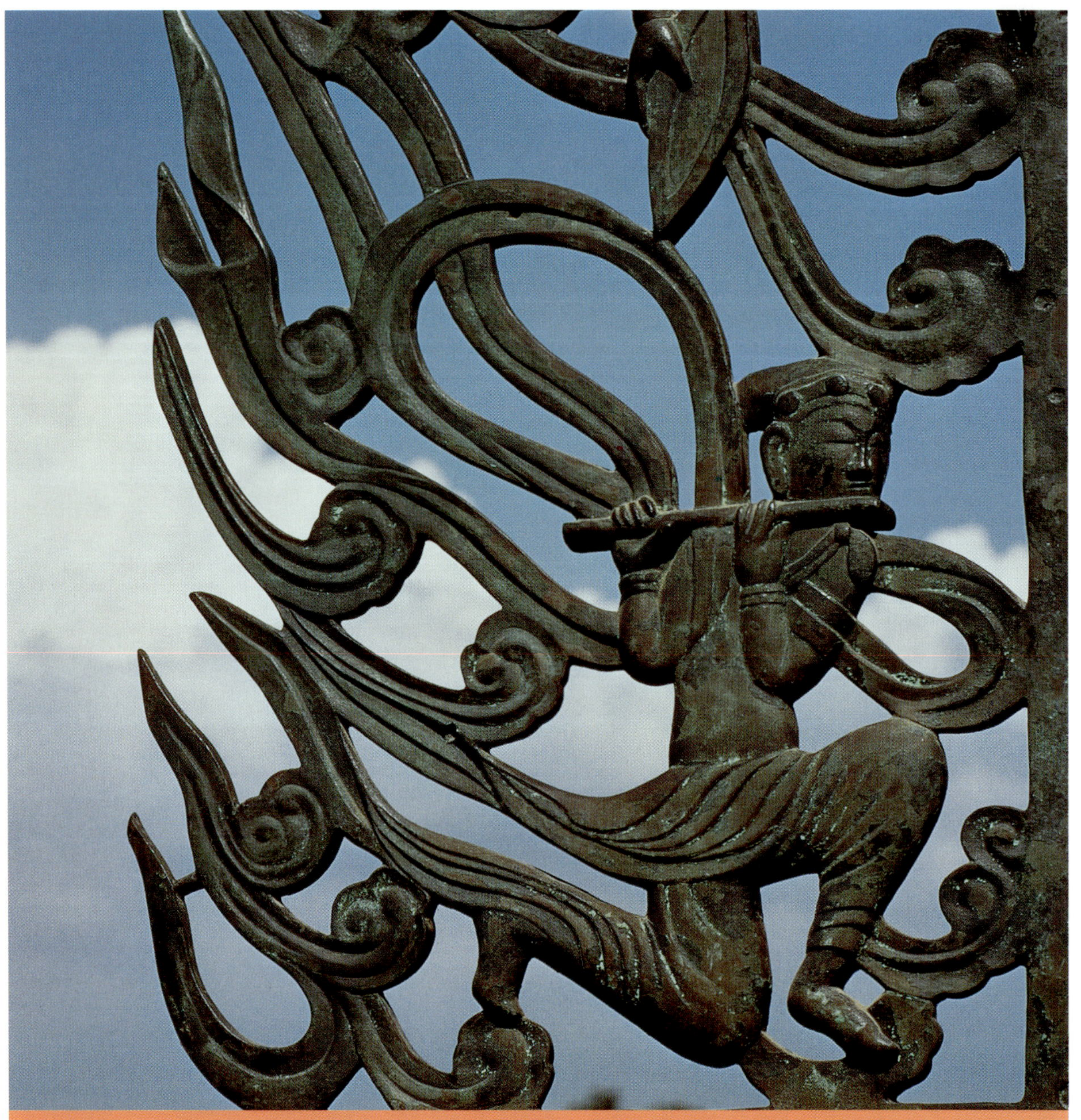

Passing autumn—

Over the soaring pagoda

Of Yakushiji

In Yamato Province,

One strand of cloud.

SASAKI NOBUTSUNA

*T*he second noteworthy thing in this place is the herd of about three or four thousand tame deer which roam through the city. Belonging to the temple, they graze in the fields and wander through the streets like dogs; they are worshipped because of their connection with the temple and the idol. Anybody killing one of these deer suffer death, his property is confiscated and his lineage cut off. If a deer should die in the street, the people living round about are obliged to report the cause of its death; failure to do so brings down heavy punishment on them.

Gaspar Vilela

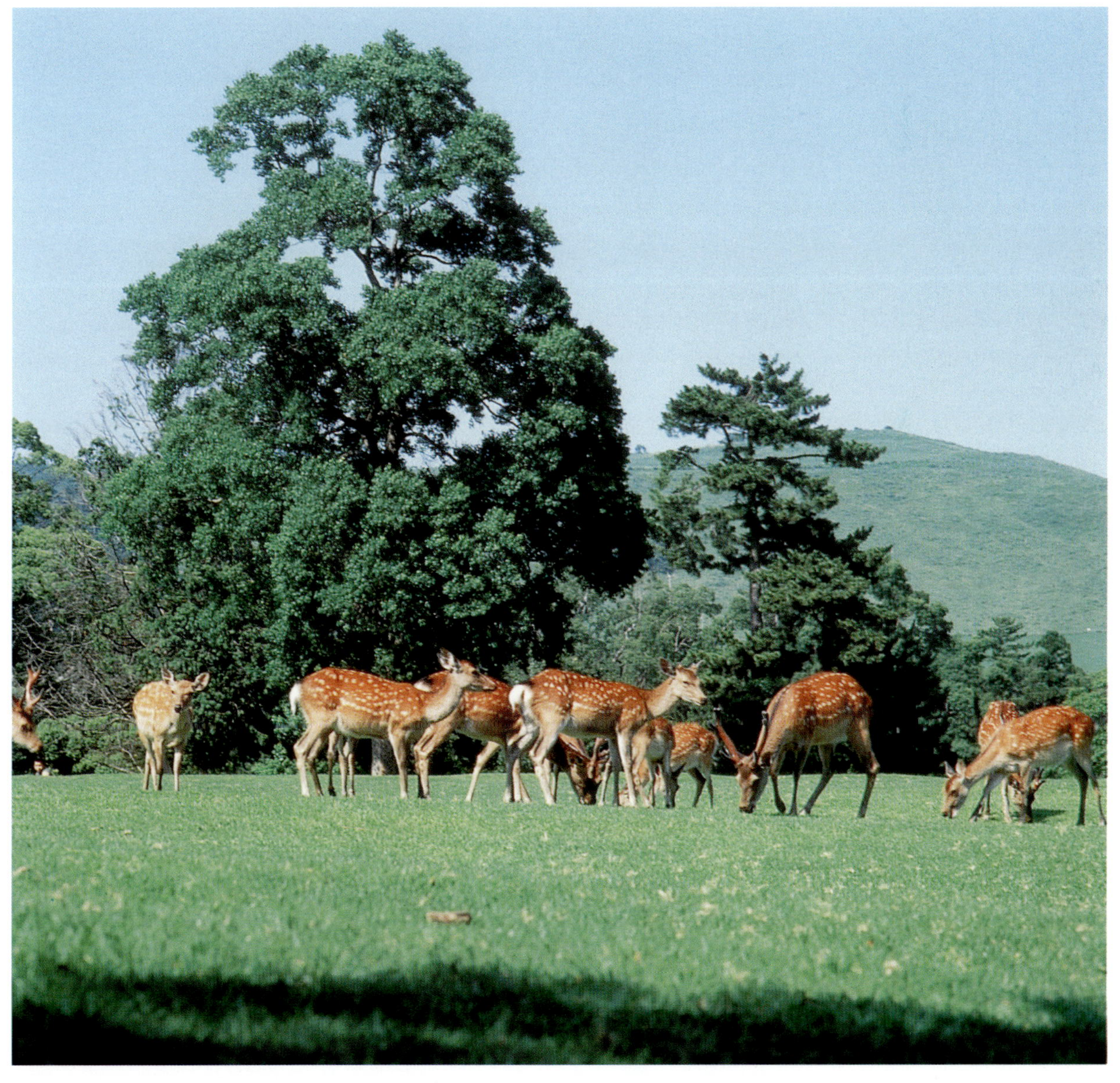

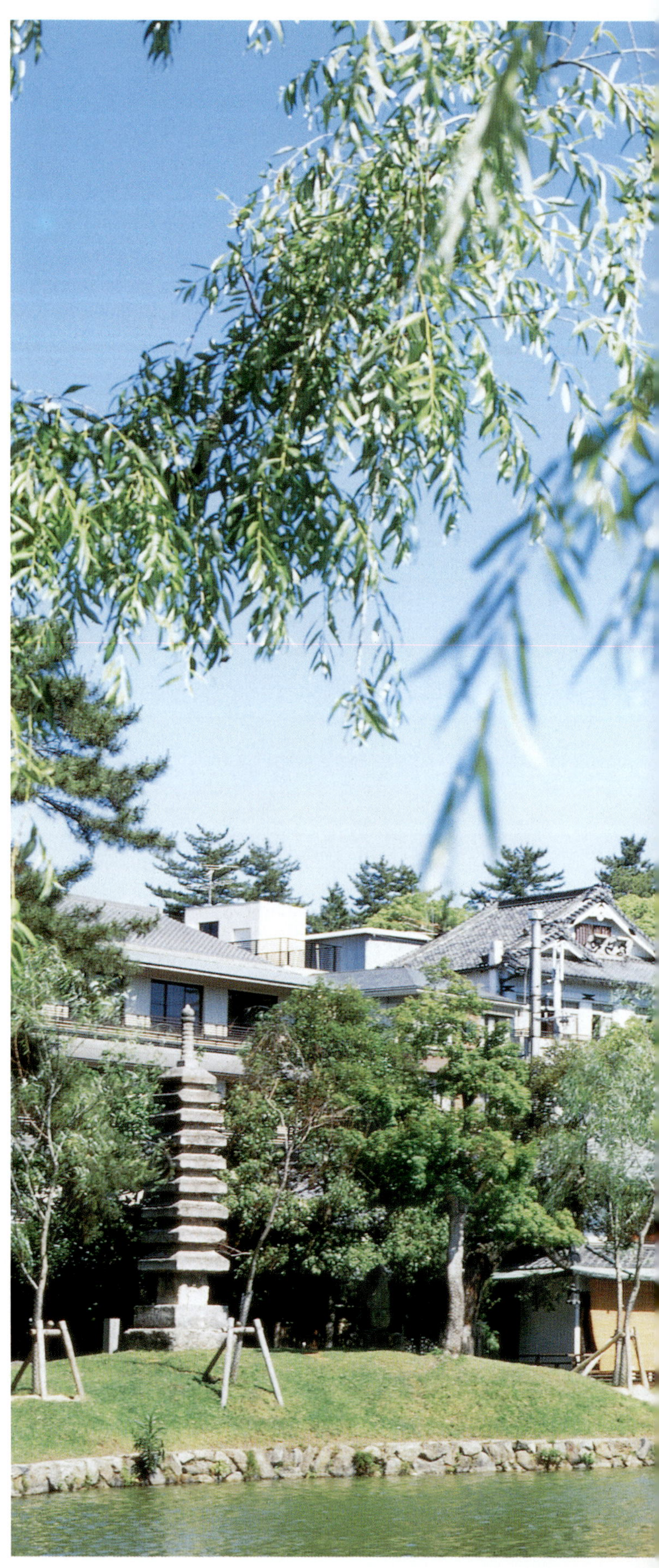

*B*lue hills and pagodas, and temples in the distance, and we came to Nara, which is but a breath, a ruin, a remnant of what it was. I have been told so often of the place, as a ruin among rice fields, that I was unprepared for the beautiful layout of what remains—for the well-planned roads and avenues, such as may well have belonged to some great capital, such as would have been heard of by travellers who, returning in days of Charlemagne from the other Eastern cities to Byzantium, might have talked of Zipango. Nothing remains but a few buildings, belonging to temples, but their approaches are splendid.

John La Farge

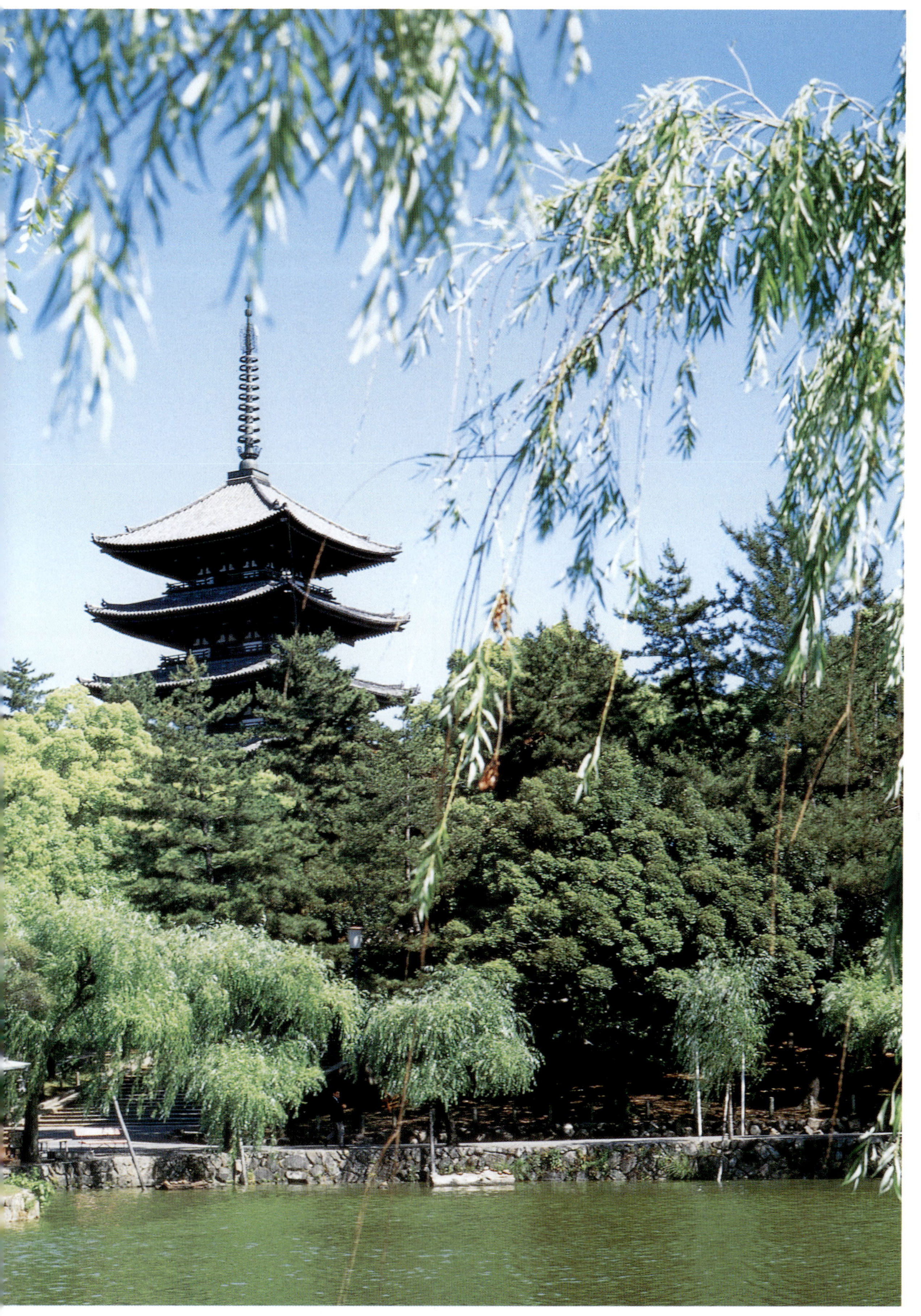

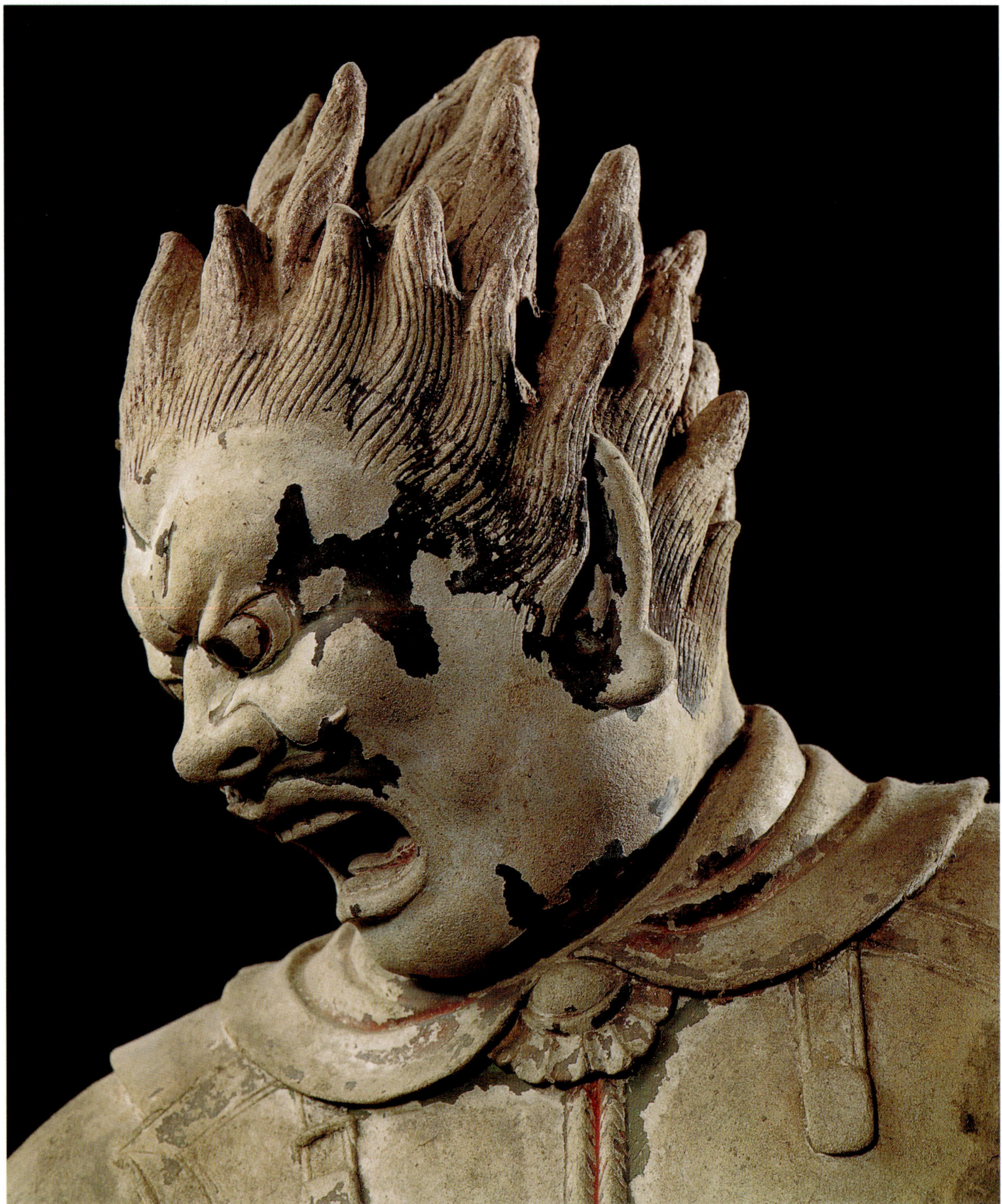

*T*hese Twelve Warriors are believed to protect the faithful by presiding over the daylight hours, the months, and the directions of space. Their armies also wage war on sickness. These twelve warriors are also representative of the twelve vows of Yakushi Nyorai. They are said to command the 80,000 pores of the skin, thus defending the health of the faithful in the name of the Buddha.

Louis Frédéric

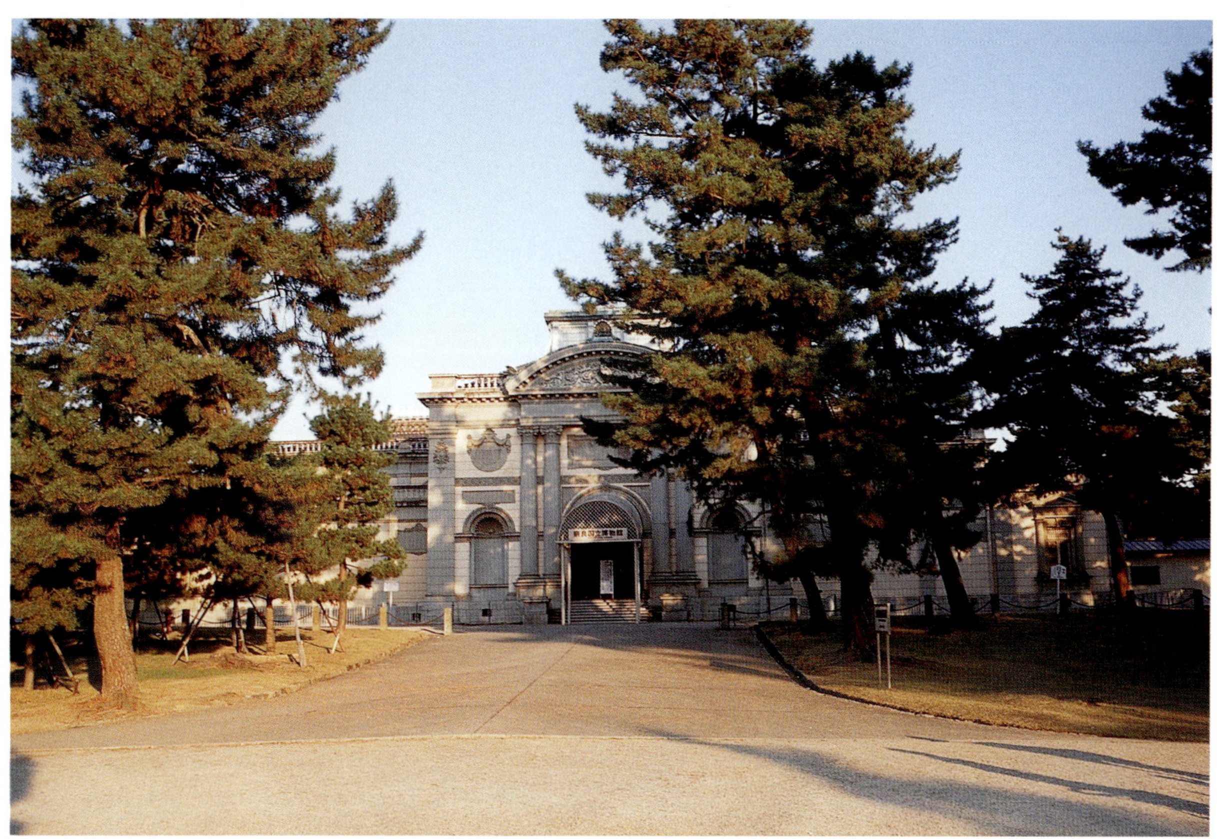

*I*t is not surprising that [Katayama Tōkuma's] Nara Imperial Museum, now a branch of the Nara National Museum, is a striking tribute to France, a grandiose neobaroque building of brick masonry sheathed in pink plaster and trimmed with grey granite. With its central door flanked by monumental double columns, its rustication, rinceau-filled arched pediment, pilasters, balustrades, niches, and swags it seems to have been dropped into this town of ancient temples without regard for the past. It would suit the forests of Marley or Fontainebleu better than the deer park at Nara. It was a bold and modern statement and…provoked controversy and an unusual architectural reaction.

DALLAS FINN

*N*ara is a lovely place, blessed with natural beauty and many fine buildings still intact. No other city comes near its harmonious blend of nature and architecture. True, present-day Nara enshrines only a surviving remnant of the ancient capital; but still, its beauty can be compared to the fragments we find so moving in old paintings by the masters.

SHIGA NAOYA

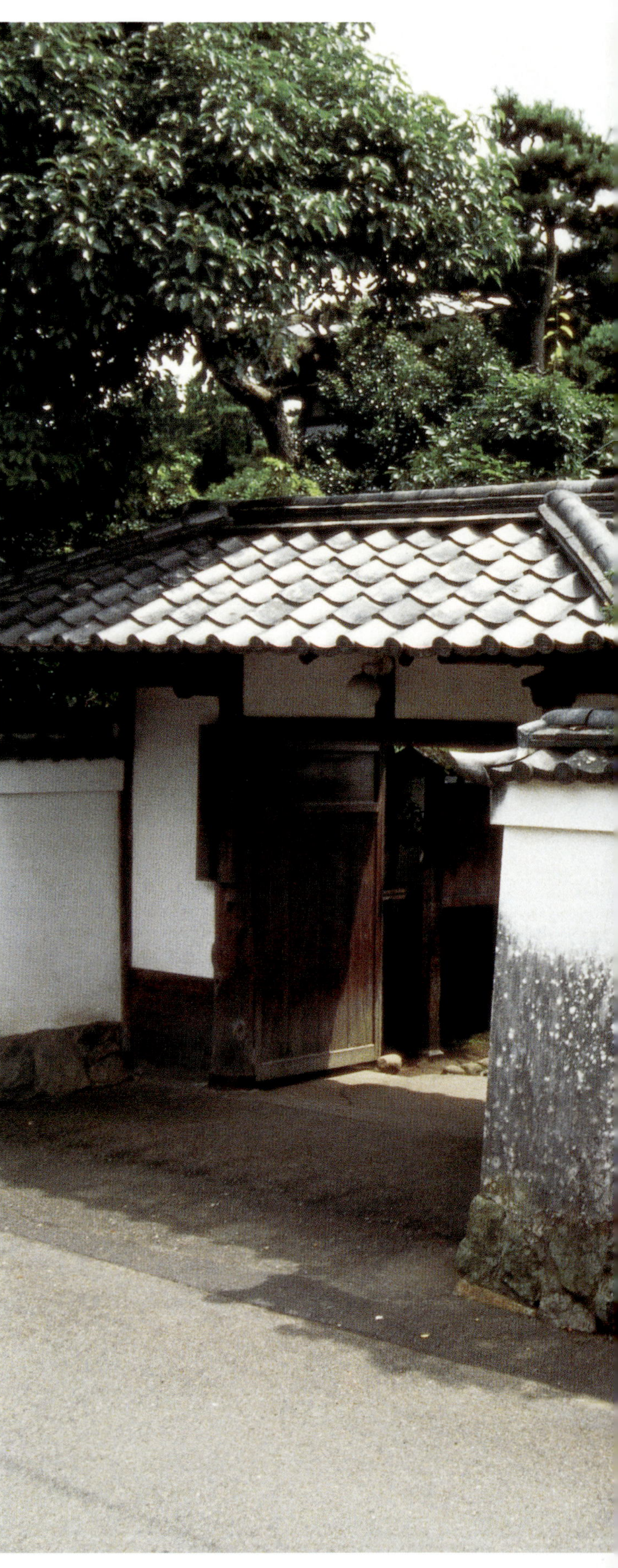

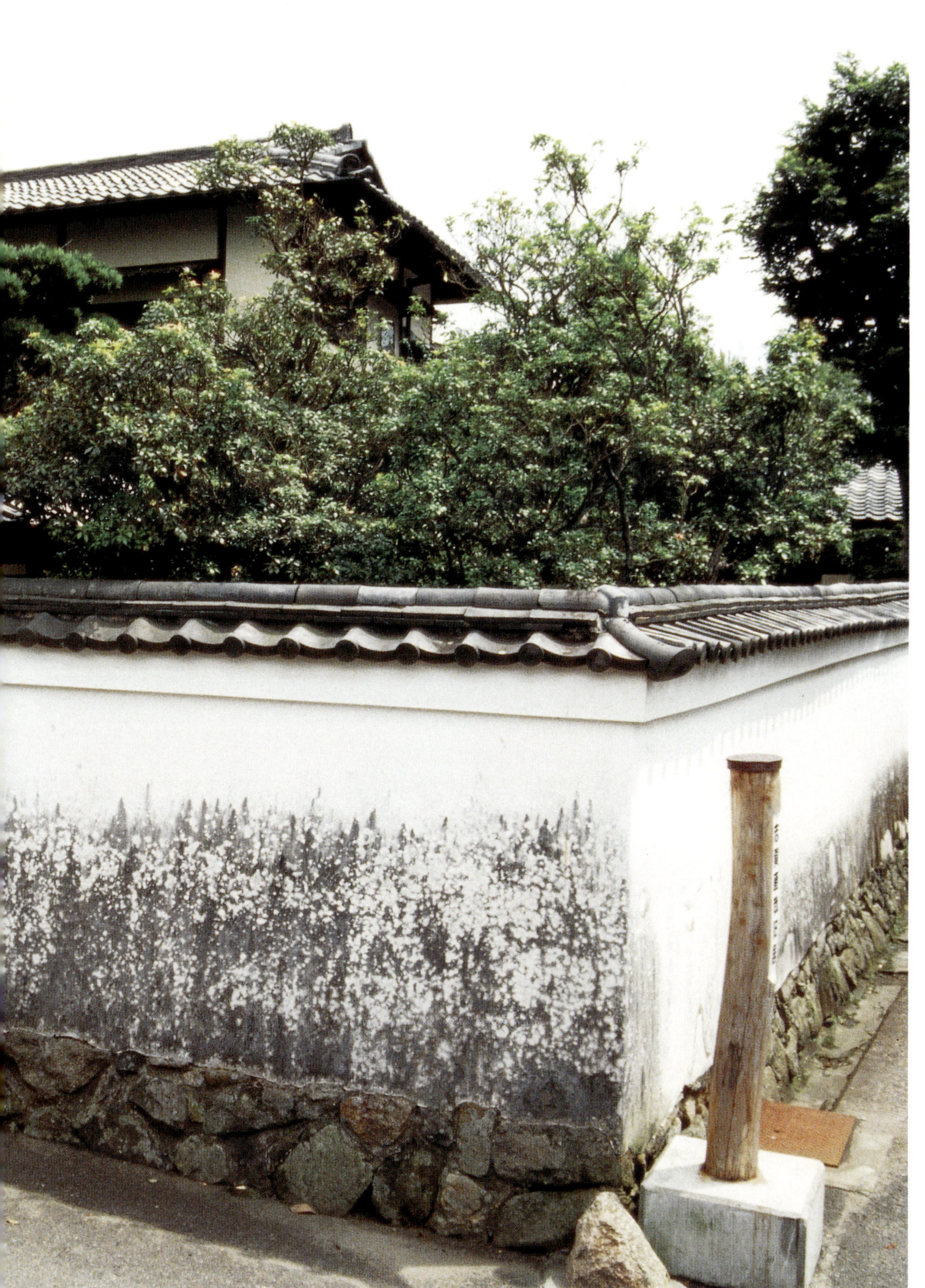

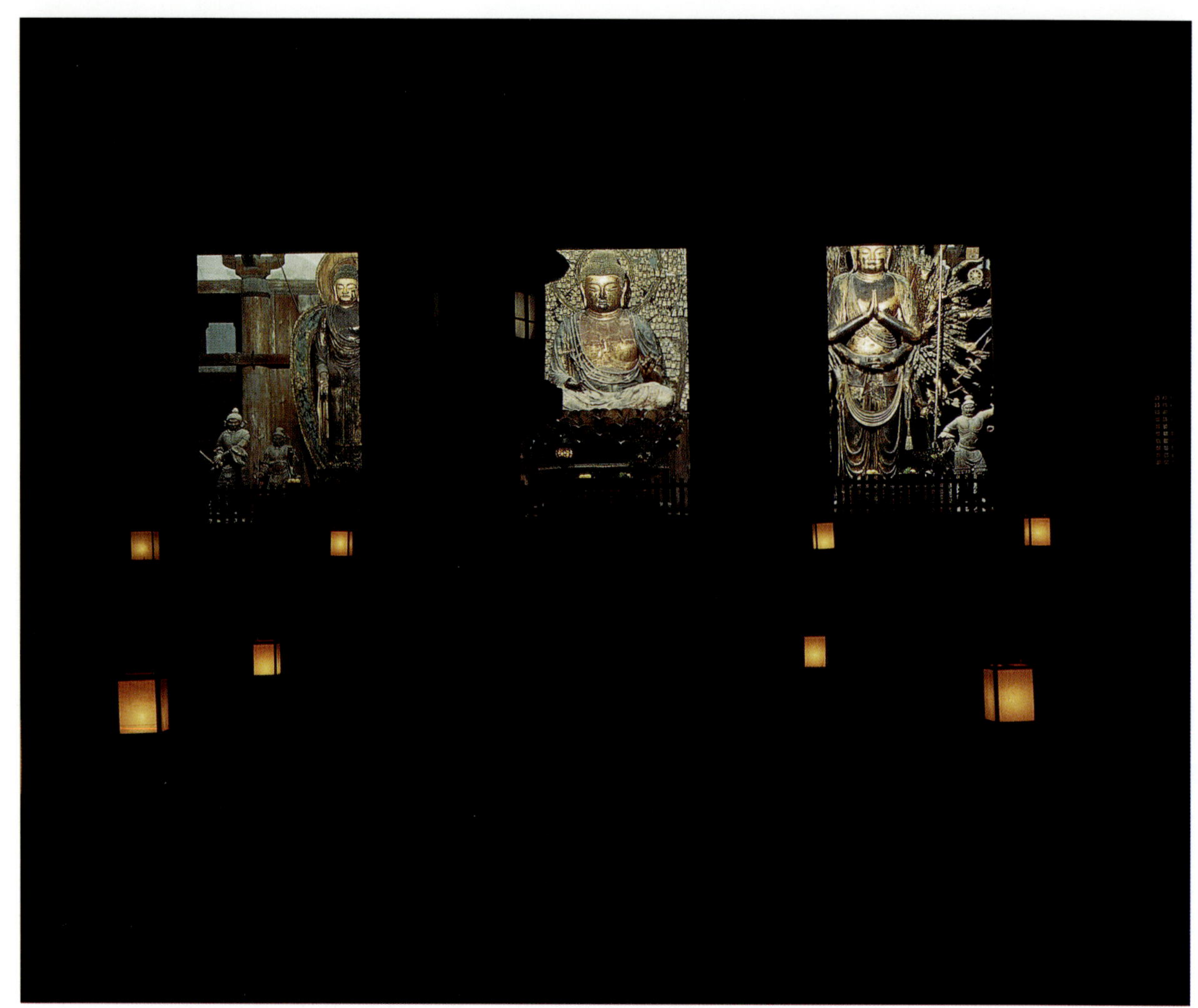

The Bodhisattva:

Sailing in the void of a cloudless sky,

How the moon shines down upon

This world of sadness.

JAKUREN

Just as a stag's antlers

Are split into tines,

So I must go willy-nilly

Separated from my friend.

MATSUO BASHŌ

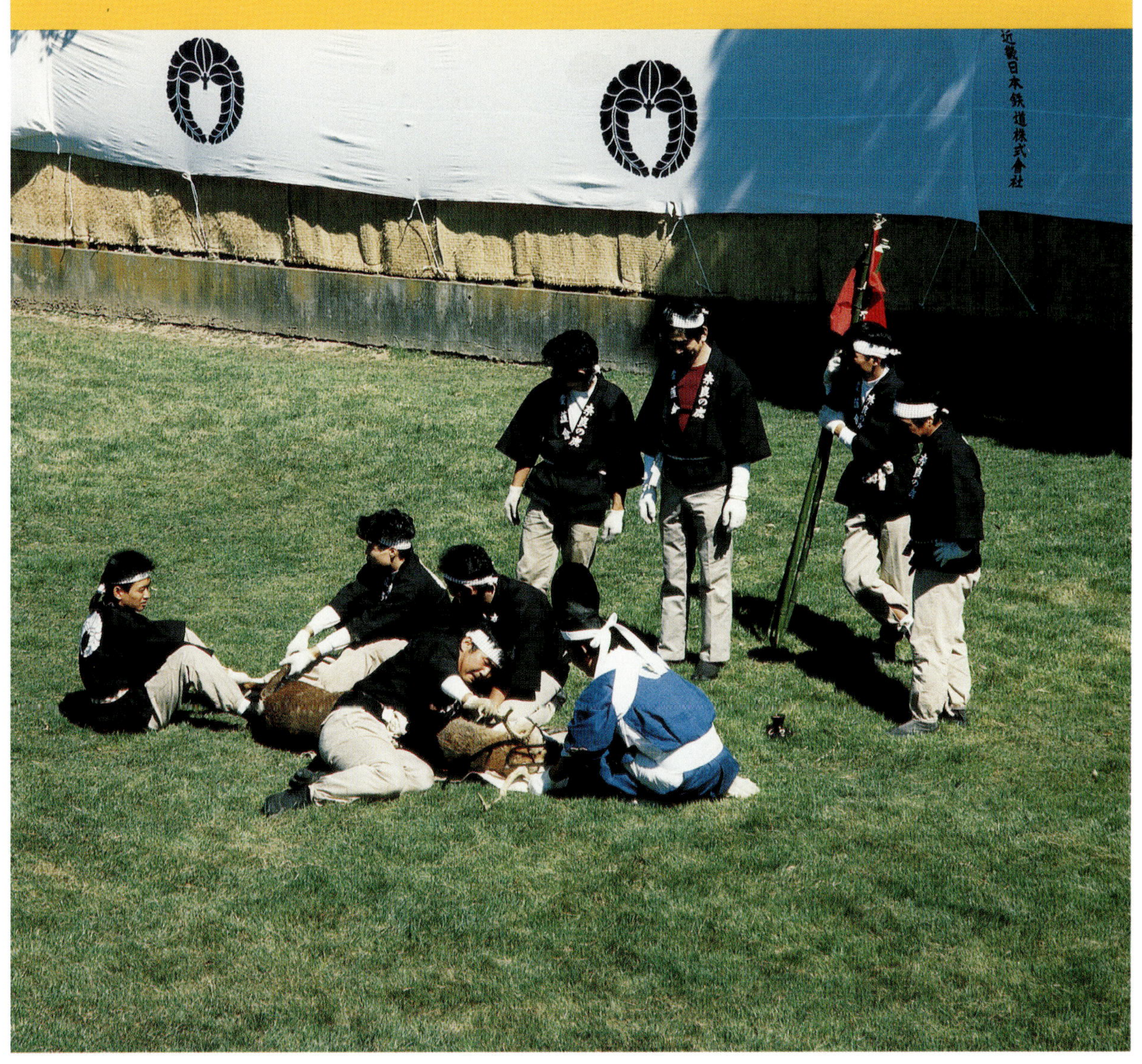

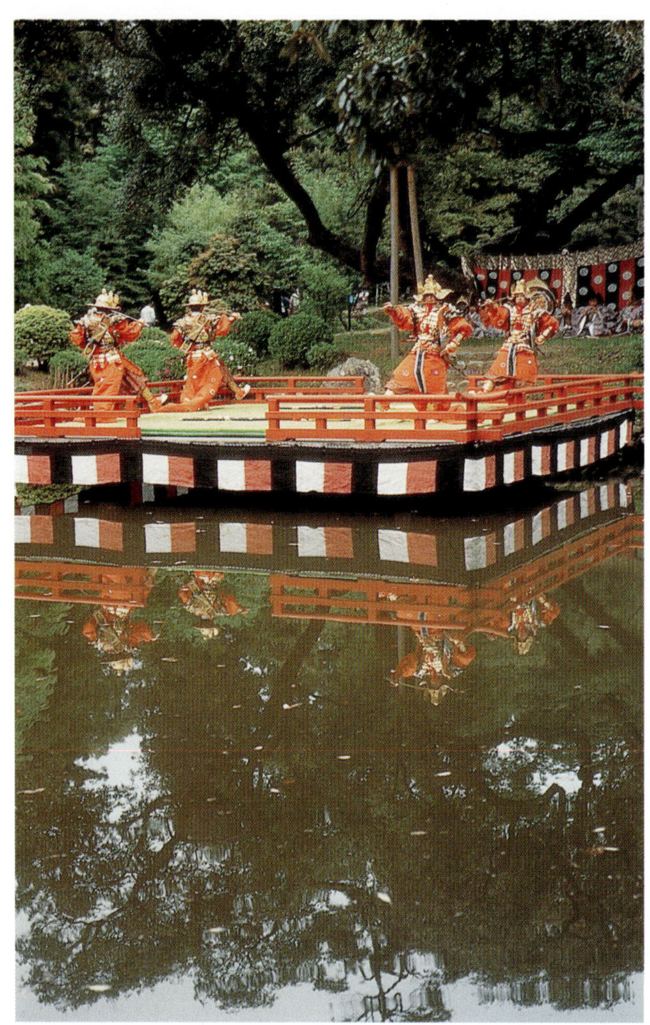

In contrast to those arts whose production actually develops in time, such as the dance, the drama, shadow puppets, even our modern films, I would like to use here the term "solid cinema" —or "solid cinematography"—to define these three-dimensional realizations in which movement is introduced from one part of an image to another, by the spectator. These works of art are, in effect, solid, yet made up of elements in such a way as to give those who see them a sense of purposeful movement in time… In this sense, the image represents an object which exists, first and finally, within *us*.

Paul Mus

The Shintō rituals were celebrated in great style. At the Coronation ceremony of 781, the Daijōsai for the Emperor Kwammu, the musical programme was very rich. Rural songs and folk dances from Echizen and Bizen entertained the assembled crowds. The courtiers from the fifth rank up were admitted to a more refined programme comprising *gagaku* as well as the traditional *ō-uta* obligatory at a Daijōsai. These had developed into a gorgeous affair. At Kwammu's Daijōsai there were dances of female shamans…to the accompaniment of flutes. Grotesque feats and characteristic dances from various provinces were performed in succession, each group marking its entry from a different palace gate.

Eta Harich-Schneider

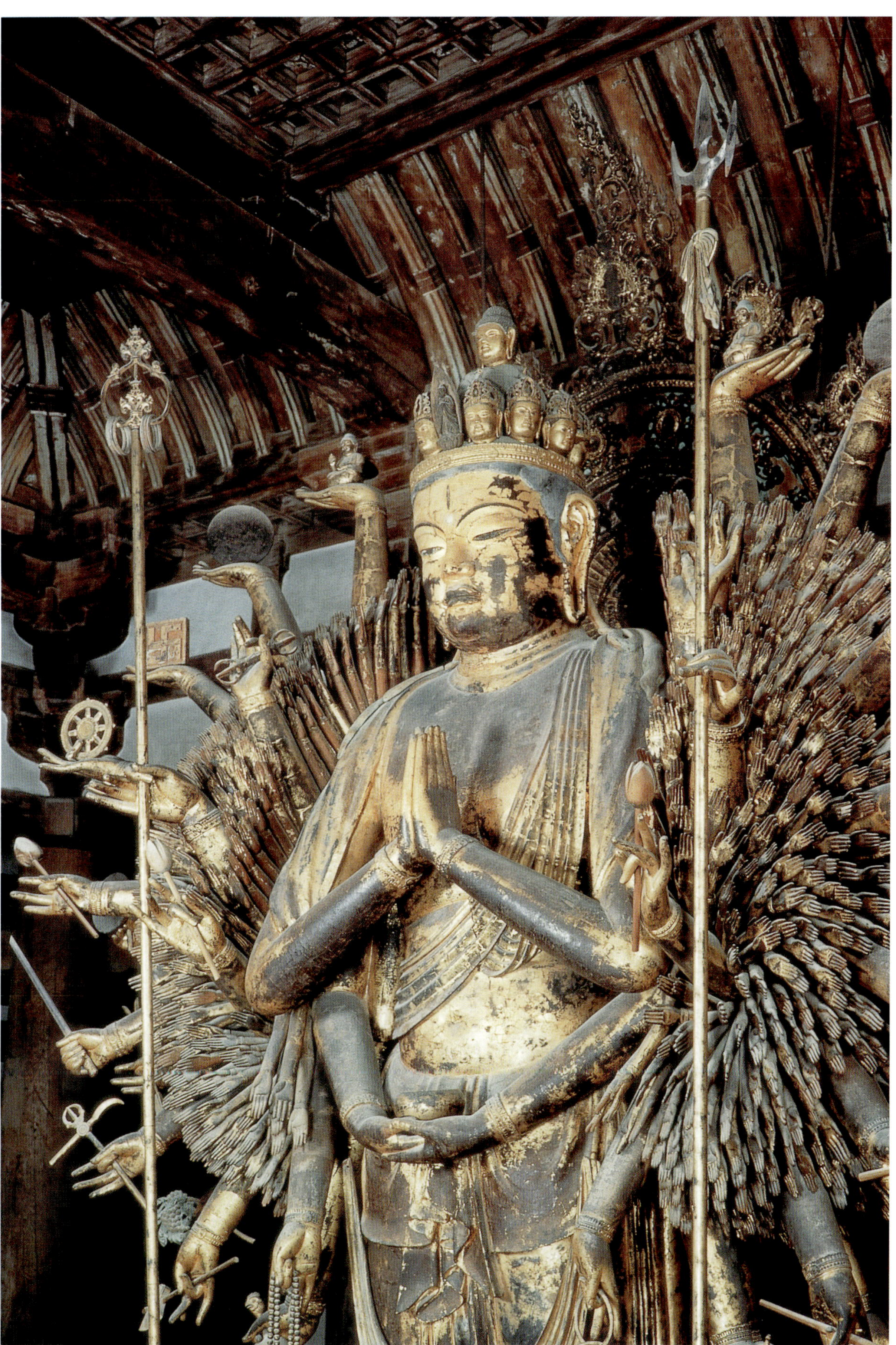

The old man began his story: In old days when I was quite young, in Nara there lived a priest called Kurodo Tokugyo who had an extraordinarily large nose. The tip of his nose shone frightfully crimson all the year around, as if it'd been stung by a wasp… I myself saw him a couple of times in the Kōfukuji temple in Nara. He had such a fine red nose that I, too, thought that he might well be scornfully called Hanazo ["Big Nose"].

On a certain night, the priest came alone to the pond of Sarusawa, without the company of his disciples, and set up, on the bank in front of the weeping willow, a notice-board which said in bold characters, "On March Third a dragon shall ascend from this pond." But as a matter of fact, he didn't know whether or not a dragon really lived in the pond of Sarusawa and needless to say, the dragon's ascension to heaven on March Third was a big lie. It would have been much more certain if he had said that no dragon would ascend to heaven. The reason why he made such needless mischief is that he was displeased with the priests of Nara who were habitually making fun of his nose, and he planned to play a trick on them this time and laugh at them to his heart's content. Your Lordship must think it quite ridiculous. But this is an old story, and in those days people who played such tricks were by no means uncommon.

AKUTAGAWA RYŪNOSUKE

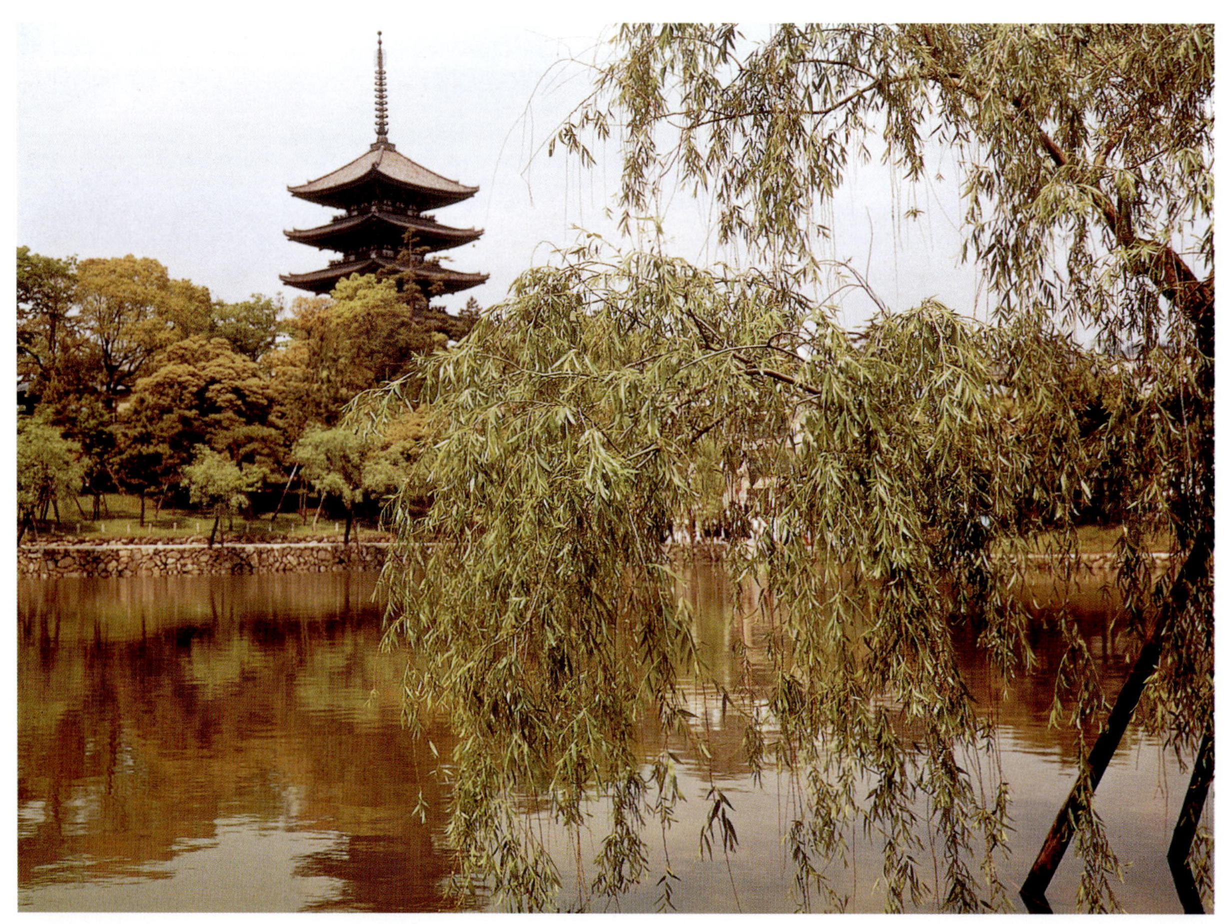

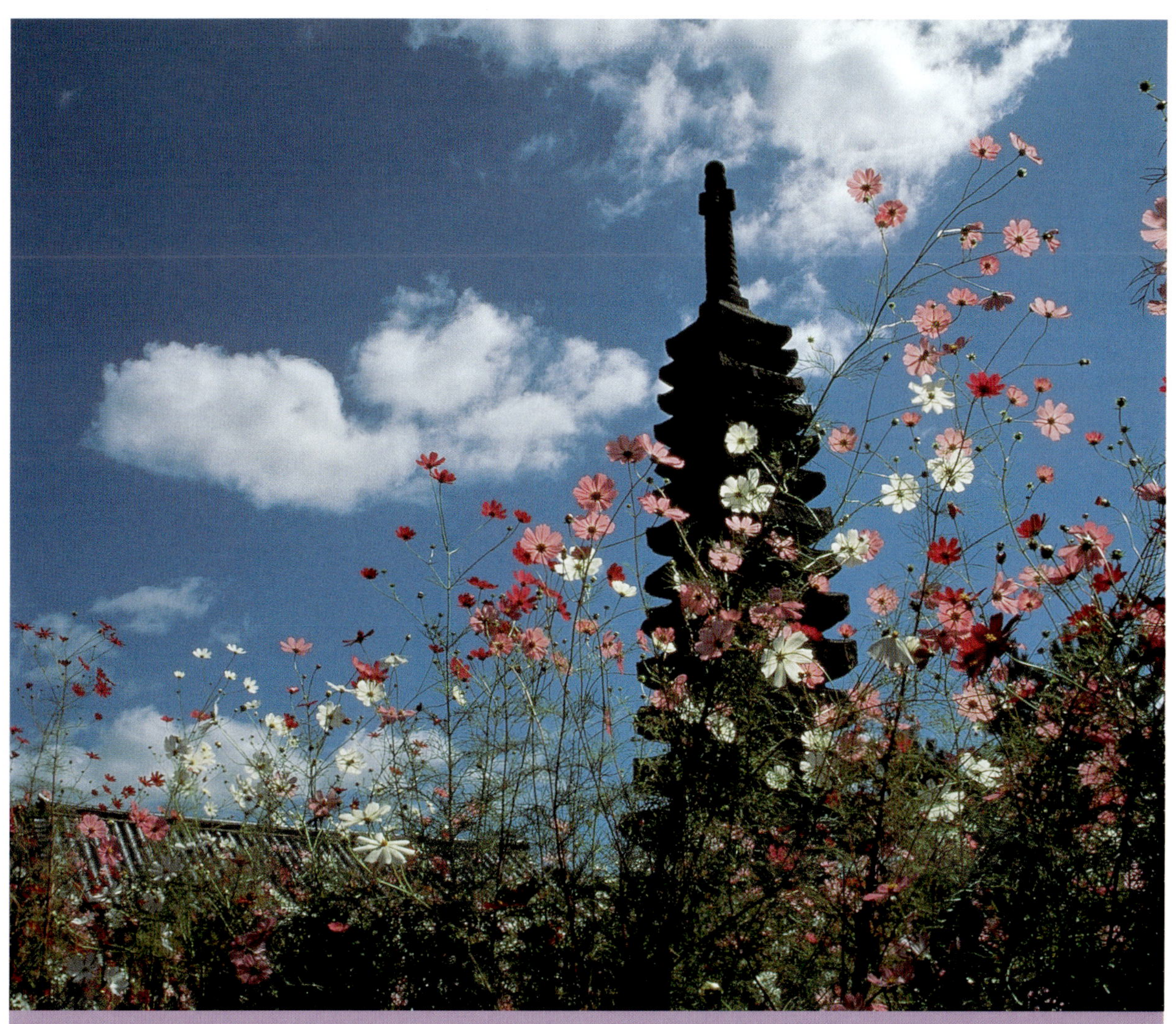

As we behold them, let us praise

The footprints trod in by

The master

Going on ahead to leave us

Until we meet directly:

Until we meet face to face.

The sixth Buddha's Footprint Poem

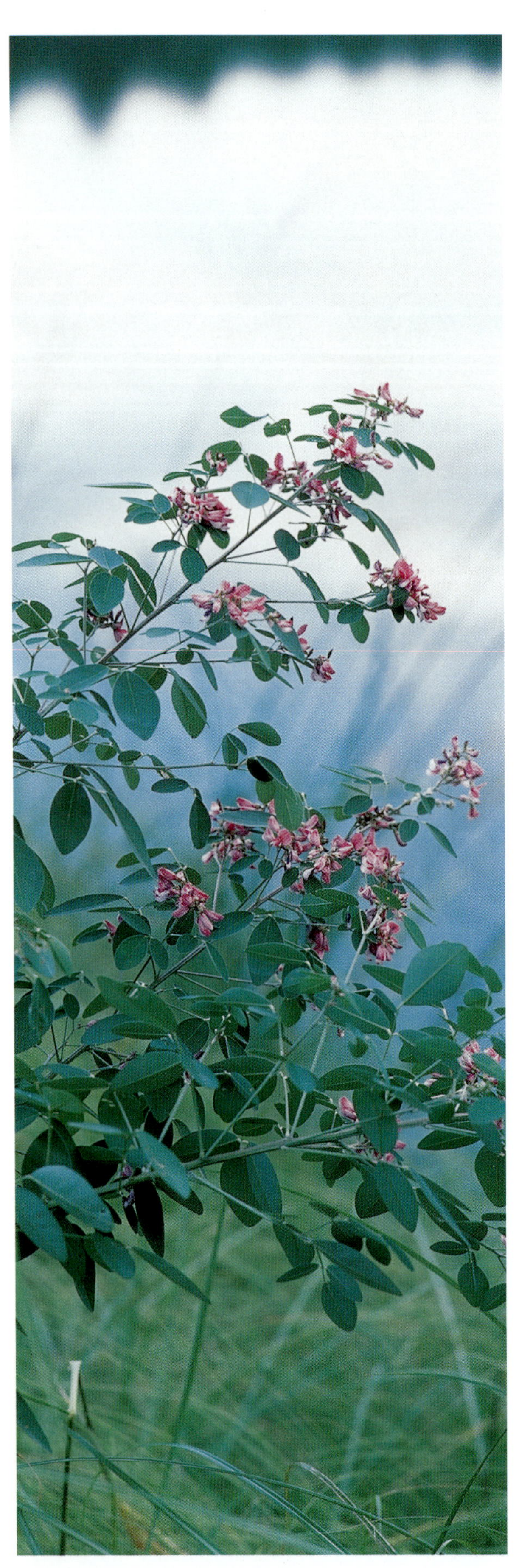

The flowers that blow

In the autumn fields,

When I count them on my fingers,

There they are—

The flowers of seven kinds.

They are the bush-clover,

The "tail flower," the flowers

Of the kuzu vine and patrinia,

The fringed pink, and the agrimony,

And last the blithe "morning face."

Yamanoue Okura

The lower leaves

Of the bush autumn bush clover

Now change their color:

From now on come

Sleepless nights, alone.

ANONYMOUS, FROM THE KOKINSHŪ

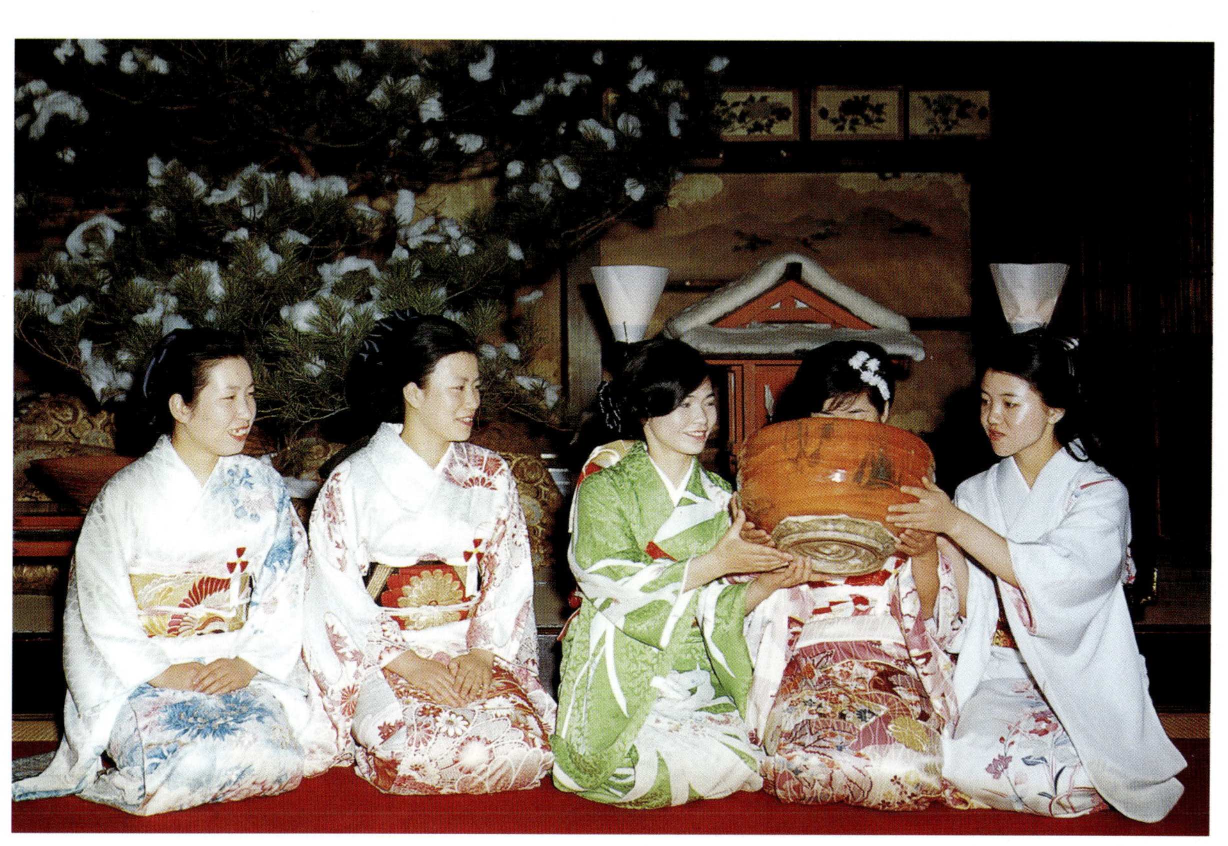

Lightning—

Coming from the north:

I turn my head in that direction.

HASHIMOTO TAKAKO

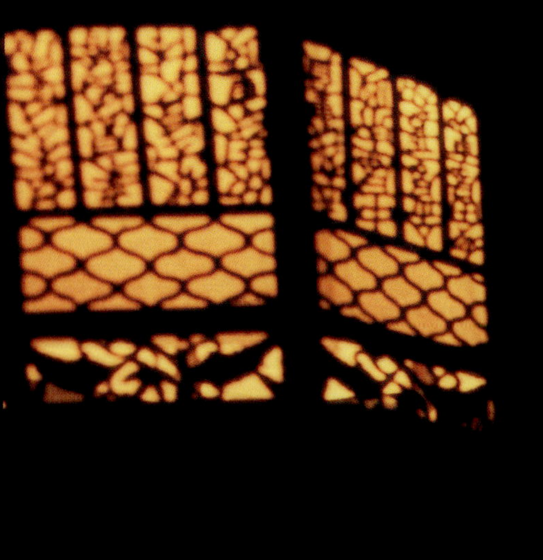
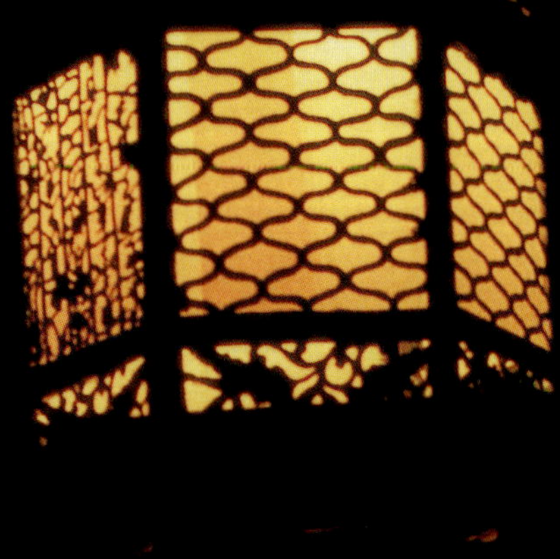
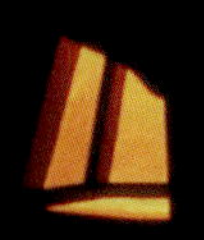
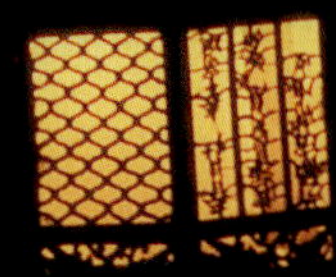
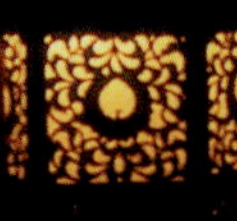
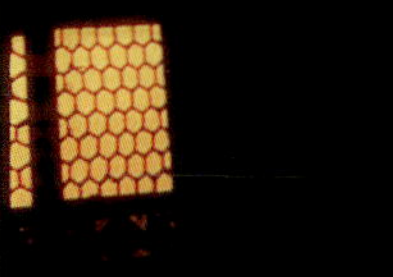
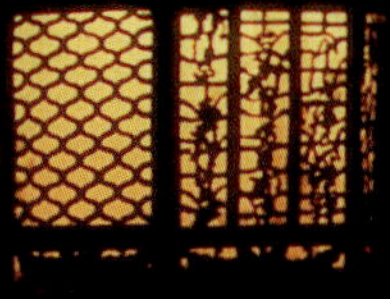

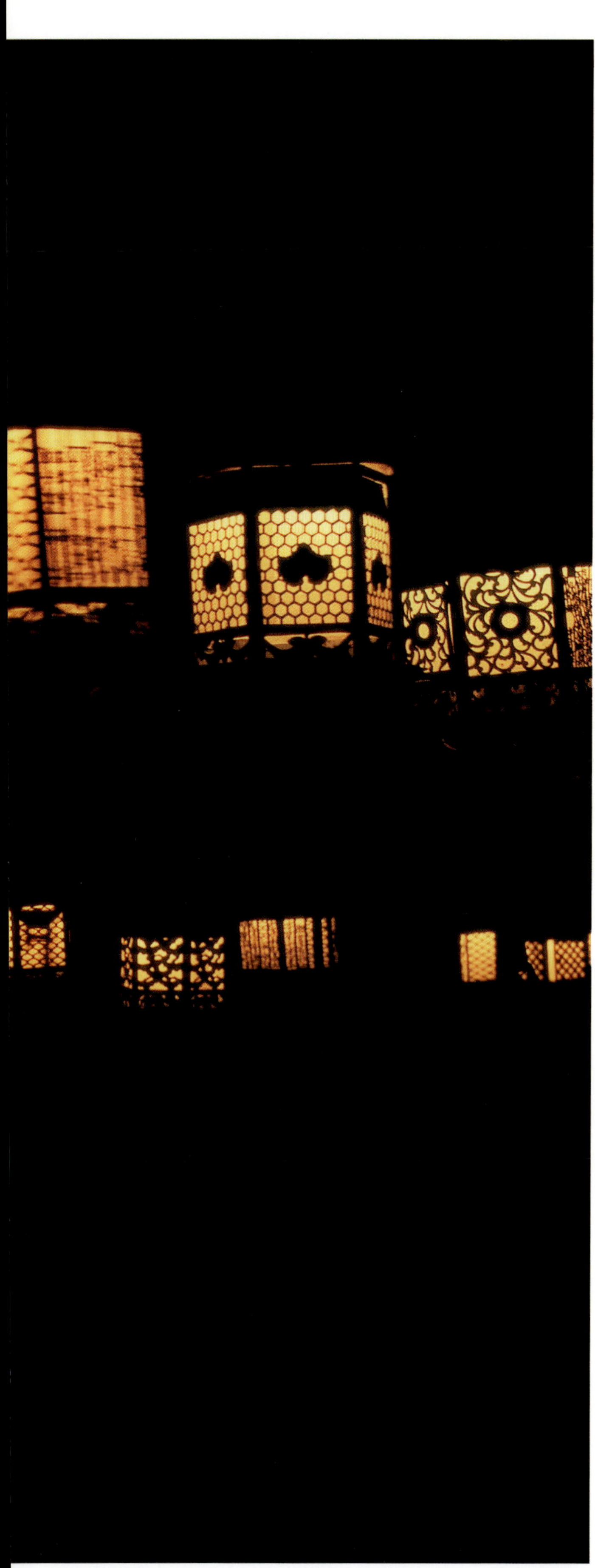

*L*ANTERNS LIT FOR THE FESTIVAL OF O-BON: That their dead should thus definitely live on to them is nothing strange. It is paralleled by the way in which the dead live on in the thought of the young generally. Actual personal immortality is the instant inevitable inference of the child-mind. The dead do thus survive in the memories of the living, and it is the natural deduction to clothe this subjective idea with objective existence.

PERCIVAL LOWELL

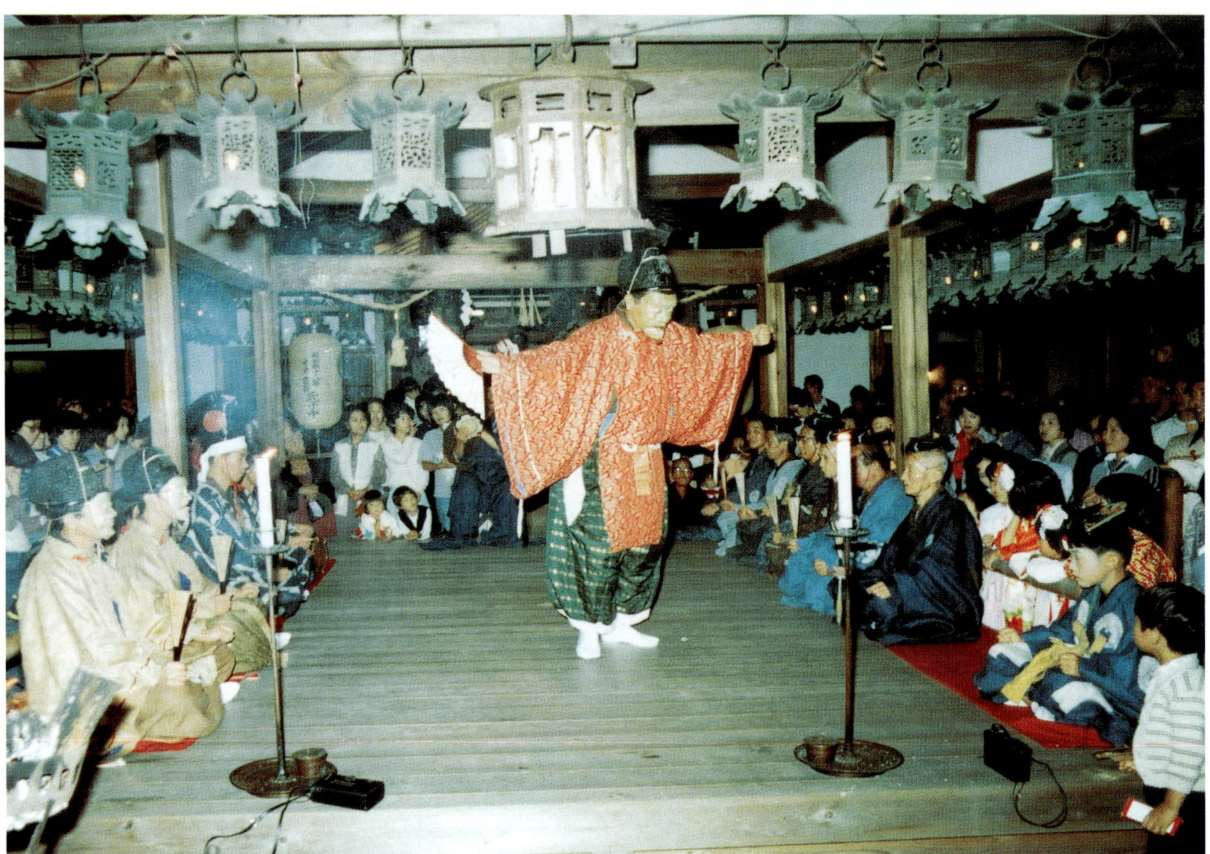

*C*oncerning the proper costume for Okina, it should not be gaudy. The performer should suggest a calm and serene atmosphere when he appears. Costumes sewn with gold thread have seldom been seen in this role. In the old days, the role of Okina was performed, according to the proper order, by the eldest actor of the troupe. At a performance [in 1374], however, the Shōgun Yoshimochi was to see the art for the first time. When the subject came us as to who should dance, only the leader of the troupe, my father Kan'ami, seemed the appropriate choice. Such was the advice given by Nan'ami, and therefore my father appeared in the role. This is how the practice began, and it has become a fundamental principle of our troupe.

ZEAMI MOTOKIYO

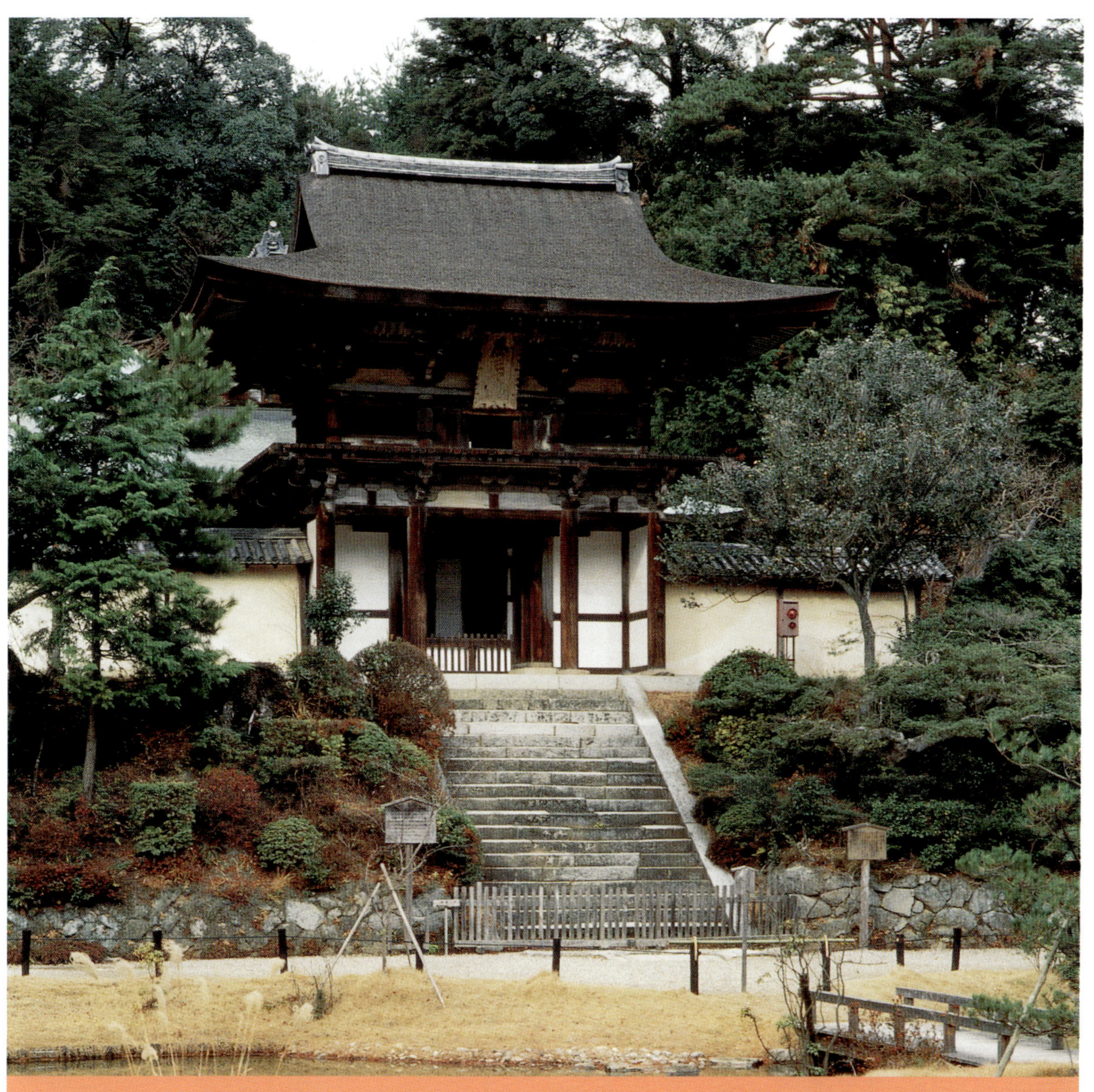

A "Paradise Garden":

The dew remains forever

Upon the flowers,

Blooming in paradise

Without regard to season.

JAKUREN

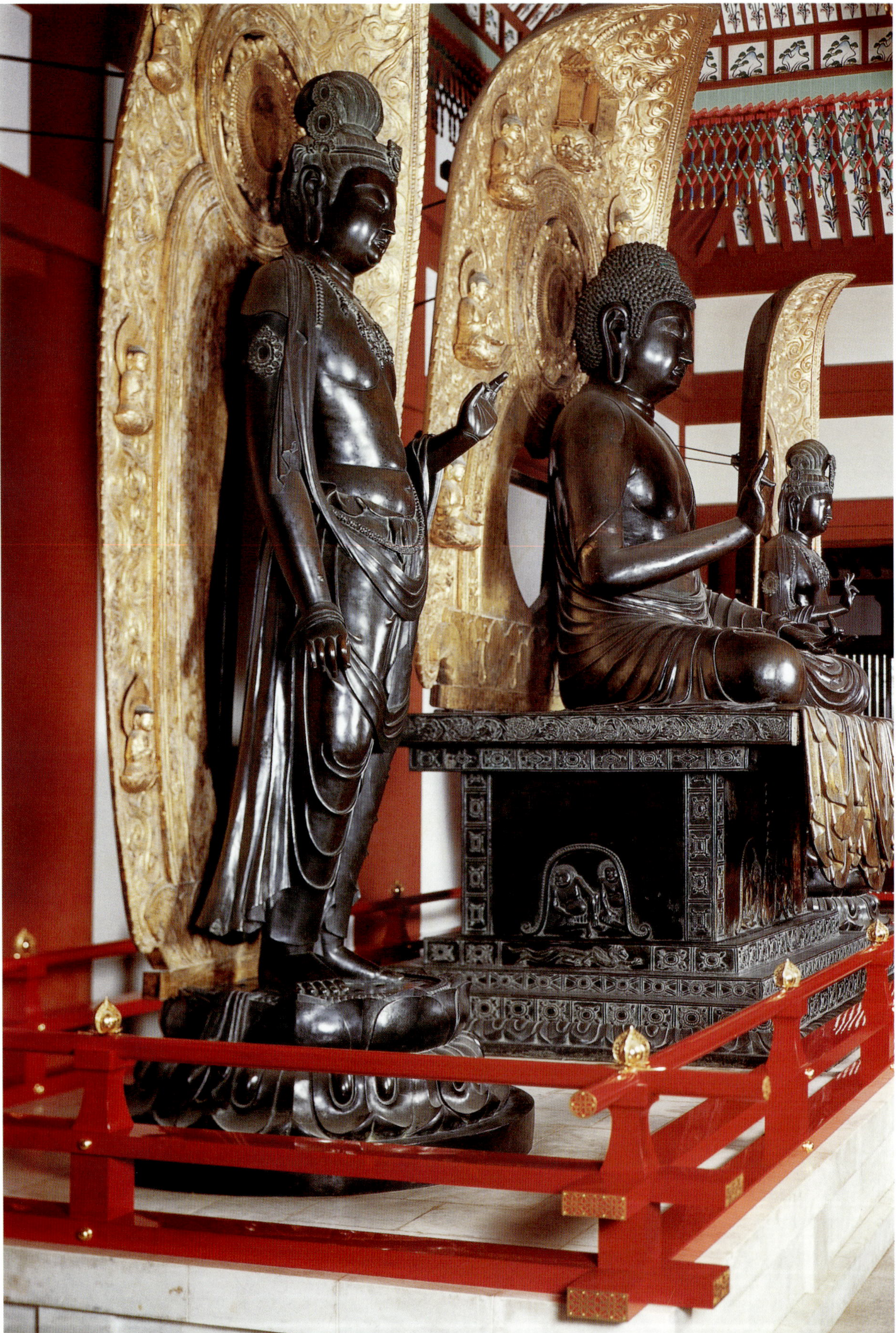

_W_hen I see the elegantly flowing lines of the Yakushi image, all the prayers offered up to it appear to blend and be absorbed by this Buddha of medicine.

The main deity is seated cross-legged on the pedestal, flanked by the Bodhisattvas of the Sun on the right and the Moon on the left. They are in perfect harmony with the Yakushi. This trinity has been fashioned to create a single sympathetic curve, a motion harmonious as music.

KAMEI KATSUICHIRŌ

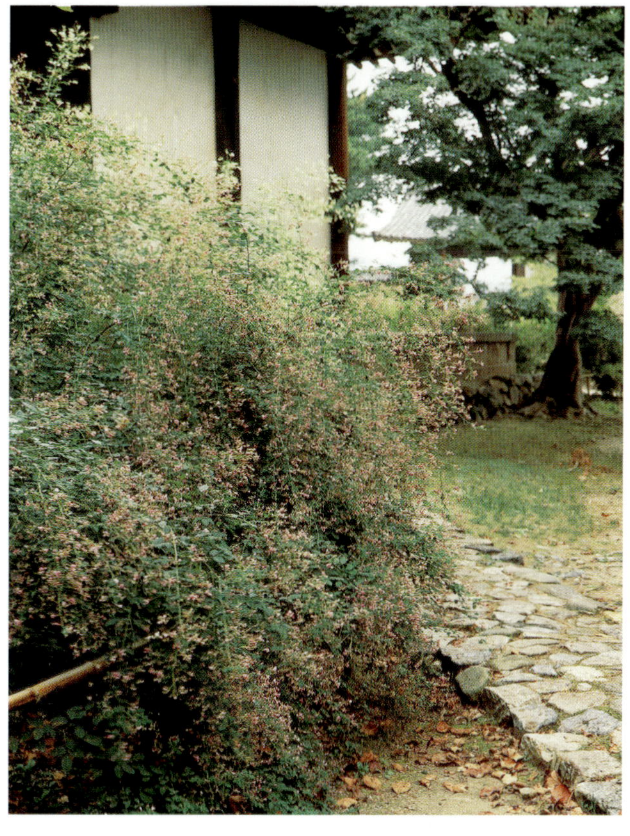

At my old home,

Ever since the sparse-leafed

Bush clover has bloomed,

Each night the moonlight

Has filled my garden.

FUJIWARA NO YOSHITSUNE

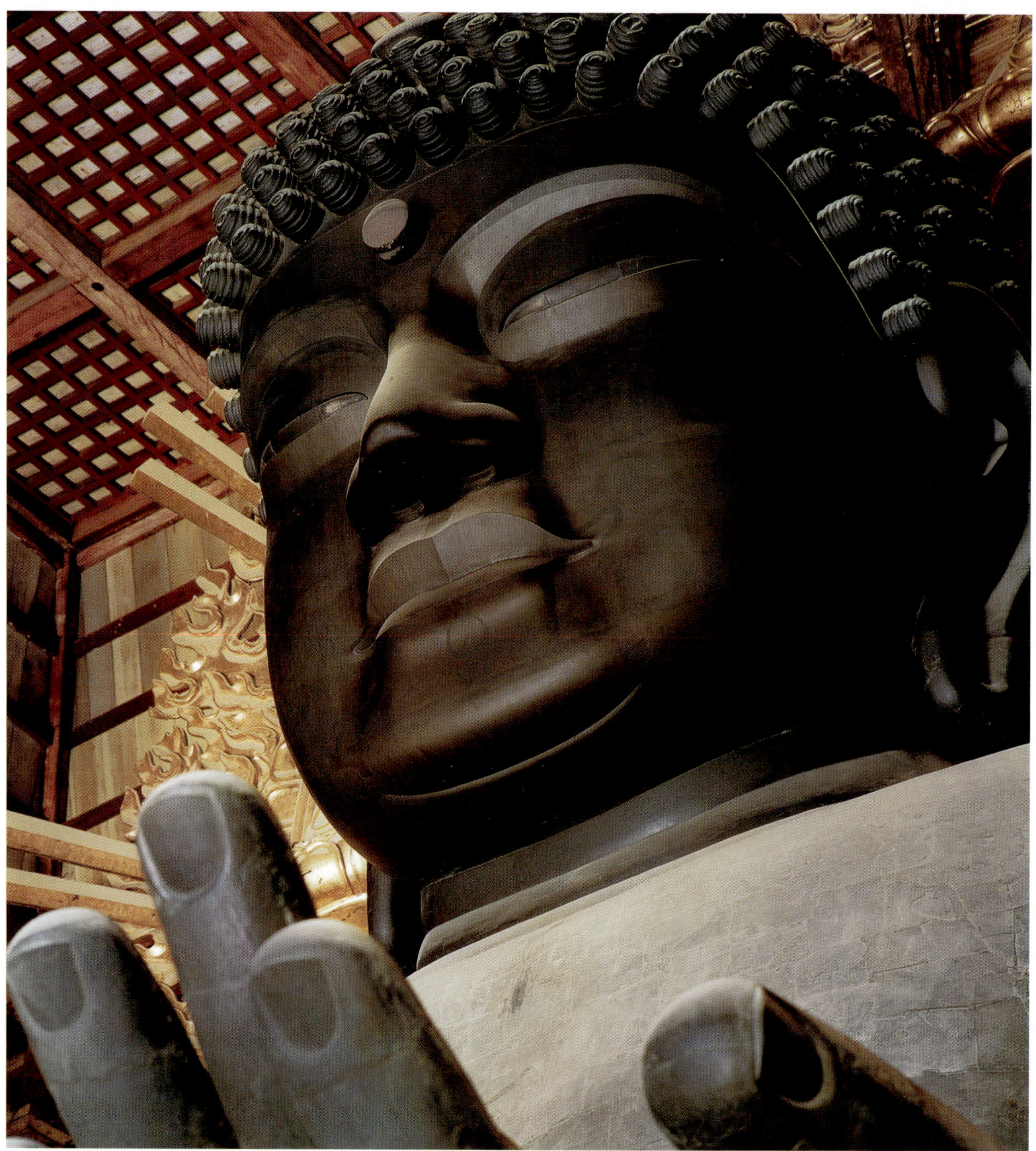

*N*ara, April 19 1923. I saw again the magnificent temple and the Great Buddha. Its foundations like a flight of the perpetual green of these two enormous roofs. The antique triangle of the pyramids, full of calculations and mysteries, form the roof by a meeting, now curved, lifted up, animated, alive. The edges of the roofs, held back and supported by those huge muscles formed by layer upon layer, are thicker towards the end. The contrast of the sharp, thin angle. The effect is obtained not through any indirect exaggeration of detail, but by a transposition in an altogether different order. Variations in the thickness of the lines, as delicate as the harmonious proportions of the columns of the Parthenon.

PAUL CLAUDEL

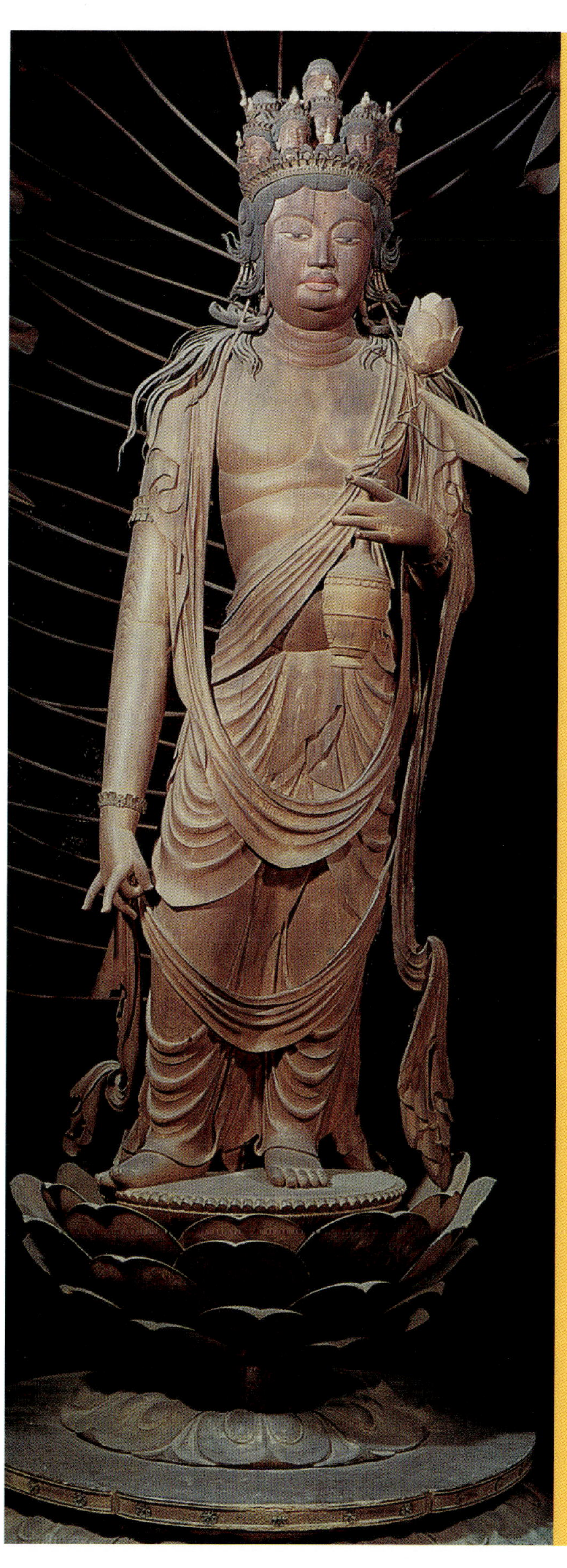

How red is the lip

Of the Goddess of Mercy!

What do I see

But a throng of

Adoring court ladies

Harkening back to the

Fujiwara.

AIZU YAICHI

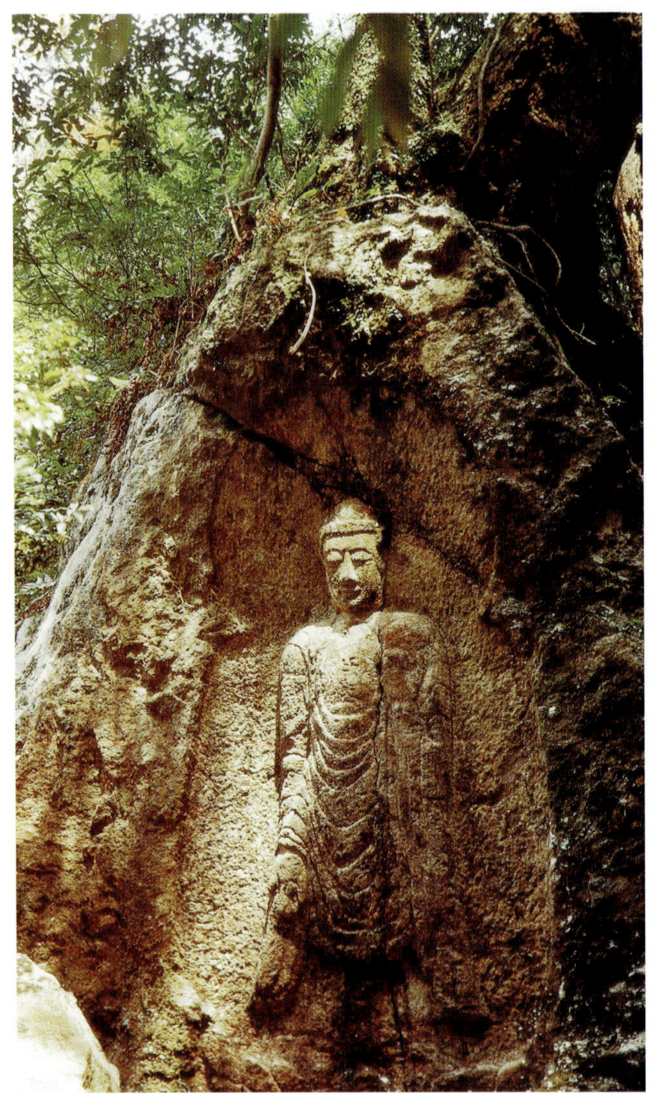

In February of 755, Ganjin was given property that had been Prince Nitabe's estate in the western part of the capital. There he built a monastery to serve as headquarters for his new Ritsu Sect. Emperor Shōmu's death halted construction of the temple, but only for a time. His successor, Empress Kōken, honored Shōmu's wishes and issued an imperial order to finish the main hall. In August of 757, the Empress presented Ganjin with the signboard reading "Tōshōdaiji" to hang on the temple gate. The main buildings of the Tōshōdaiji complex were completed two years later…

Every time Fushō entered the precincts of Tōshōdaiji, he looked up at the roof of the main hall. There he would see, mounted on both sides, the tail of the bird he had received as a gift from China and dedicated to this building.

INOUE YASUSHI

The "Twilight Buddha:"

Now, seeing

The setting sun,

The evening sky of Buddha's paradise

Comes into my mind.

FUJIWARA NO TOSHINARI (SHUNZEI)

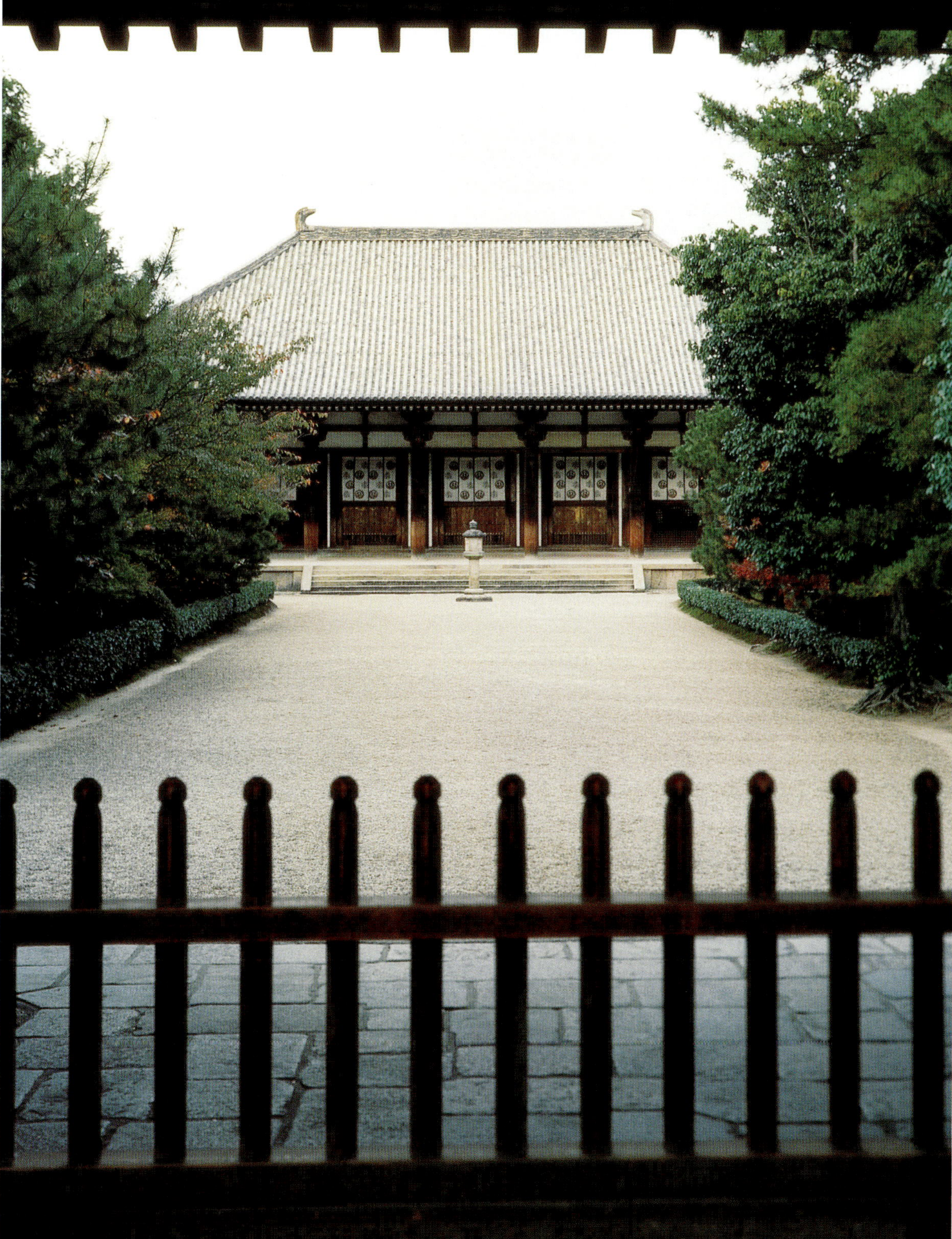

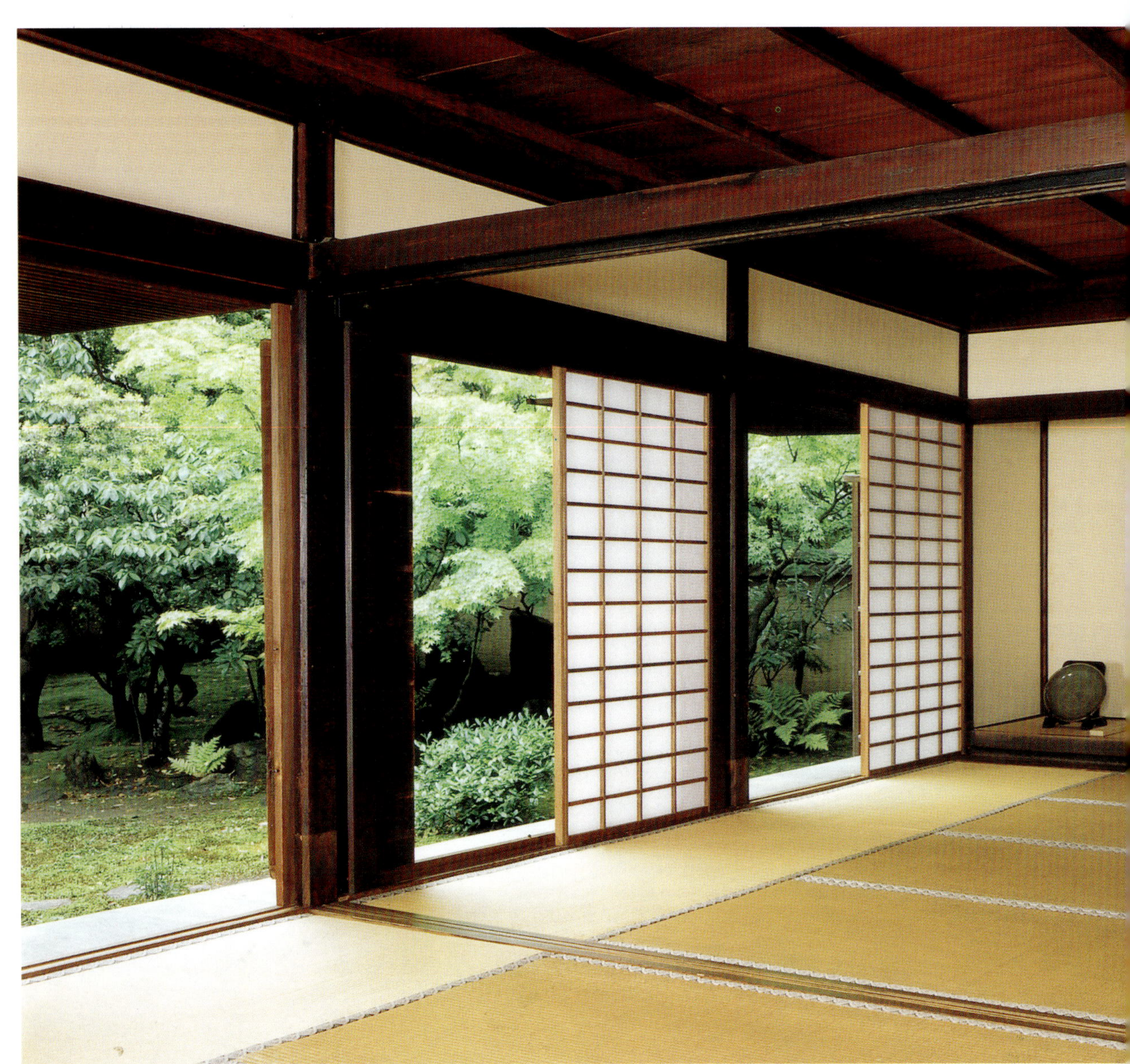

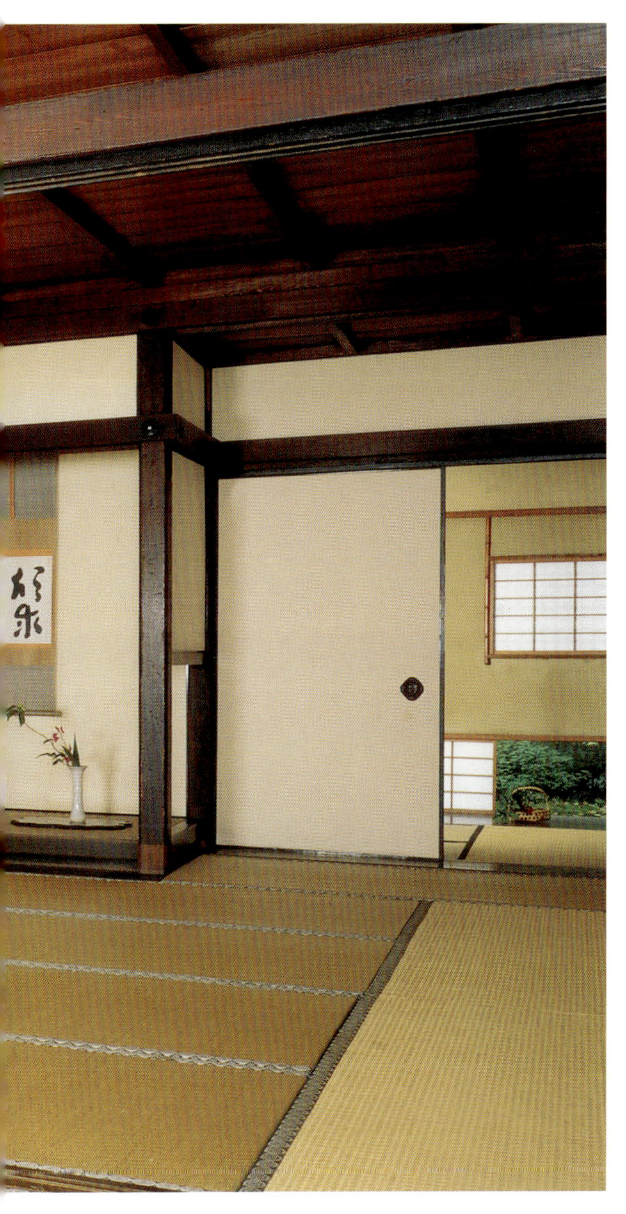

*O*ne of the chief points of difference in a Japanese house as compared with ours lies in the treatment of partitions and outside walls. In our houses these are solid and permanent; and when the frame is built, the partitions form part of the framework. In the Japanese house, on the contrary, there are two or more sides that have no permanent walls. Within, also, there are but few partitions which have similar stability; in their stead are slight sliding screens which run in appropriate groves in the floor and overhead. These groves mark the limit of each room. The screens may be opened by sliding them back, or they may be entirely removed, thus throwing a number of rooms into one great apartment. In the same way the whole side of a house may be flung open to sunlight and air.

Whatever is commonplace in the appearance of the house is towards the street, while the artistic and picturesque face is turned towards the garden, which may be at one side or in the rear of the house — usually in the rear. Within these plain and unpretentious houses there is often to be seen marvels of exquisite carving and the perfection of cabinet work; and surprise follows surprise as one becomes more and more fully acquainted with the interior finish of these curious and remarkable dwellings.

EDWARD S. MORSE

I was thankful to spend a couple of quiet days in Nara, a fine old city. I stayed at the Nara Hotel: like the old Oriental in Kobe and the Park at Matsushima, it is one of those solidly Edwardian places that remind me so much of Somerset Maugham. In my spacious room there were two massive mahogany beds, wardrobes and chests of drawers, archaic light fittings, ponderous arm-chairs. In the hotel there were endless, lofty red-carpeted interiors; I was always getting lost in them and being helped back to my room…

JAMES KIRKUP

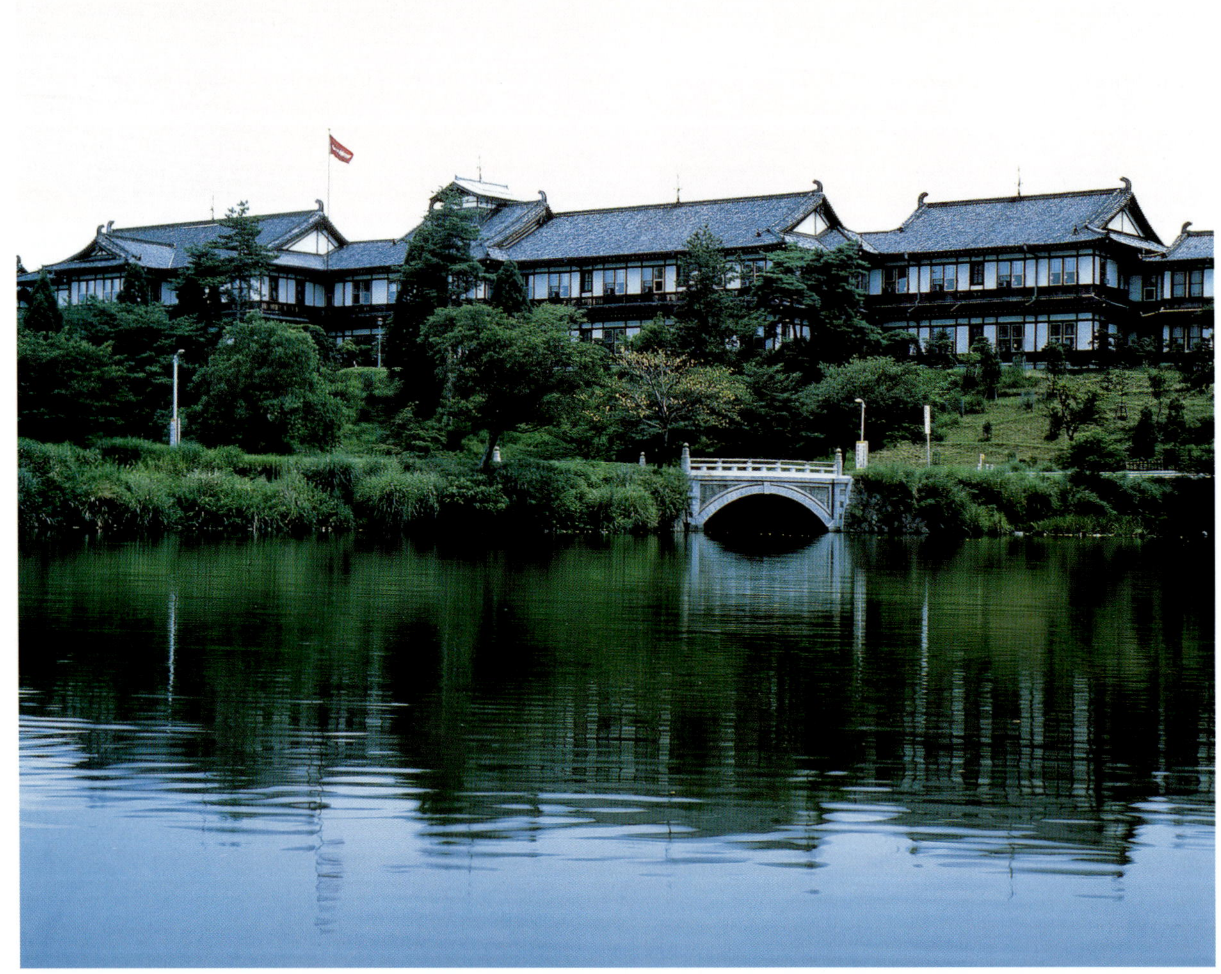

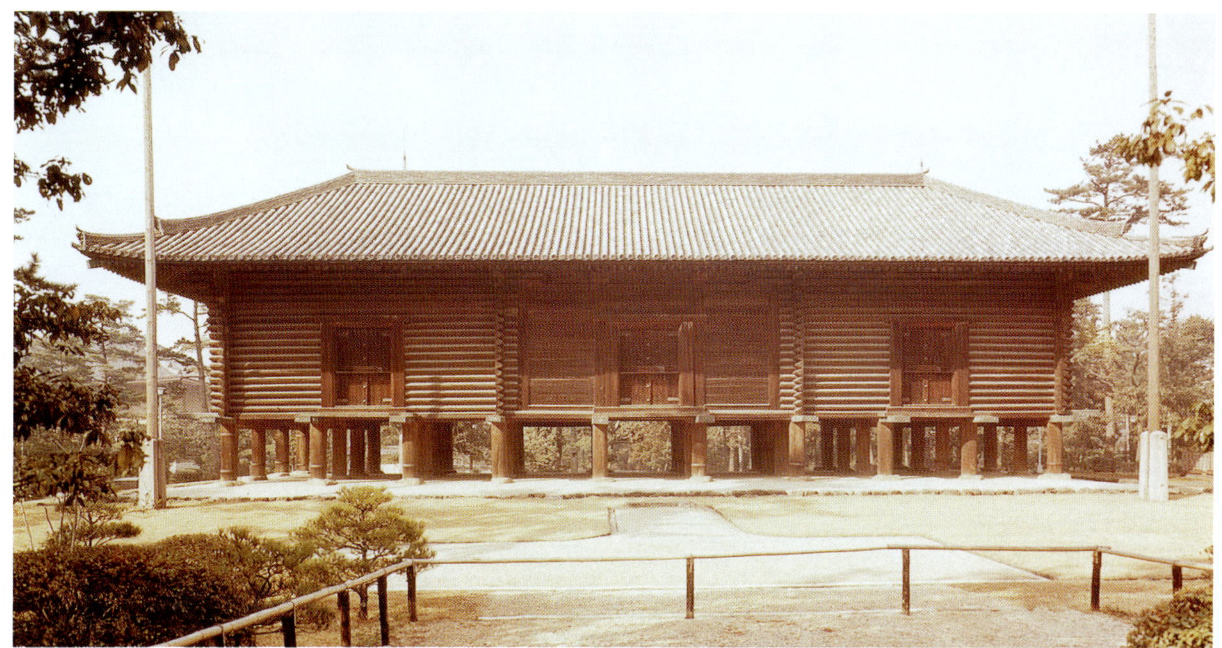

That storehouse is the famous Shōsōin of Nara, erected in 749 and still existing; and the articles therein are by far the larger parts of the deposits of that year, as can be seen by comparison of the original inventory. It is the greatest palace of its kind in the world, a unique domestic museum; the only competitor being the combination of Pompeii itself with the unearthed Roman treasures stored in the Naples Museum. But there the articles are only those that could defy damp and heart—stone, metal, earthenware, and frescoed plaster. Whereas in the Shōsōin every kind of article is represented, however perishable: writing paper in rolls from the Emperor's own desk, garments of every grade from his wardrobe, the perishable furs and fair feather slippers of the Empress; jewels *ad libitum*, including an infinite variety of stone and glass beads; all the utensils of housekeeping, pans for cooking, bowls for eating, spoons and knives and forks and, yes, glass finger bowls; bedsteads and couches, and vases and boxes, and cabinets, and floss silk for embroidery, and accoutrement for horses, and court banners, and rare manuscripts, and painted screens, and metal mirrors, and musical instruments, and weapons of war, and a thousand other articles of unique interest. Nowhere else exists such an opportunity for studying the daily life and art of a vanished civilization.

Ernest Fenollosa

*L*ong ago there was a lady attendant who served the Nara Emperor. She was a very attractive woman, and many men—among whom were several courtiers— wooed her, but she refused to accept any of their proposals. The reason why she kept herself so aloof was that she was deeply in love with His Majesty, admiring him above all other men.

The Emperor had once summoned her to him, but since he failed to call for her again, she felt truly wretched. Night and day she brooded over her unhappy fate, never ceasing to feel unhappy and to long for him.

His Majesty had indeed summoned the lady attendant on one occasion, but he had not been particularly attracted to her. Nevertheless, she continued to appear as usual before him. Realizing that she loved him in vain, the woman had no desire to go on living and one night stole out of the palace and threw herself into Sarusawa Pond.

The Emperor did not learn of her tragic death for some time. One day, however, someone happened to mention the tragedy. Deeply saddened by her untimely death, His Majesty made an imperial visit to the banks of the pond where he had members of his retinue compose poems in her memory. Kakinomoto no Hitomaro composed this poem:

> How sad it makes me
> To see the disheveled hair
> Of my beloved,
> Resembling so the water plants
> In Sarusawa Pond.

His Majesty composed this poem:

> How I detest the Sarusawa Pond!
> I wish its waters had vanished
> When my beloved
> Threw herself in and was enveloped
> By the water plants.

It is said that His Majesty gave her a proper burial near the pond before returning to the palace.

FROM TALES OF YAMATO

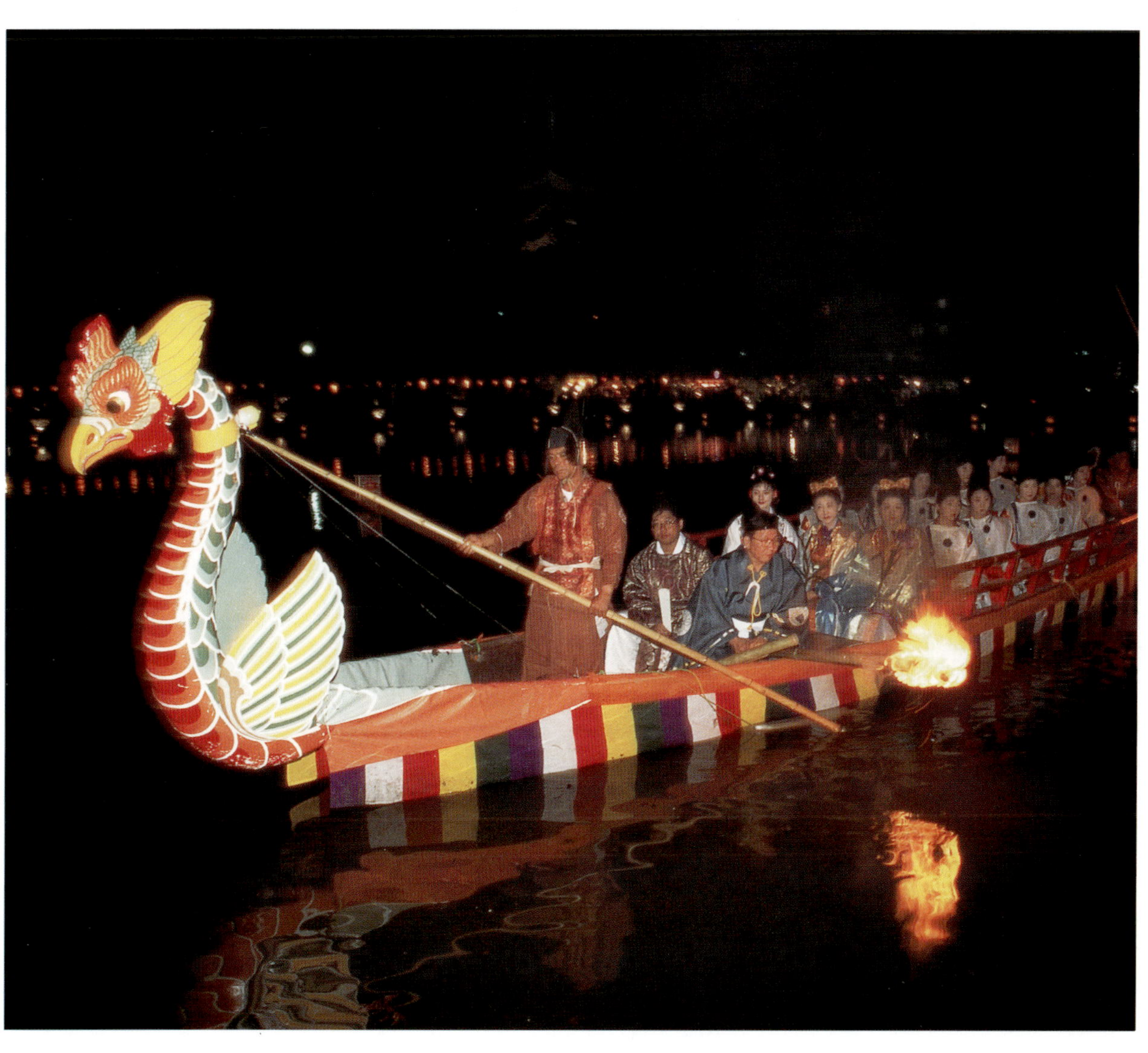

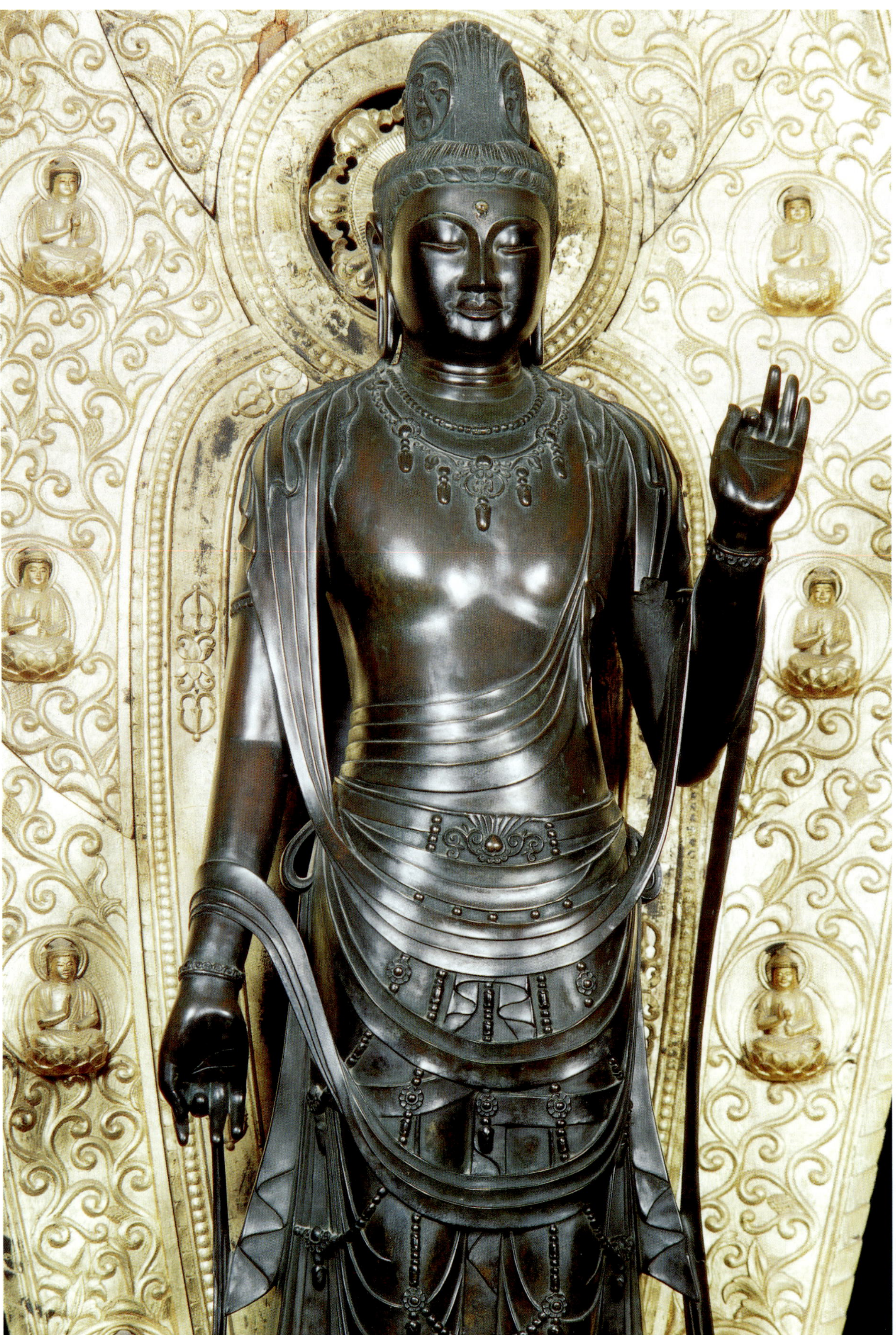

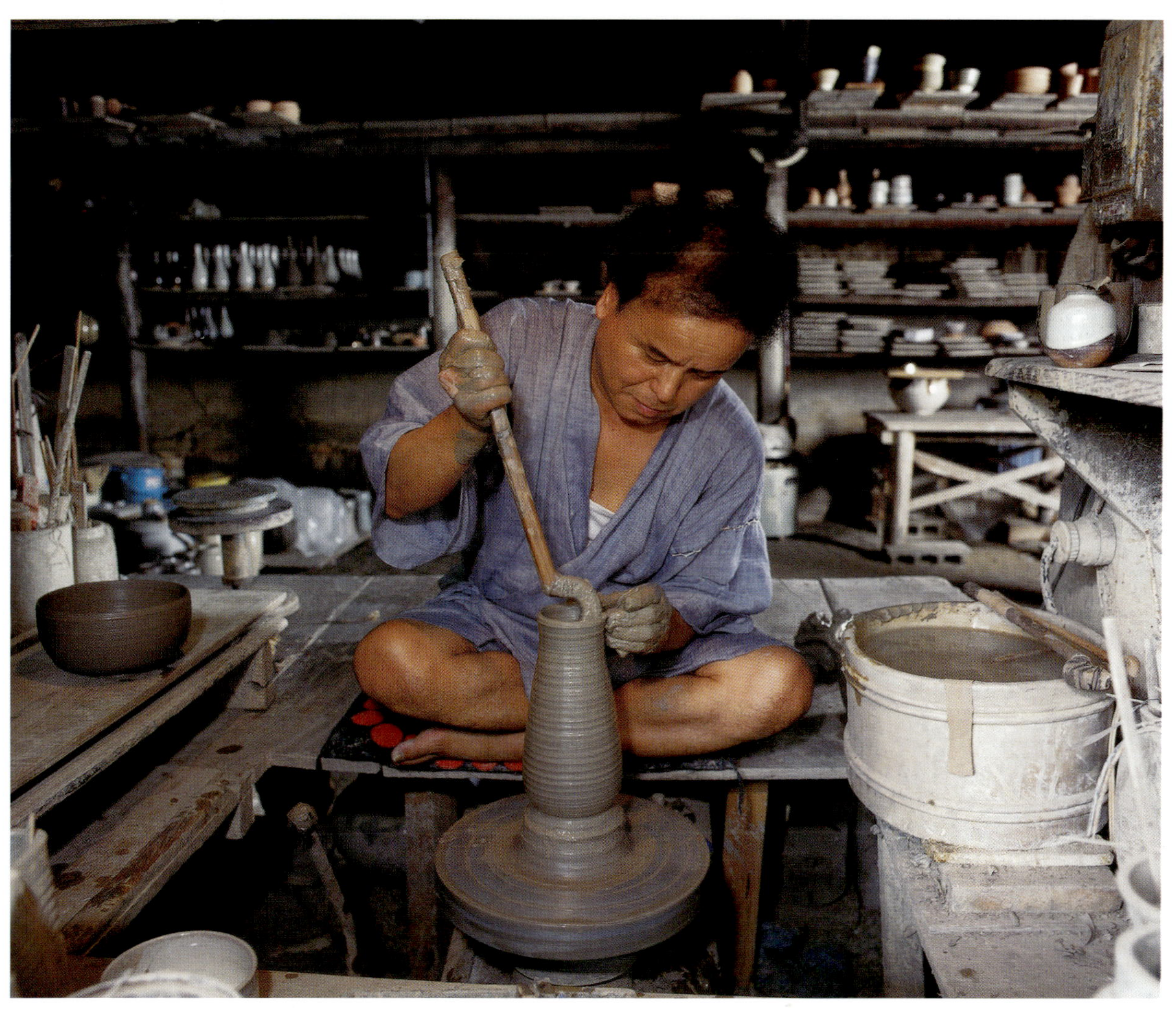

The Shō Kwannon, the lotus-bearing divinity of com-passsion, is a magnificent sculpture, human in proportions and composed of feature…The complicated folds of the draperies, the suggestion of the full wrinkles of the materi-al, and the transparency of the garments which reveal the conformations of the body all add up to a degree of realism not attempted before. Divinity is thought out in human form, full in face and stout in limb.

ROBERT TREAT PAINE

"You come to see?" The manager took us along a veranda of polished wood to the kilns, to the clay vats, and the yards…There are differences many and technical between Japanese and English pottery in the making, but these are of no consequence. In the moulding house, where they were making the bodies of the vases, the wheels, all worked by hand, ran true as a hair. The potter sat on a clean mat with his tea things at his side. When he turned out a vase-body he saw that it was good, nodded appreciatively to himself, and poured out some tea ere starting the next one.

RUDYARD KIPLING

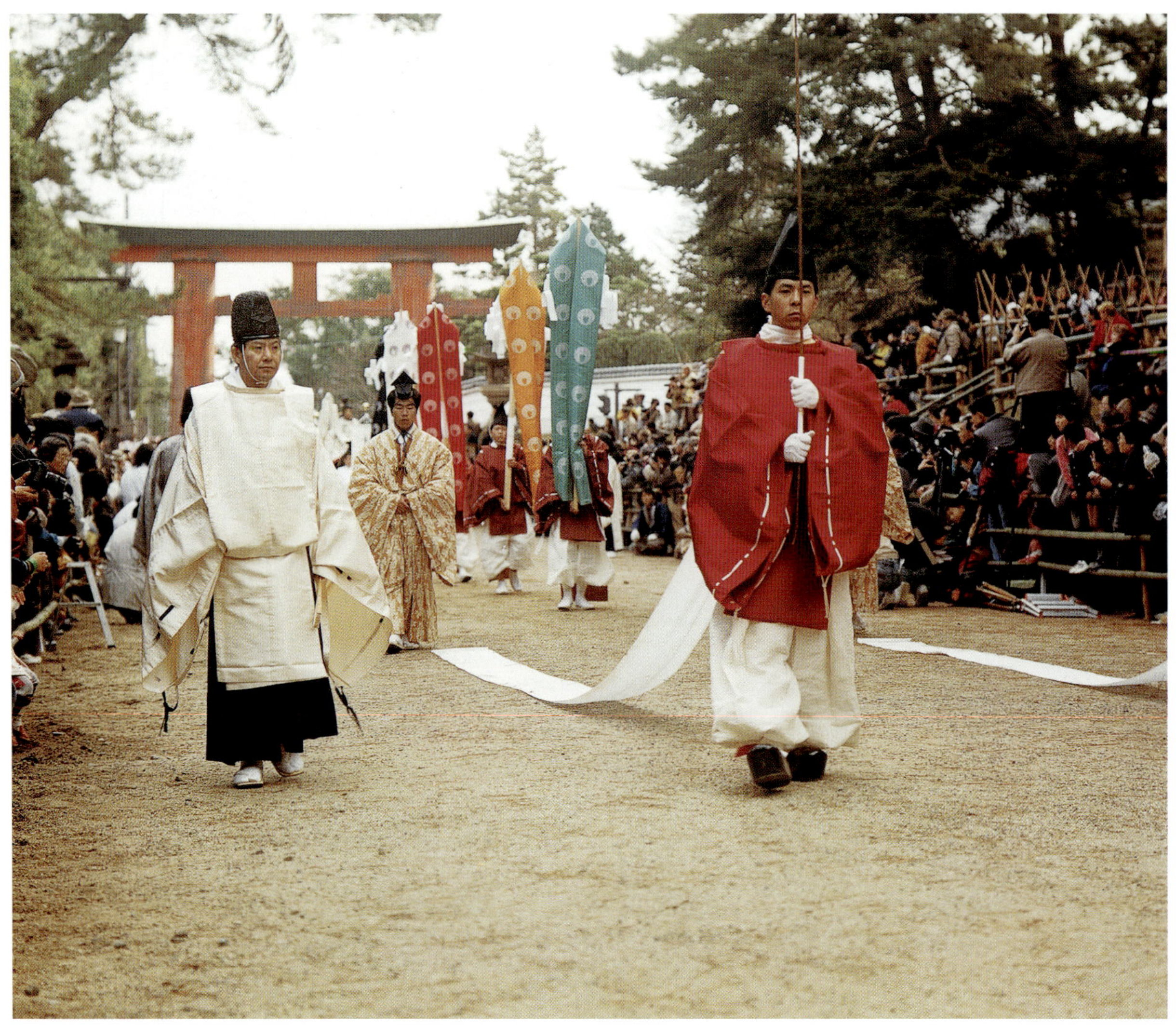

*T*he *Onmatsuri*, the festival of the Wakamiya, was actually a celebration for the whole shrine. It began on the 17th day of the 9th month. Kōfukuji levied funds for it from the entire province of Yamato, so that it had the character of a province festival as well. It involved (as it still does) bringing the Wakamiya deity down from his permanent sanctuary to a "travel place" (*tabisho*) along the avenue from Kōfukuji to the main sanctuary complex, and presenting various offerings and entertainments there for the pleasure of the deity and the assembled crowds.

ROYALL TYLER

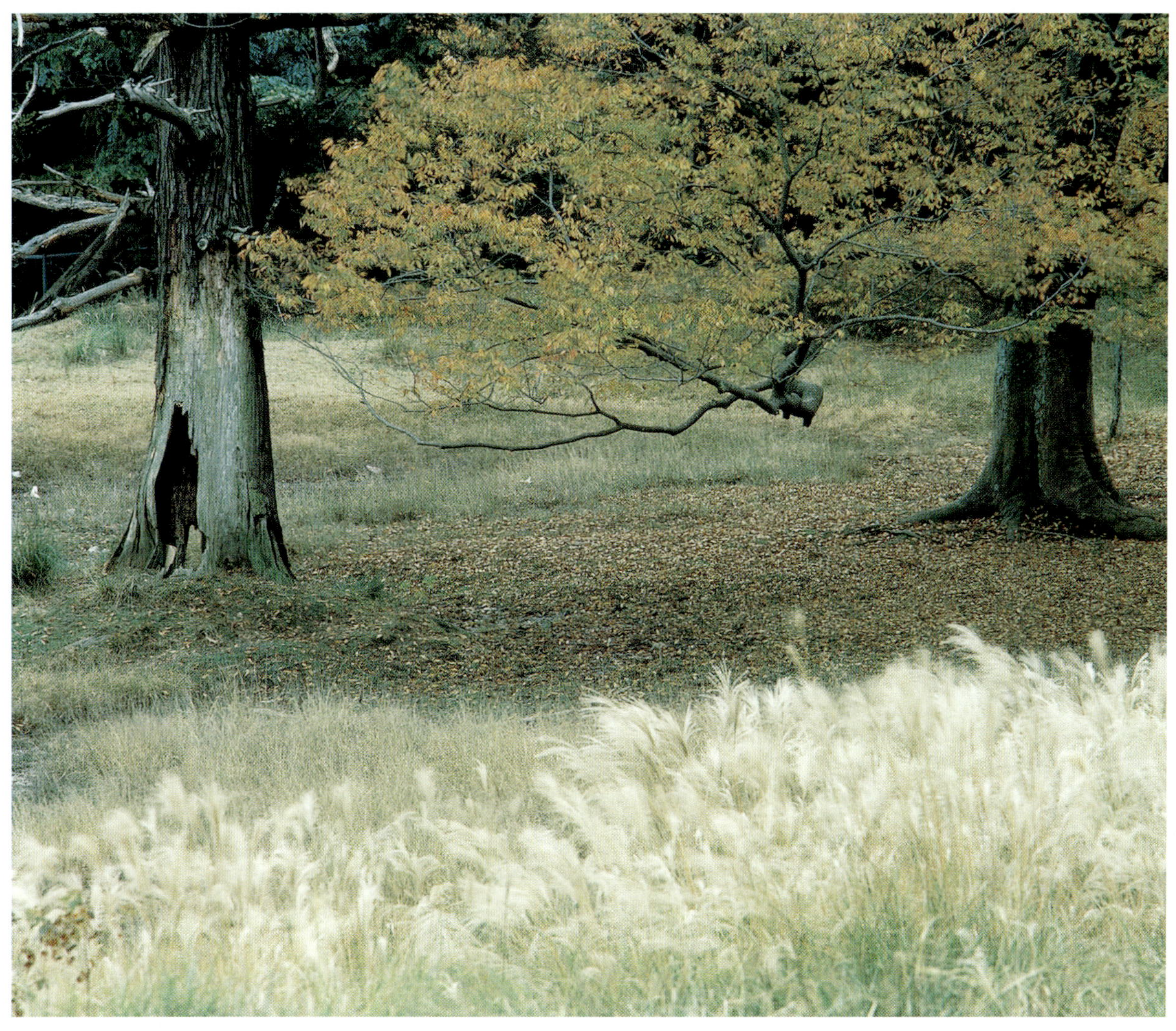

*T*he room I stayed in was near the entrance to Asachigahara. It was in fact near the first torii gate on the path leading to Kasuga Shrine. The room was a small one. Even then it was very old. Now, thirty years later, I found it just as it was back then…

Speaking of finding no sign of change, I must say that Nara itself seems not to have changed in the last thirty years. There must have been some small changes; but the city looks the same. I can't think of any other city so unaffected by the passage of time. Nara's unchanging sameness is what revives these feelings of nostalgia, which also never change.

Hirotsu Kazuo

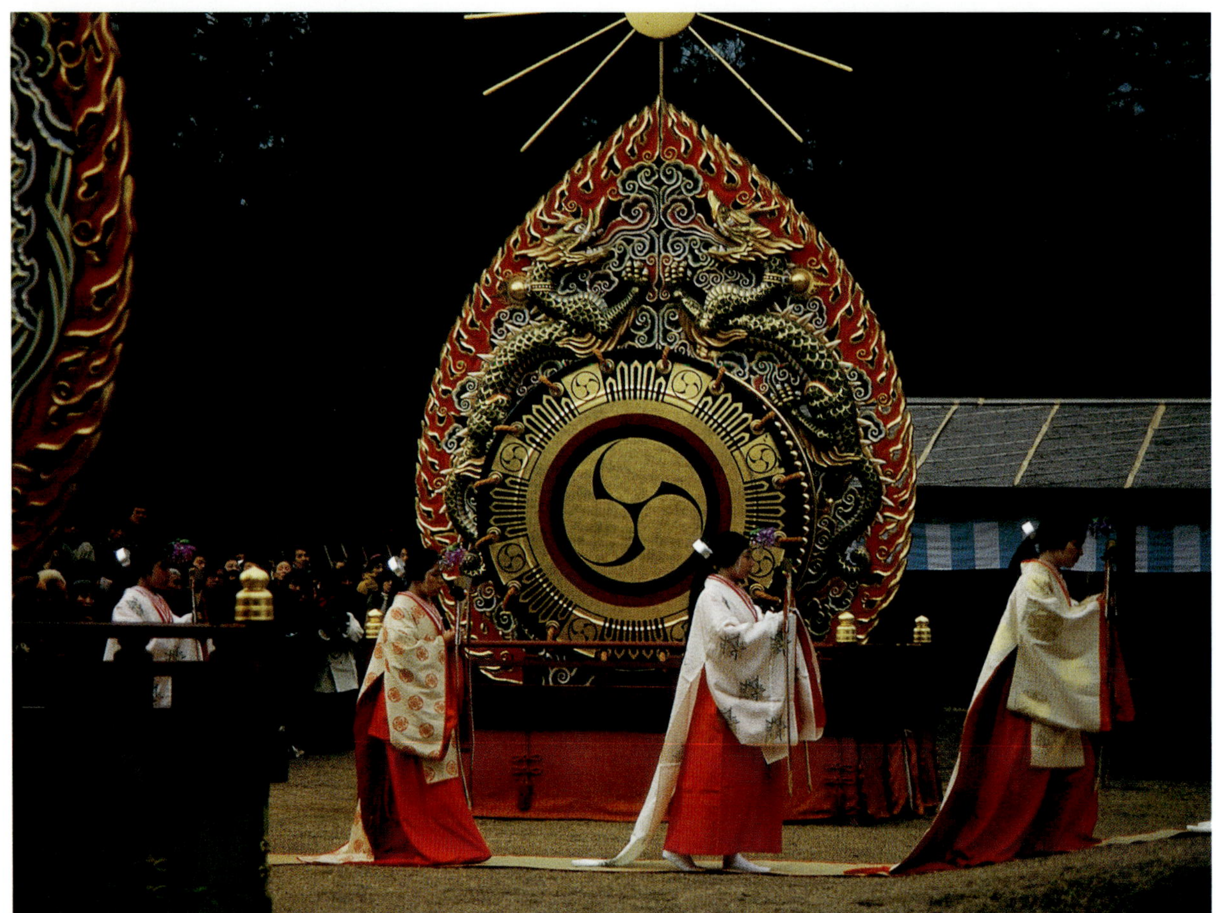

It is the night of a sacred festival, and all Nara is astir. The streets are also decorated, as the Mikado is expected to visit the town within the next day or two. Bamboos stand at either side of the streets at distances of about twelve feet apart, and these are connected by festooned straw bands which hang at a height of six feet from the ground. From these straw bands hang the cut papers symbolizing the Shinto religion. We now turn into an avenue of gigantic cryptomeria trees—the grandest avenue I have ever seen—where are stalls rendered gay with lanterns, on which are sold toys, sweet stuffs, and other trifles. Leaving this by an avenue turning on the right, we behold a sight which I shall never forget. Here is one of the most lovely of groves, formed of colossal trees, with innumerable stone monumental lanterns at either side. These lanterns vary in height from four to ten feet, and nearly every one is lit. (I afterwards learned that there are two thousand two hundred lanterns in this grove.) Every now and again we come to little flights of rude steps, for the avenue ascends the slope of a rounded hill. This rising ground, the flocks of gaily dressed people who are going to the temple to pray, and the strange aspect of this vast forest of stone lanterns, produce a scene in the highest degree surprising.

At the top of this beautiful grove, amidst a vast crowd of lanterns, rises the temple called Wakamiya. It is celebrated for its thatched roof, the thatch being very thick and regular, and consisting of layers of the inner bark of a fir-tree. This roof is the most perfect of its kind in Japan; and near the temple is a shrine containing a god, which is so sacred that even a priest may not enter its abode.

CHRISTOPHER DRESSER

When it comes to admiring temples, what I love most of all is to see their pagodas rising in the distance. Back when one could ride the bus from Nara to Horyūji, I often took that route. It gave me exquisite pleasure to see the pagodas that came into sight one after another as the bus passed across the fertile Yamato plain.

After passing the Heijō capital, now nothing but a field, I begin to see the Eastern Pagoda of Yakushiji. I see it growing, rising up to soar above the green pine forest. The splendor of that vision deepens the joy it is to visit the old capital once again.

KAMEI KATSUICHIRŌ

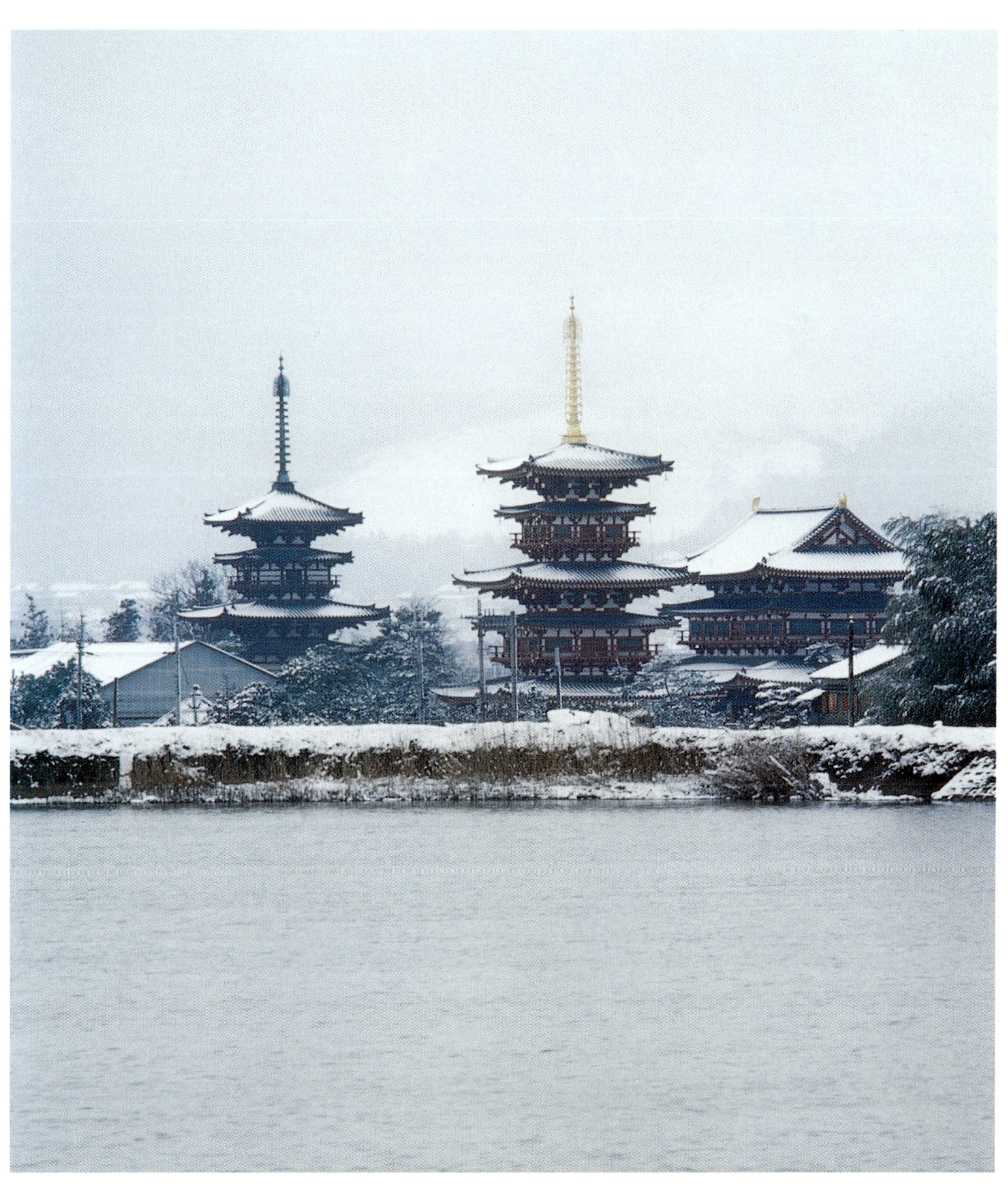

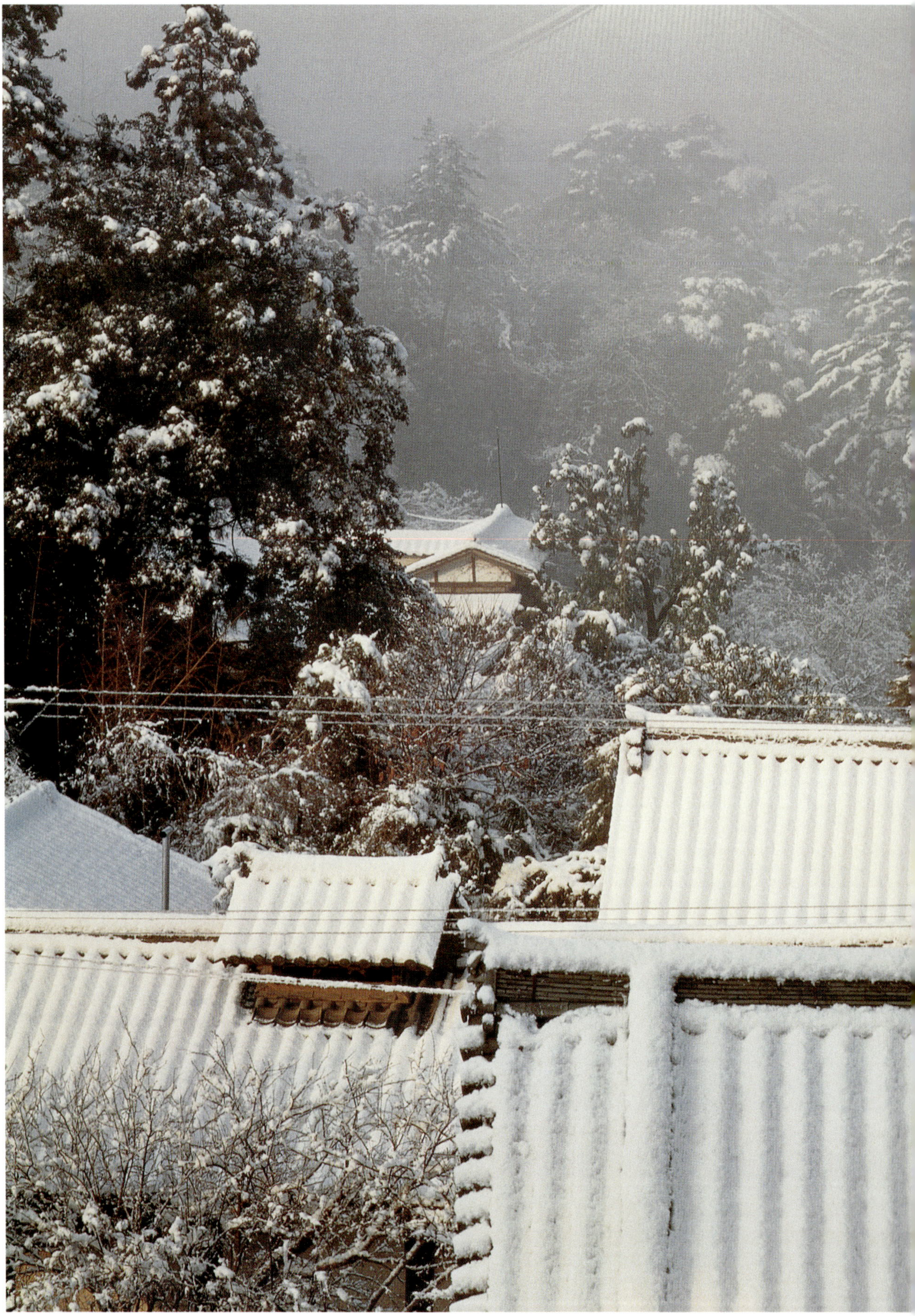

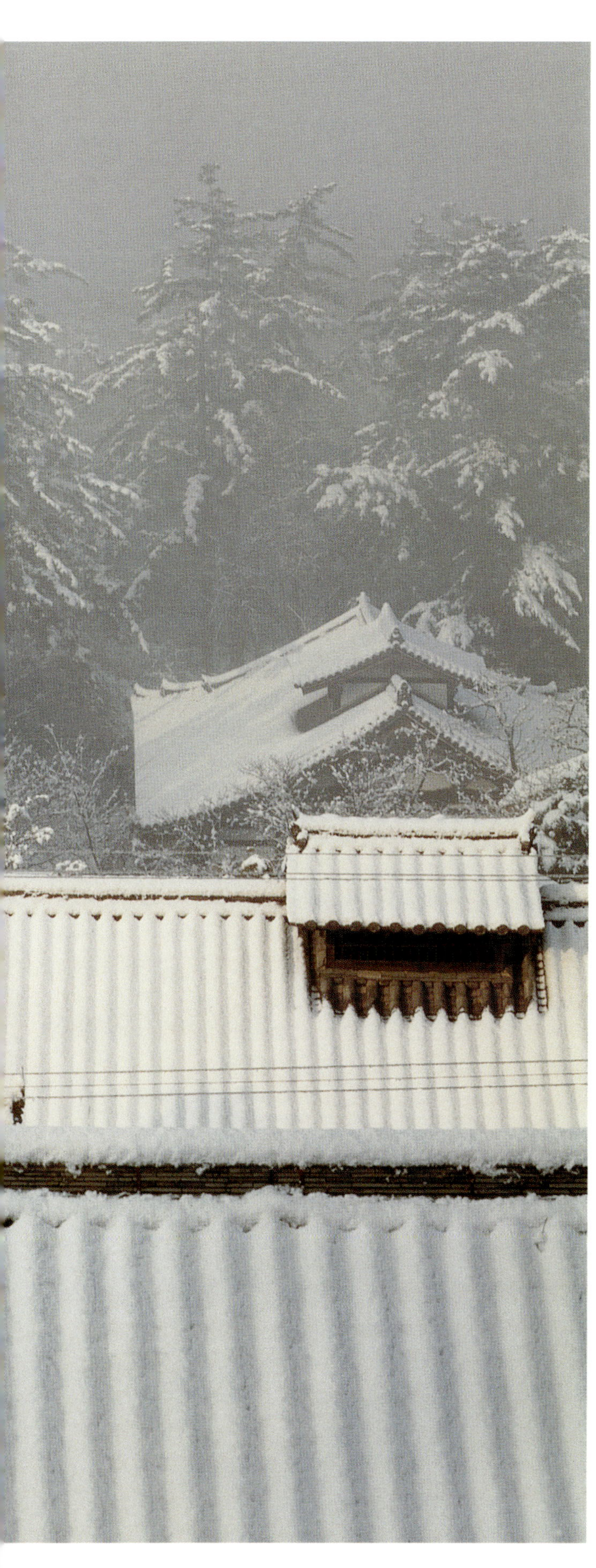

*A*s the train emerged from the Mount Ikoma tunnel, the scenery suddenly changed. It became the scenery of Nara: smaller mountains with rounded tops and gentle slopes now clothed in a wintery landscape tinged with bright brown. He felt as if the world of Japanese myth were still alive.

Ishikawa Tatsuzō

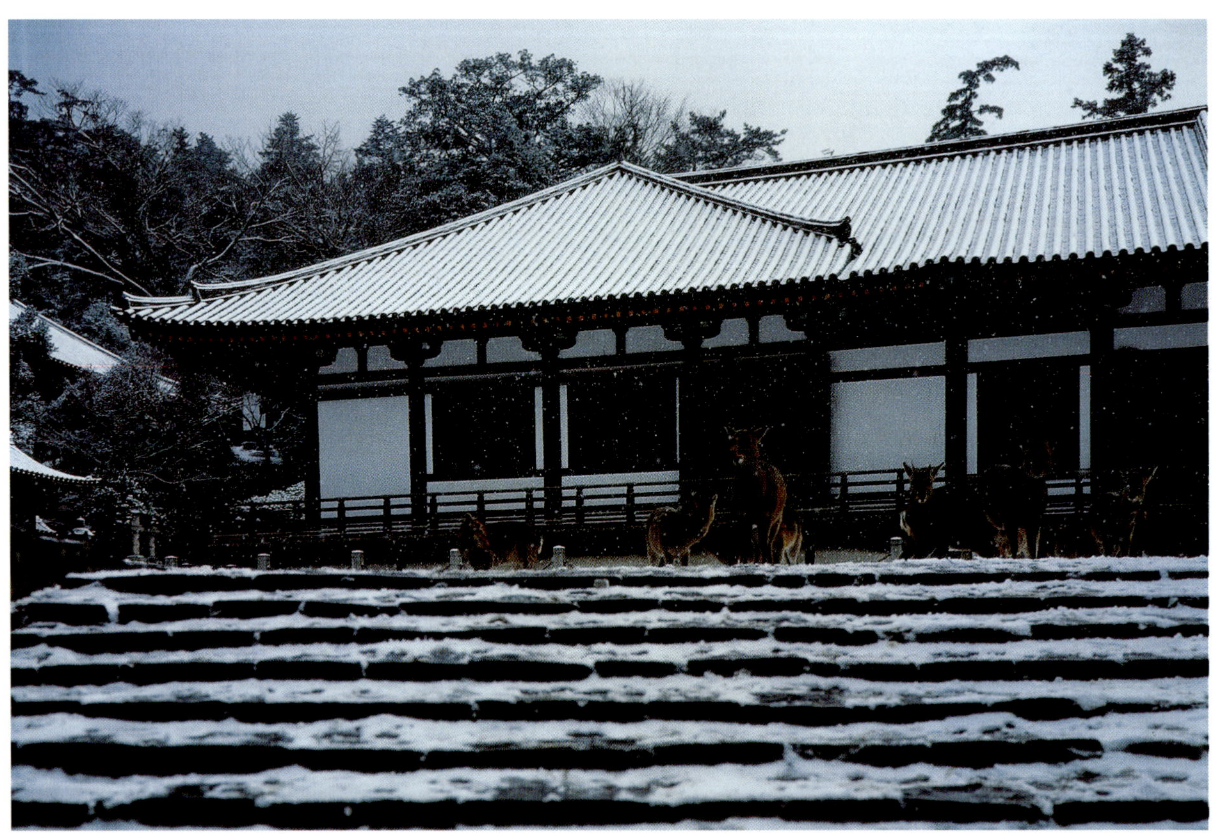

Dazzled by the light of the moon, I climbed the flight of stone steps. My eyes had grown accustomed to the darkness of the forest. Now the Sangatsudō stood bathed in bright moonlight.

What a refreshing sight! The fine, light roof reflected a delicate silvery radiance. The eaves cast beautiful shadow lines, those to the left from the Tempyō period, those to the right from the Kamakura era. Even that difference gave one a sense of harmonious variation.

WATSUJI TETSURŌ

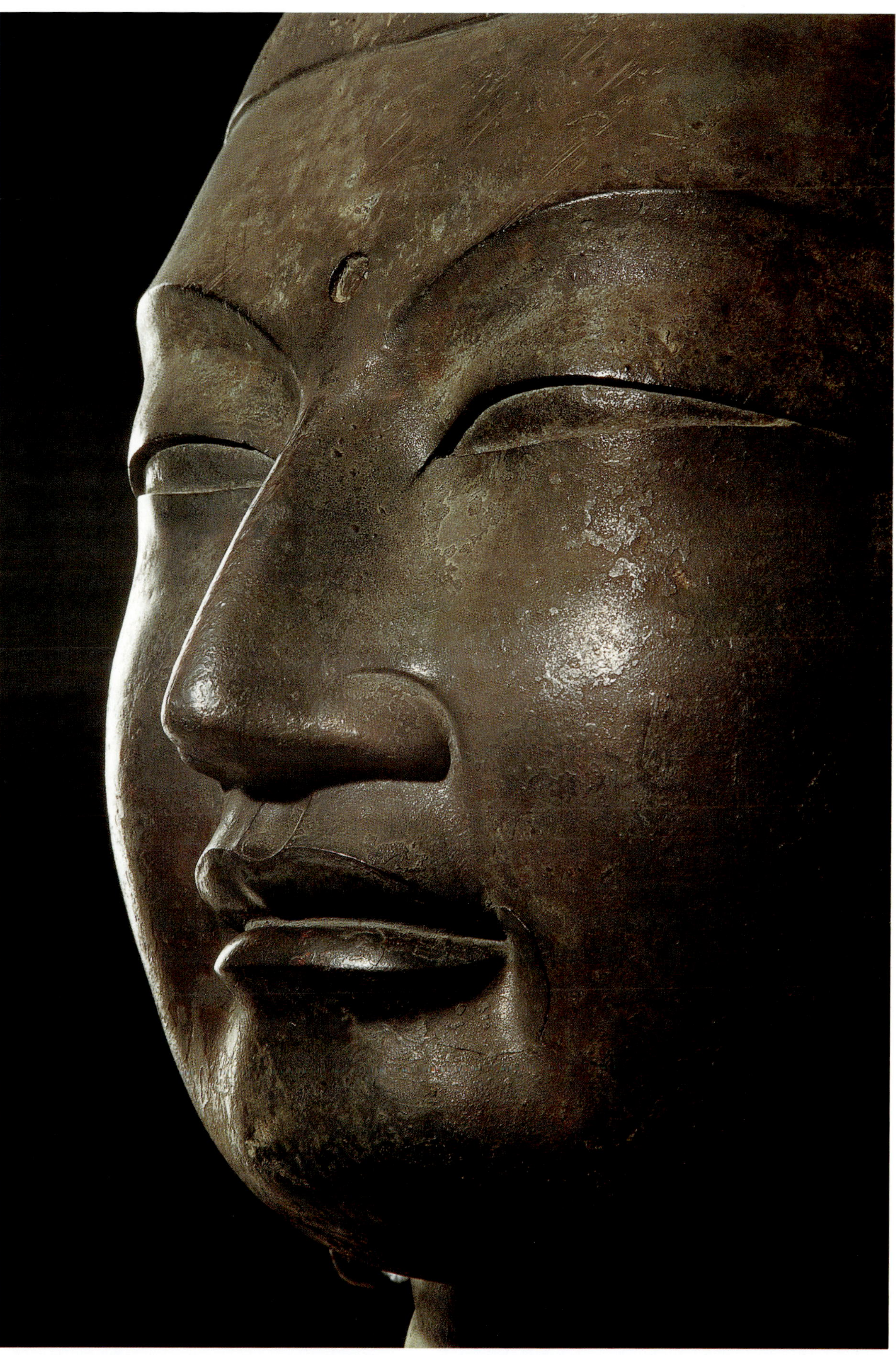

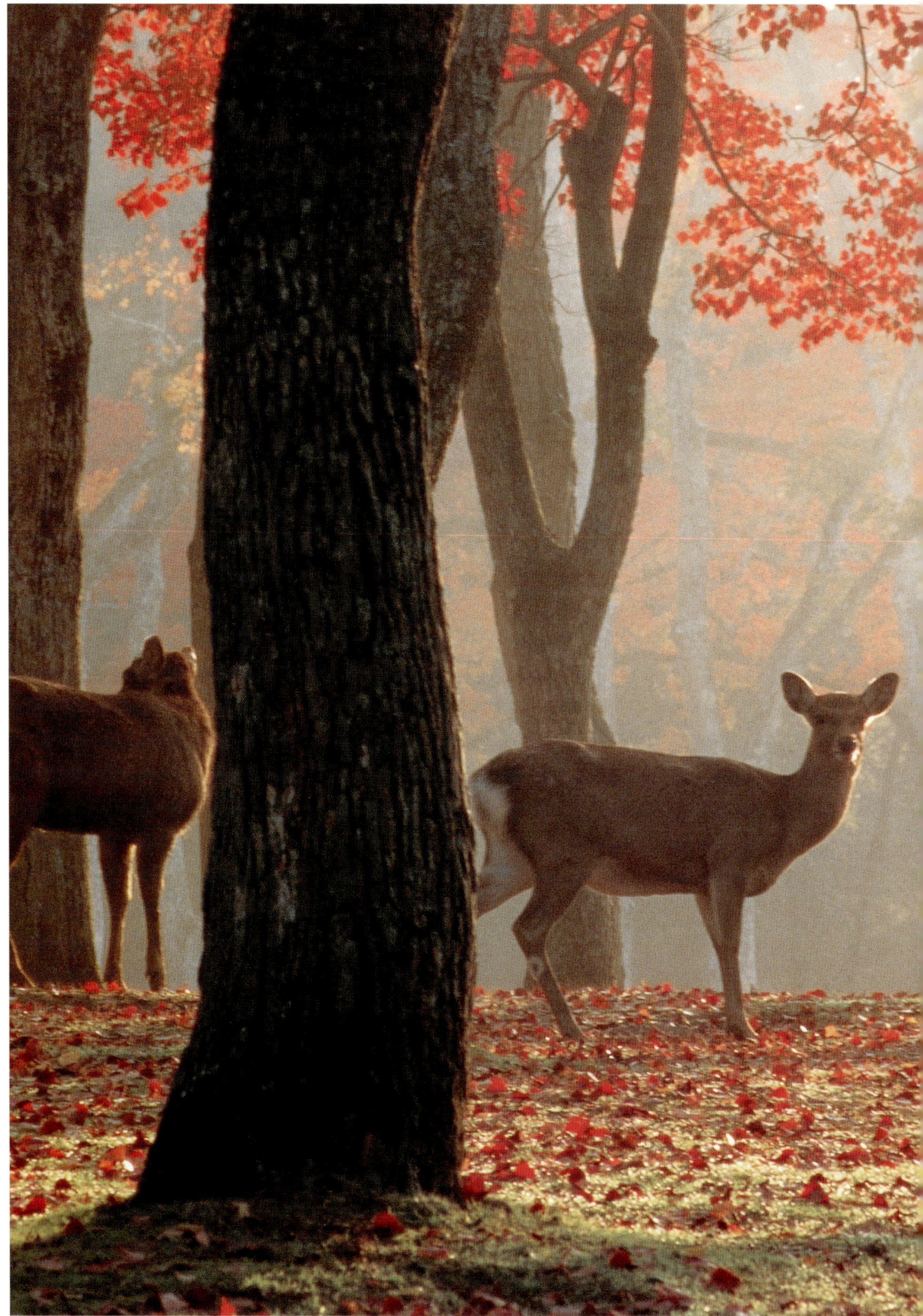

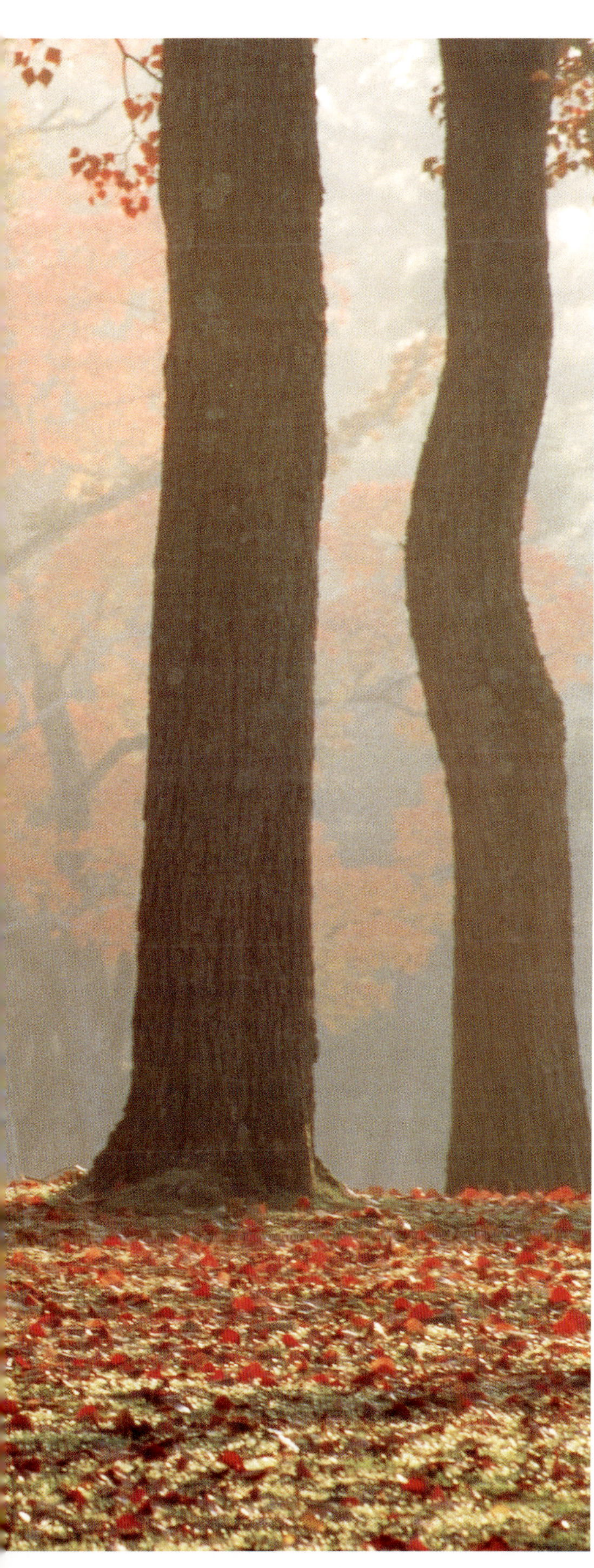

I passed through the red doors of Shinto into the park and I shivered, thinking of the vast power we [in the West] would have if we had a great faith. Now we either smile idly and eruditely or spin fiercely in the hell of individuality, uprooted, without coherence, without hope. The Japanese believe in an illusion, perhaps, but they reach great, fruitful, practical results; while we who do not believe in anything live miserably and die forever…In this park my heart becomes wild.

Nikos Kazantzakis

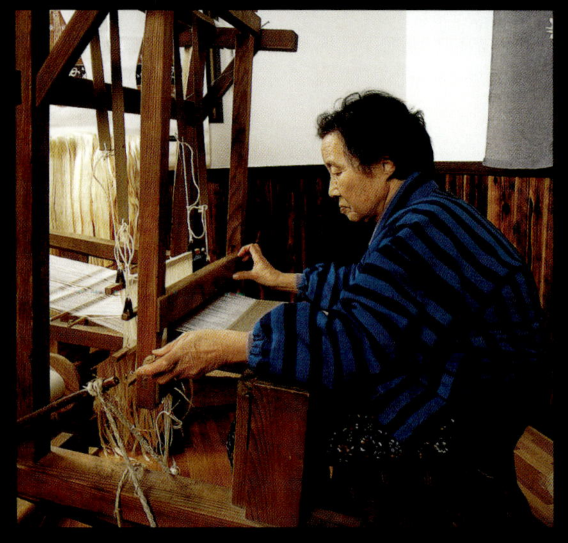
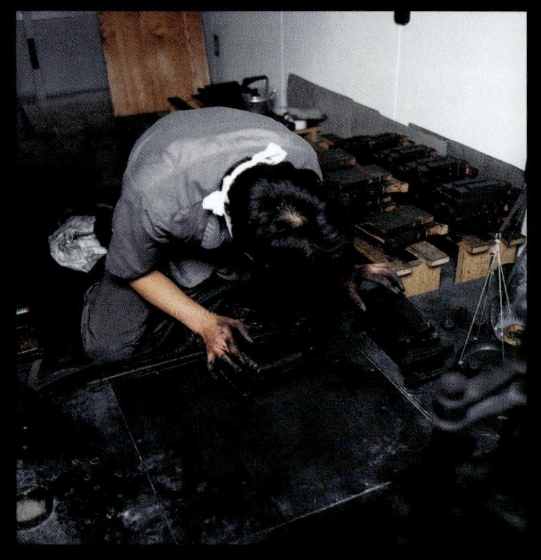
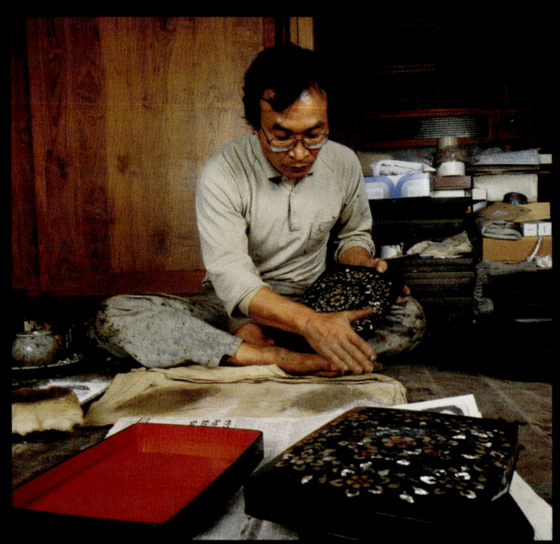
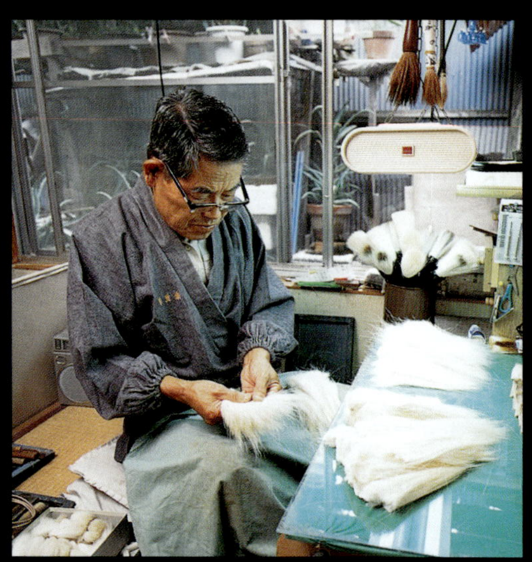
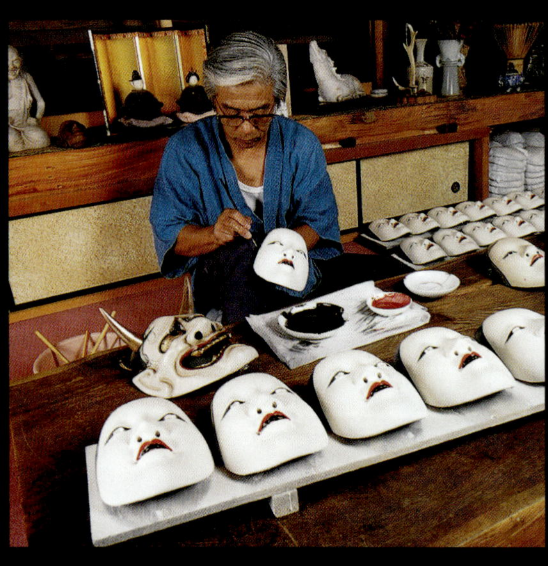
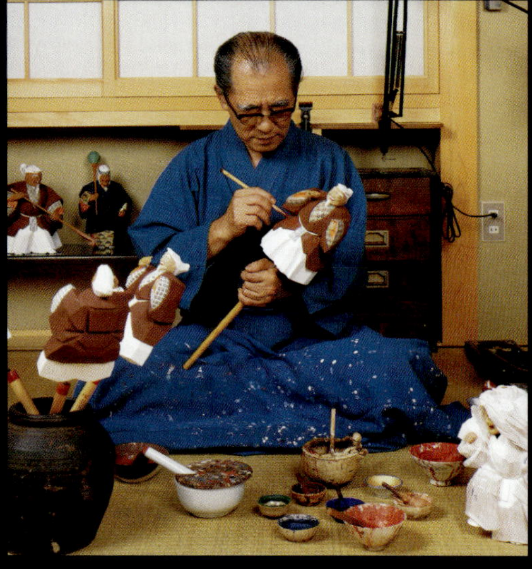

*I*n our vocabulary to-day the word "artisan" has a much less dignified connotation than its cognate "artist." It refers to a handicraftsman definitely low in status and without refinement. The artist is often a pleasant subject for conversation, but we discuss the artisan only hesitantly. In like manner, in the expression "arts and crafts" it is customary to give a far higher honour to the former than the latter.

Let us remember, however, that all these opposing ideas such as "artist and artisan" and "arts and crafts" are only products of the Age of Individuality Worship. In modern times when the genius and the hero were worshipped, it was necessary that a line should be drawn between "artist" and "artisan." Naturally enough, history has been eloquent in recounting the lives of great artists, but it has been indifferent to the lot of artisans. The history of art is the biography of a few geniuses, and the works of the great multitude of artisans are forgotten before they are recorded on the pages of history. But is that as it should be?

YANAGI SŌETSU

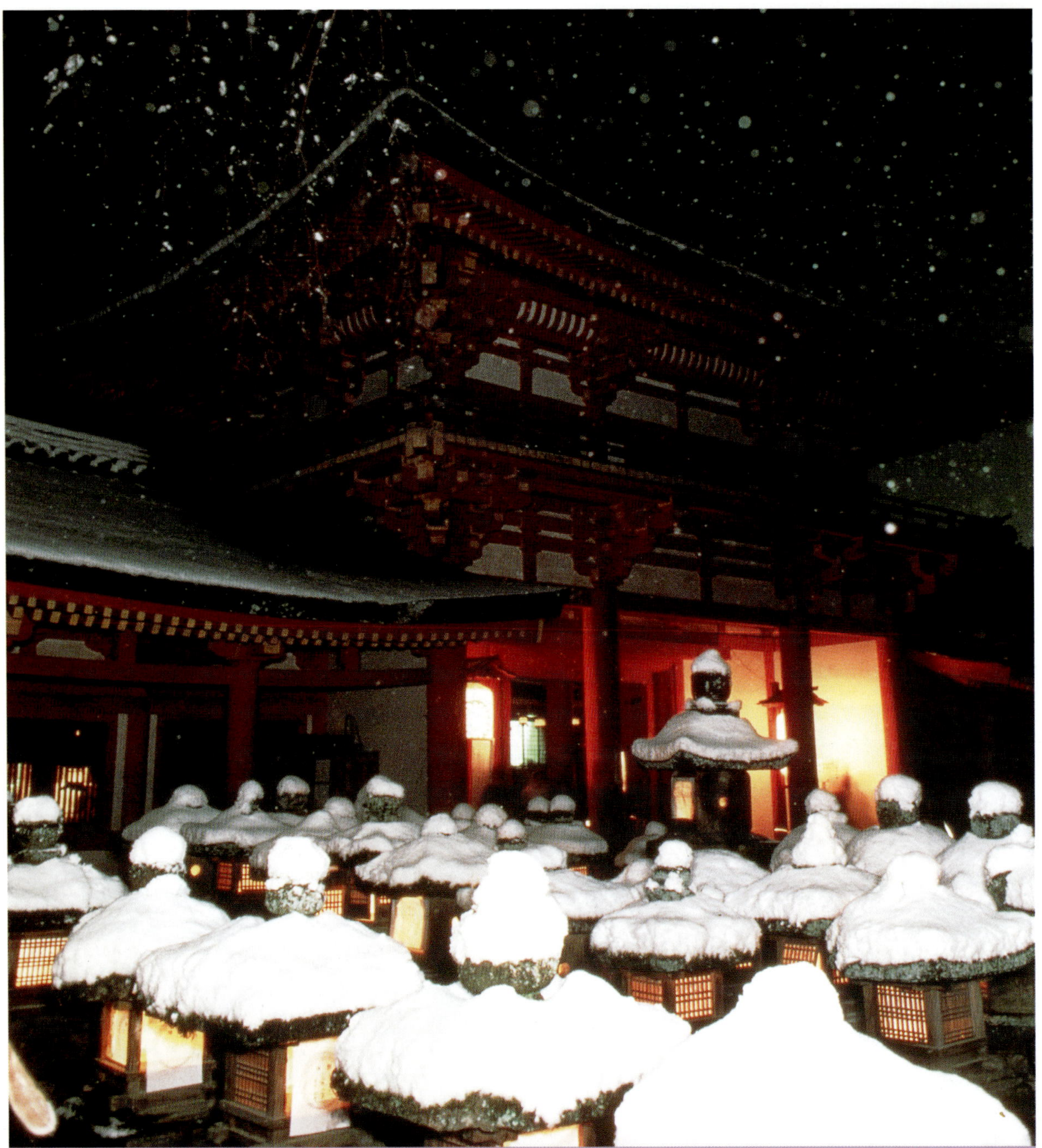

Even as the snow falls today

    At the commencement of the New Year

    And with the new-born spring,

    Ever thick come, good things!

Ōtomo Yakamochi

Notes on the Images and Authors

All translations, except where noted, are by the editors. (KM) indicates Keiko I. McDonald; (TR) indicates J. Thomas Rimer

Cover. The Daimonji Mountain-Burning Festival.

The yearly festival on Mt. Takamado, north of Nara, takes place on August 15 and takes its name from the bonfire which is lit high on the hillside. The pieces of wood to be burned are arranged in the shape of the character *dai* ("great"), while the word *monji* means "writing." Here, the first character refers to the vastness of the universe, and setting fire to the pieces of wood so arranged betokens a purification of the human spirit.

Page 3. The Lantern Festival at Kasuga Shrine.

Among the many splendors of this important shrine are a thousand hanging bronze lanterns and at least twice that many in stone. They are lit twice a year, on February 4 for Setsubun (a spring festival) and on August 15 for O-bon (the festival of the dead).

Donald Keene, long the premier scholar of Japanese literature and culture in the Western world, has written a number of travel essays, including one on Nara, which are contained in a recently published collection of his writings entitled *The Blue-eyed Tarōkaja* (Columbia University Press, by permission).

Page 5. Shōryakuji and its surrounding countryside.

The area is sometimes referred to as "the village of brocade," because the maple trees planted there turn such brilliant colors in the fall. It is believed that Emperor

Ichijō built a temple there between 990 and 995. At the height of its prosperity, it boasted a number of impressive buildings, but over the centuries all but a few have vanished.

Page 6. Sunset over Nara, from the Nigatsudō.

The Nigatsudō was founded by the priest Jicchu in 752. Its name, literally the "Second-Month Hall," derives from the fact that religious rites involving prayers for the health of the nation are held there annually during the second month of the lunar calendar. Its hilltop location gives the Nigatsudō a commanding view of the city of Nara (see page 36).

Sir Alfred East (1844–1913), an eminent painter of the Victorian period, visited Japan in 1889 on a commission from the Fine Art Society of London. His journal, *A British Artist in Meiji Japan*, unpublished until 1991 (In Print, by permission), provides a number of evocative descriptions of Japan at the end of the nineteenth century.

Page 8. Asebi flowers blooming in Nara Park.

Asebi flowers, sometimes called "lily of the valley bushes," clothe Nara Park and the Kasuga Shrine in the early spring season. Since deer have long been considered divine messengers at Kasuga, *asebi* trees were planted, tradition has it, to protect the deer from wolves and wild boars.

Shūōshi (1892–1981) began his studies as a medical doctor but by the 1920s had become a major force in the renovation of the 17-syllable *haiku* form. (KM)

Page 13. The Drum-Dancing Festival at Yagyū.

This folk festival, held annually on August 17, began as

a dance in honor of the rain god. Today it survives only in a version dedicated to a deity related to a higher-ranking god of the nearby Yamaguchi Shrine. This Drum Dancing festival is designated as Intangible Folk Cultural Asset by the Nara Prefectural government.

Santōka (1882–1940) was a remarkable Buddhist monk. Ordained at the age of forty-four, he then traveled as a medicant monk throughout Japan. The translation, by John Stevens, is from *Mountain Tasting* (Weatherhill, by permission).

Page 14. Camellias in bloom at Byakugōji Temple.

Founded by the priest Gonsō in 715, the temple prospered as a place of worship for commoners during the medieval period. Its camellias are famous for their great age (some upwards of four hundred years) and their beauty in bloom. Some bear blossoms in five different color patterns.

The *Kojiki* (Record of Ancient Matters), completed in 721, is the oldest written text of its kind in Japan, and provides a remarkable collection of myths, historical material, poems, legends, and genealogies. Among them is this evocative poem, translated by Donald L. Philippi (University Press of Tokyo, by permission).

Page 16. Mountain-Burning Festival at Mount Wakakusa.

Mount Wakakusa, commonly known as Mount Mikasa, commands a splendid view of the city of Nara. Its park and walking paths are open to the public from March 21 to June 15, and from September 10 to November 25. The Mountain-Burning Festival of January 15 is one of the most spectacular of the historic commemorations held in Nara.

Yamabe no Akahito (fl. 724–737) is, after Hitomaro, the best-loved poet of the eighth-century poetry collection, the *Man'yōshū*. This translation, by Ian Hideo Levy, is from his *The Ten Thousand Leaves* (University Press of Tokyo, by permission).

Page 17. Cherries blossoming at Kōfukuji Temple.

Originally built as a tutelary temple for the powerful Fujiwara clan, Kōfukuji temple enjoyed imperial patronage in the Nara period. At the height of its prosperity, it housed over a hundred and seventy priests. Much of the temple was destroyed in 1180, when Nara was sacked by a large army of the Taira clan during the civil wars of the time.

The passage cited is from *The Tale of the Heike*, the great account of those civil wars, and describes the burning of Nara. The translation is by Helen McCullough (Stanford University Press, by permission).

Page 18. Forsythia blooming at Futaiji Temple.

Futaiji Temple, on the Saho river, is noted for its springtime show of forsythia. The buildings were first constructed as a residence for the Emperor Heizei a year after his retirement in 810. They were made into a temple in 847 by one of his grandsons, the celebrated poet Ariwara no Narihira.

Lady Ōtomo (c. 700–750) is one of the leading women poets in the *Man'yōshū*. Her son-in-law, Ōtomo no Yakamochi, edited this famous early collection. This translation is also by Ian Hideo Levy (see page 16).

Page 20. Yellow roses blooming at Hannyaji Temple.

These yellow roses (*yamabuki*) bloom in a garden surrounding a three-tiered pagoda. The temple is said to have been founded by the Priest Ekan from the Korean kingdom of Koguryö as early as 627. It was greatly expanded in 735, during the reign of Emperor Shōmu. The pagoda was reputedly rebuilt in 1240, after the razing of the temple, like so much else in Nara, during the 1180 civil wars.

Hattori Ransetsu (1654–1707) was an important disciple of the greatest of the *haiku* poets, Matsuo Bashō; after his master's death in 1694, he helped carry on the Bashō tradition in Edo. (TR)

Page 21. *Bugaku* dancing at the Kasuga Shrine.

Bugaku (which might be translated as "dance entertainment") is a performance art originally introduced from China as part of a series of elaborate court rituals. It became a sophisticated art form during the Heian period, but declined in medieval times. *Bugaku* survives today in Nara as part of an annual ceremony performed at the Kasuga Shrine on January 15.

Faubion Bowers has been for thirty years or more an informed commentator on many aspects of Japanese theatre and culture. His *Theatre in the East*, from which this extract is taken, was first published in l956 and still remains a useful account of performance arts in Japan, Southeast Asia, and India (Grove Press, by permission).

Page 22. The Setsubun Festival.

The Setsubun Festival (literally "the changing of the season"), anticipates the first day of spring in the traditional Japanese calendar. Many events are held to celebrate this seasonal change, among them a ceremony of exorcism performed at Kōfukuji temple, in which a Buddhist deity defeats six devils, a dramatic enactment accompanied by the traditional saying, "Fortune in! Devils out!"

Page 23. The Kōnin Ceremony.

This ceremony is held at the Daianji Temple on January 23. Its origin was an occasion when prayers were offered for the longevity of the Emperor Kōnin, who came to the throne in the year 770 at the age of sixty-two. After the priests perform their annual ritual, they offer sake in bamboo stalks to their visitors. Believers consider such offerings a useful preventive for cancer.

Shiga Naoya (1883–1971), one of the great novelists of modern Japan, lived for many years in Nara, where he visited and described a remarkable variety of sites in his stories and essays. (KM)

Page 24. Gangōji Temple.

Before the founding of Nara in 710, the area now referred to as Fujiwara-kyō, south of the city, served for a time as imperial capital. The Asuka Temple, built in that area in 588, was highly revered as one of the earliest Buddhist temple constructions in the nation. After the capital shifted to Nara, the now historic structure was relocated there and renamed Gangōji. Destroyed in the civil wars of 1180, the temple was rebuilt, but in the medieval period its power declined. Now only the priest's quarters, added in the fourteenth century, and a few associated buildings are all that remain of this once glorious complex.

Satō Aiko (born 1923) is a leading woman novelist in contemporary Japan, and a step-sister of the noted poet Satō Hachirō. *The Actress Aiko*, from which this excerpt is taken, chronicles her own mother's stormy career as a performer. (KM)

Page 26. Camellias in bloom at Denkōji Temple.

Denkōji Temple was founded in 771 by the priest Shitaku Risshi, an important disciple of Ganjin (Chien-chen), the Chinese cleric who first brought Tendai Buddhism to Japan. The temple was established as a branch of the famous Tōshōdaiji, where Ganjin served as chief priest and teacher. The temple gradually lost importance until it was restored in 1585 by the mother of Tsutsui Junkei, a powerful warrior of the time. The Tsutsui clan was among the most distinguished in Nara, its family members serving since the medieval period as heads of the congregation at Kōfukuji, a role which made them, in effect, chiefs of police.

Shōha (?–1771) was a close disciple of the great *haiku* poet Yosa Buson. (TR)

Page 27. Kairyūōji Temple.

This temple was built under the patronage of the Empress Kōmyō, probably in 731. The West Main Hall survives as an original structure of the period, and the grounds also contain a small five-story pagoda constructed in the Nara period.

Hori Tatsuo (1904–53), one of the outstanding writers of the interwar period, was heavily influenced by modern French literature and wrote a number of evocative stories and short novels still widely admired. Later in his career, his trips to older cultural sites in Japan produced a series of evocative writings, including *A Visit to Yamato*, from which this excerpt is taken. (KM)

Page 28. Spring flowers in the village of Yagyū.

The picturesque village of Yagyū, headquarters of the famous clan of the same name during the Edo period, is now a part of the city of Nara.

Eiji Yoshikawa (1892–1962) is one of the most famous of popular Japanese novelists, whose exciting accounts of samurai adventures have thrilled generations of Japanese readers. This extract, translated by Charles Terry, is taken from *Musashi: An Epic Novel of the Samurai Era* (Kodansha International, by permission).

Page 30. Kasuga Shrine.

This beautiful and dignified shrine (see pages 3 and 66) constitutes a major historical site of the city of Nara. Founded in 766 as a tutelary shrine of the ascendant Fujiwara Clan, the shrine expanded, along with the ever-increasing power of the clan, during the Heian period.

Sacheverell Sitwell (1897–1988), the poet and art critic, was the youngest member of the famous Sitwell family, all of whom were writers of note in England over a period of several generations. His long-anticipated trip to Japan produced an evocative 1959 travel account *The Bridge of the Brocade Sash*, from which this excerpt is taken (World Publishing Company).

Page 31. Magnolias blooming at the Akishino Temple.

The Akishino Temple was founded in 780, under the patronage of the Emperors Kōnin and Kan'mu. Much of the temple has been destroyed over the centuries, but one original structure, now the Main Hall, remains, containing a beautiful dry-lacquer statue of a Buddhist deity.

Tachihara Masaaki (1927–80) was a much-admired writer of popular fiction, whose literary career was solidly established after 1966, when he received the prestigious Naoki Prize. After that, his astonishing creative energy yielded a number of novels, virtually all of which turned out to be best-sellers. He made a number of trips to Nara in preparation for *The Life of a Flower*, from which this excerpt is taken. (KM)

Page 32. The Hokkeji Temple Garden.

This beautiful temple served as a national headquarters for various nunneries established in the Nara period. The renowned strolling garden is open to the public in the spring and the fall. Visits are particularly popular in early May, when the iris are in bloom.

Another quotation by Sacheverell Sitwell, from his visit to Nara (see page 30).

Page 34. Fan-Throwing Ceremony at Tōshōdaiji Temple.

This ritual ceremony, held every year on May 19 at the famous Tōshōdaiji, is dedicated to the priest Kakusei, credited with reconstructing the temple in the thirteenth century. The fan is believed to exorcise evil spirits.

Basil Hall Chamberlain (1856–1935), a British educator who taught for a time at Tokyo University, was the first European scholar to describe many aspects of Japanese life. This description of the origins of the fan is taken from his *Things Japanese*, first published in 1890.

Page 35. A distant view of Mount Wakakusa with Kōfukuji Temple in the foreground.

This mountain overlooking the city takes the form of three gently-rounded peaks. A popular monument at the top commands a fine view of Nara and vicinity.

Yosano Akiko (1878–1941) was a major force in making the traditional 31-syllable *waka* form a vehicle for the expression of modern feminine sentiment. Despite the fact that she most often used such a traditional form, she remains one of the most innovative poets of the modern period. (KM)

Page 36. Purification Ceremony at Nigatsudō.

This quotation, which describes so eloquently the ceremonies held annually since 752 in the second lunar month at this temple in the Todaiji complex, is taken from the 1960 novel *After the Banquet* (Knopf, by permission) by one of Japan's leading writers of the postwar period, Mishima Yukio (1925–70).

Page 37. The Kasuga Festival.

The festival, held annually on March 13, re-enacts a series of shrine rituals pictured on a famous medieval narrative scroll, in which an official messenger is chosen from among the descendants of the Fujiwara Clan, whose task it becomes to offer food and prayers to the chief deity of the shrine before dining with the gods themselves.

The *nō* dramatist Komparu Zenchiku (1405–68?) wrote the play *The Kasuga Dragon God* in order to extol the importance of the Kasuga Shrine, whose priests were, and remain, important sponsors of *nō* performance. The translation is taken from the English-language version of the play by Royall Tyler, which appears in his collection *Japanese Nō Dramas* (Penguin Classics).

Page 38. Willow trees around Sarusawa Pond.

Sarusawa Pond, near the Kōfukuji temple in the east of the city, has long been a favorite spot for visitors. Filled with carp and turtles and surrounded by willow trees, legend has placed dragons there as well.

Uejima Onitsura (1661–1738), a talented *haiku* poet, was a younger contemporary of Matsuo Bashō, and the two shared similar aesthetic views. (TR)

Page 39. The Buddha-Viewing Ceremony.

The ceremony, performed annually on April 8, takes place in a small pavilion set up in the grounds of the Tōdaiji, Nara's most famous temple. This four-hour ritual begins at eight o'clock in the morning and runs until noon. Sweet tea is poured over the statue and then offered to visitors.

Another poem by Santōka (see page 13), whose travels took him all over the country. This translation is also by John Stevens, from *Mountain Tasting*.

Page 40. Statue of Ashura at Kōfukuji Temple.

This triple-faced dry lacquer statue with three pairs of arms is representative of the dynamic style of Buddhist sculpture achieved in the eighth century.

The description is from one of the classic accounts of the Japanese visual arts, Hugo Munsterberg's *The Arts of Japan*, first published in 1957 (Charles E. Tuttle Company, by permission).

Page 41. Wisteria blooming at Kasuga Shrine.

Hanging bronze lanterns and pendant wisteria in bloom lend an air of elegance to the complex of shrine buildings, with their predominant vermillion hue.

Emperor Godaigo (reigned 1313–36), a noted poet, suffered exile as a result of intrigues relating to his attempts to restore direct imperial rule. (TR)

Page 42. The Buddha's footprints in stone at Yakushiji Temple.

The carved footprints of the Buddha represent a venerable sculptural theme. This pair is reputedly the oldest in Japan, dating from 753. Said to have been imported from Paikche (Korea), it is believed to atone for the sins of those who worship it.

The Buddha's Footprint Poem reproduced here is the first of sixteen such poems carved on stones which now are kept at the Yakushiji Temple in Nara. These texts, probably composed in the eighth century, are considered to be among the earliest of their kind in the history of Japanese literature. The translation is from a monograph-length study of these intriguing poems undertaken by Roy Andrew Miller, *"The Footprints of the Buddha: An Eighth-Century Old Japanese Poetic Sequence"* (American Oriental Society, 1975, by permission).

Page 43. Crepe myrtle blooming around Sagi Pond.

The crisp papery textures of these blossoms seem a fine accompaniment to a distant view of the Floating Pavilion (Ukimidō) in Sagi Pond.

Masaoka Shiki (1867–1902) is a much-admired Meiji *haiku* and *waka* poet who stands at the forefront of his contemporaries in his experiments with subject matter and language. (TR)

Page 44. The Floating Pavilion and Sagi Pond.

Sagi Pond and its beautiful Floating Pavilion are located in Nara Park. The water, flowers, and hills behind combine to make a striking visual composite.

Ogiwara Seisensui (1884–1976) is a celebrated essayist and *haiku* poet noted for his experiments in writing *haiku* in a free, untraditional rhythm. This excerpt is taken from the sequence *Pilgrimage to Kannon*. (KM)

Page 45. The Festival of Emperor Shōmu.

The festival is held annually on May second in order to honor Emperor Shōmu (reigned 724–49) for his role in expanding and beautifying the city of Nara, particularly the areas surrounding the Tōdaiji temple, which he ordered constructed in 756.

Jien (1155–1225) a prominent Tendai Buddhist cleric and poet, left many moving poems of a devotional nature. (TR)

Page 46. Firelight *nō* at the Kōfukuji Temple.

Performances of *nō*, the elegant masked medieval drama, have been held at Kōfukuji since medieval times. Today, on May 11 and 12 of each year, the medieval atmosphere is recreated by four major troupes that perform in the ruins of the great South Gate of the temple.

Zeami Motokiyo (1363–1443) first brought the *nō* to perfection and remains the greatest playwright and theoretician in the history of the form. The quotation is taken from his memoir "Reflections in Art," taken down by his son Motoyoshi. (TR)

Page 47. Cosmos at Hannyaji Temple.

The thirteen-story pagoda at Hannyaji Temple (see page 20) is one of the finest of its kind in Japan.

This poem by the Emperor Heizei (reigned 806–809) is found in the first great collection of 31-syllable *waka* poetry, the *Kokinshū* (Collection of Old and New Poetry), c. 920. (TR)

Page 48. Takisaka Path.

This path, also called Yagyū Highway despite its sometimes slender width, remained the main thoroughfare between Nara and the village of Yagyū (see page 28) during the Tokugawa period. Rising into the hills, it is rich in wayside Buddhist statues, carved and placed there over a long span of history, from the Nara period onwards. Maples help to provide spectacular views of autumn scenery.

Fujiwara no Yoshitsune (1169–1206) was a noted court poet also gifted in calligraphy and the composition of poetry in classical Chinese. This particular poem can be found in the important collection *Shinkokinshû* (New Collection of Old and New Poetry), compiled early in the thirteenth century, which surpasses even the *Kokinshū* in its beauty and profundity. (TR)

Page 49. The Great Buddha Purification Ceremony.

On August 7 of each year, the great Buddha at Tōdaiji is given a ceremonial cleaning, a prodigious task given the huge mass and height of the sculpture. Over one hundred and fifty priests, all clad in white, participate in this ceremony. Using chains hung from the ceiling, they clean the gigantic statue, yielding, according to some accounts, some fifty buckets of accumulated dust.

Gaspar Vilela, S.J. (1525–72) was born in Portugal and eventually became a Catholic missionary in Japan, where he was able to travel to a number of sites, including Nara. The translation is by Michael Cooper, from his *They Came to Japan: An Anthology of European Reports on Japan, 1563–1640* (Center for Japanese Studies, The University of Michigan, by permission).

Page 50. Spire of the pagoda of Yakushiji Temple.

This beautiful figure of a musician is one of four that grace the top of the nine-ringed spire of the Yakushiji's famous three-storied pagoda, and are said to represent angels dancing and playing musical instruments.

This elegant poem, in the 31-syllable classical *waka* style, is by the much-respected literary scholar and poet Sasaki Nobutsuna (1872–1963). (KM)

Page 51. Deer roaming near the Kasuga Shrine.

The deer living in Nara Park have been considered divine messengers since the twelfth century. They have been designated by the government as a "national monument," and are happy to munch on special crackers sold to tourists for this purpose.

Another quotation from Gaspar Vilela, an early Portuguese visitor to the city (see page 49).

Page 53. Sarusawa Pond and Kōfukuji Temple.

At the founding of Nara in 710, the Umasaka Temple in the Asuka area was moved to the new capital and given its present name. During the Nara period, the temple prospered through the support of the Fujiwara clan, but in 1180, many of its buildings were destroyed in the civil war. The great five-story pagoda was rebuilt in the fifteenth century and stands as the second highest pagoda in Japan. Among its holdings are some of the finest Buddhist sculptures in Japan.

John LaFarge (1835–1910), the American artist, was an early and enthusiastic visitor to Japan, and the record of his impressions, *An Artist's Letters from Japan*, first published in 1897, remains fresh today.

Page 54. One of the figures of the Twelve Warriors at Shin-Yakushiji Temple.

Shin-Yakushiji contains a celebrated statue of the titular deity, Yakushi Nyorai (the Buddha of Medicine). The figure is guarded by twelve warriors known as Ashura. The statue here, which stands erect, is armed with swords and arrows and shows a wrathful gaze. The statue has been designated a National Treasure.

Louis Frédéric, a leading European scholar of Buddhism, finished his definitive French-language guide to Buddhist iconography in 1989. The English version, from which this entry is taken, was published in 1995 (Flammarion Publishers).

Page 55. The Nara National Museum.

The museum, located in Nara Park, contains one of the finest collections of Buddhist art in the world. To the famous main building, constructed in the Meiji period has been added an elegant annex, opened in 1973. In addition to its superb permanent displays and other special exhibitions, an exhibition of selected treasures from the Shōsōin (see page 79) is presented each fall.

Katayama Tōkuma (1854–1917), one of the first Japanese architects to build in the Western style, designed in addition to the Nara Museum other remarkable buildings such as the Kyoto National Museum and the Akasaka Detached Palace in Tokyo. This citation on his work is taken from Dallas Finn's *Meiji Revisited: The Sites of Victorian Japan* (Weatherhill, by permission).

Page 56. The former residence of the novelist Shiga Naoya, near Shin-Yakushiji.

Shiga Naoya (see page 23), long considered a leading figure in modern Japanese literature, lived in Nara from 1925 to 1938. His most important novel, *A Dark Night's Passing*, was written in this house. The quotation is from an essay by Shiga entitled simply "Nara." (KM)

Page 58. The Moon-Viewing Festival at Tōshōdaiji Temple.

This ritual is meant to celebrate the coming of the harvest moon. The main hall of the temple is opened to visitors, and crowds gather outside to admire the fantastic effects created by the moonlight falling on Buddhist statues and the ceramic figures of the dolphins who ride the rooftops.

Jakuren (?1139–1202), a Buddhist priest and poet, wrote verse on religious topics of a special poignancy. This particular poem can be found in the *Shinkokinshū*, which contains some thirty-eight of his poems, indicating the significance of his work to his contemporaries. (TR)

Page 59. Cutting the antlers of the deer.

The antlers of the sacred deer of Nara Park (see page 51) are cut once a year, in October, a tradition dating back to 1671.

This *haiku* by Matsuo Bashō, translated by Yuasa Nobuyuki appears in *The Narrow Road to the Deep North and Other Travel Sketches* (Penguin Books, by permission).

Page 60. *Bugaku* concert at the Botanical Garden.

These popular concerts, sponsored by Nara's Manyō Botanical garden, take place on May fifth and November third of each year. A special stage is constructed in the middle of a small pond, in order to better evoke the courtly atmosphere of the Tempyō period (729–49).

Eta Harich-Schneider (1897–1986) first studied the harpsichord under Wanda Landowska and gave the first performances of Bach's great "Goldberg Variations" in Berlin in the 1930s. Fleeing the Nazis, she went to Tokyo, where eventually she took up the study of Japanese music. Her 1973 *History of Japanese Music*, from which this extract is taken (Oxford Universtity Press, by permission), still remains definitive.

Page 61. The Thousand-Armed Kannon at Tōshōdaiji Temple.

This statue, nearly eighteen feet high, is the largest of its type in Japan. Originally created in the eighth century, it still retains 953 of the original thousand arms. The statue is a National Treasure.

Paul Mus (1902–69), the famous French savant of Buddhism and an expert on Southeast Asia, wrote widely on various topics connected with Asian art, religion, and culture. This excerpt is taken from an article "Un Cinéma Solide," published in the journal *Arts Asiatiques* in 1964. (TR)

Page 62. The five-story pagoda of Kōfukuji Temple, with the Sarusawa Pond in the foreground.

The pagoda, one the great sights of Nara, is often photographed with its reflection in the pond and is often described in literature.

Akutagawa Ryūnosuke (1892–1927), one of the most sophisticated of modern Japanese storytellers, often used historical material in his pungent satires. "The Dragon," the story from which the excerpt was taken, was published in 1919. The translation by Takashi Kojima can be found in *Rashomon and Other Stories* (Liveright Publishing Corporation, by permission).

Page 63. Cosmos flowers blooming at the Hannyaji Temple.

This temple and its famous pagoda (see pages 20 and 47), one of the most venerable in Nara, is well known for the various flowers that bloom there in successive seasons.

The poem is the sixth of the Buddha's Footprint Poems (see page 42).

Page 64. Bush clover blooming at Byakugōji Temple.

Hundreds of bush clover plants surround the Byakugōji Temple, another ancient Buddhist site founded by the priest Gonsō, in 715. Bush clover is a plant with powerful emotional and literary associations in Japan. As summer passes into fall, each bush appears to become a rising and falling mountain of blooms in white, or in shades of purple or rose. This graceful flourish at harvest time suggests both the summer's bounty and the fleetingness of life itself, and Japanese poets have long been drawn to compose verses on the bush clover in bloom. The *Man'yōshū*, the great early anthology of Japanese poetry, contains some 137 poems on this plant.

Yamonoue Okura (660–c.733) is among the poets most widely included in the *Man'yōshū*. Among his most famous poems are those relating to his visit on an official mission to T'ang China and those recounting his suffering at the loss of a dead child. The translation is taken from the edition of the *Man'yōshū* edited by the Nippon Gakujitsu Shinkōkai (Columbia University Press, by permission).

The second, anonymous poem is from the first imperial anthology of 31-syllable *waka* poems, the *Kokinshū*, commissioned around 905. Like the earlier *Man'yōshū*, this anthology includes a number of striking verses on the subject of bush clover.

Page 65. The Great Tea Bowl Ceremony at Saidaiji Temple.

This ceremony is held four times a year: January 15, on the second Saturday and Sunday of April, and on the second Sunday in October. On those occasions, the priests of the temple brew tea in a gigantic bowl and offer it to the faithful. This particular ceremony dates back to 1239, when it was first undertaken by the priest Eison.

The poem that accompanies the photograph is carved on a famous stone pillar at the temple, and was written by one of the outstanding women *haiku* poets of this century, Hashimoto Takako (1899–1963).

Page 66. The Lantern Festival at Kasuga Shrine

As noted earlier (see page 3), the Kasuga Shrine is adorned with some three thousand or more lanterns donated by benefactors from every part of Japan, some dating back as far as the eighth century. The lanterns are lit twice a year, in February, for the Setsubun Festival, and, as here, on August 14 and 15, for the traditional festival of O-bon, which venerates the souls of the departed.

Percival Lowell (1855–1916), a member of the famous Lowell family of Massachusetts, was one of the first visitors to Japan in the Meiji period to take a serious interest in traditional Japanese religions. The extract is taken from his pioneering study *Occult Japan*, first published in 1895. Lowell's research is said to have been very influential on the work of William James, whose *The Varieties of Religious Experience* of 1902 remains a classic of American letters.

Page 68. The dance of Okina at the Nara Zuhiko Shrine.

This festival, held on October 8, originated in the dances presented to the main deity of the shrine. Residents of the nearby community preserve these forms of dance, which predate the *nō* of Zeami, in order to present them at the festival.

Zeami (see page 46) points out in this citation from the treatise "Reflections on Art" that the ancient dances performed by the character of Okina (which might roughly be translated "Old Man") were considered both ancient and sacred even in his lifetime. (TR)

Page 69. The "Paradise Garden" of Enjōji Temple.

This temple is thought by some to have been founded by the order of the Emperor Shōmu, while others believe it was built by the priest Korō, who came from China along with Ganjin (see page 26). The main hall contains a number of famous Buddhist statues carved by the famous sculptor Unkei (?–1223). The strolling garden is laid out in a quiet, natural style, as befits a representation of Buddha's paradise.

The poem, another by the cleric Jakuren (see page 58), extols the beauty of Buddha's gardens, which transcend the seasons. (TR)

Page 70. The Yakushi Triad at Yakushiji Temple.

The main deity of the temple, Yakushi, sometimes referred to as the Healing Buddha, stands thirty feet high in the center of the group, in a robust pose characteristic of late seventh-century Buddhist art. To the right and left are the Bodhisattvas of the Sun and Moon. They too adopt characteristic poses, exquisitely rhythmical as their twisting torsos and graceful hands echo the motions of their flowing garments.

Kamei Katsuichirō (1907–66) was a writer imprisoned for his Marxist views of society in the 1930s, and who eventually turned to writing on various aspects of traditional Japanese culture. The quotation is from his *A Record of Temples in Old Yamato*. (KM)

Page 71. Bush Clover at Shin-Yakushiji Temple.

This is another renowned spot in Nara where these famous blooms can be found.

The *waka* is by Fujiwara no Yoshitsune (see page 48), who, considered by some as the most gifted young poet of his day, died at a relatively early age. This poem is also found in the *Shinkokinshū*. (TR)

Page 72. The Great Buddha at the Tōdaiji Temple.

The Daibutsu, or Great Buddha, is one of the wonders of Japan, visited by pilgrims and sightseers from all over the world. The figure took seven years to build and was dedicated in 752 by the Emperor Shōmu, in a magnificent ceremony attended by visitors from as far away as India. The figure seen today is actually a replacement of the original, which was badly damaged over the centuries in a series of fires.

One of the most distinguished visitors to the Great Buddha and the temple which houses it was Paul Claudel (1868–1955) the noted French playwright and poet who served as France's Ambassador to Japan from 1921 through 1926. These notes from his diaries, published by Gallimard, capture his impressions in an unpolished but striking form. (TR)

Page 73. Eleven-Headed Kannon at Hokkeiji Temple.

Legend has it that an Indian sculptor modeled this Kannon (Goddess of Mercy) on the Empress Kōmyō, who founded the temple. The statue, a little over three feet in height, is carved from a single block of sandalwood. Its partly colored and sensuous surface conveys a sense of individual personality markedly different from other contemporary statues. Eleven small faces adorn the top of the head.

Aizu Yaichi (1881–1956) remains well-known for his innovative calligraphy and his modern *waka*, many written to describe the beauties of Buddhist art in Nara. (KM)

Page 74. A carved-rock statue of a Buddhist image on the Takisaka Path.

Along this path (see page 48) many beautiful carved images have been placed over the centuries. None is more lovely than this so-called Yūhi Kannon, or "Twilight Bodhisattva," so named because the statue, which faces west, looks most beautiful at sunset.

Fujiwara no Toshinari (1114–1204), also known as Shunzei, was a great poet in his own right and the father of Fujiwara Teika, often considered the finest poet in the *waka* tradition. This poem is taken from the *Shinkokinshū*. (TR)

Page 75. Tōshōdaiji.

One of the great temples of the early Nara period, its founding is well-described in the quotation by the distinguished writer Inoue Yasushi (1907–1991) in his evocative novel of 1957 *The Roof Tile of Tempyō*, from which this extract is taken. (KM)

Page 76. The Imanishi Family Residence.

Nara was spared bombing attacks during World War II, so the city retains a number of houses dating back to the medieval period, and their present residents are given financial incentives to aid them in preserving the historical character of their buildings. The Imanishi Family

Residence is a famous surviving example of architecture created in the *shōin* style of the Muromachi period (1333–1573).

Edward S. Morse (1838–1925) came to Meiji Japan to teach zoology and biology at Tokyo University. He was a man of wide cultural interests, ranging from anthropology to architecture. This quotation is taken from his pioneering study *Japanese Homes and Their Surroundings*, first published in 1886.

Page 78. The Nara Hotel.

Built for foreign visitors in 1909, the hotel had all the accoutrements expected by wealthy tourists. Its so-called Japan Revival Style of architecture, still carefully preserved, has given it a classic status among Western-style buildings of the period. The planning and construction of the hotel is well-described in Dallas Finn's *Meiji Revisited: The Sites of Victorian Japan.*

James Kirkup (born 1918) the well-known British poet, stayed in the hotel in the 1950s, and recorded his favorable reaction in his 1962 *These Horned Islands*, from which this extract is taken (The Macmillan Company).

Page 79. The Shōsōin.

The Shōsōin, built to house the treasures presented at the time of the consecration of the Great Buddha in 752, was built in the *azekura* or "log cabin" style of construction, which, through an ingenious system using logs cut in triangular cross-sections that permit some circulation of air, has preserved these treasures until today. As noted earlier, selected items from the collection are shown in rotation on a yearly basis at the Nara National Museum during late October to early November, when the building itself is open to the public.

Ernest Fenollosa (1853–1908), an influential figure in the art world of Meiji Japan, first came from Boston as a teacher of philosophy but soon concerned himself with the traditional Japanese arts. His account of the development of East Asian art, *Epochs of Chinese and Japanese Art*, was first published after his death in 1912.

Page 81. The Festival of the Lady Attendant at Sarusawa Pond.

This famous festival to honor the tragic death of a Lady Attendant (*uneme*) is held in September, in the evening. The Emperor in the tale has been variously identified as Heizei or Shōmu, among others.

The account reproduced here is Number 150 in the *Tales of Yamato*, a tenth-century poem-tale. The translation is by Mildred Tahara (University Press of Hawaii, by permission).

Page 82. The Sacred Kannon (Shō-Kannon) at Yakushiji Temple.

Designated as a National Treasure, the figure shows great refinement and grace.

The distinguished art scholar Robert Treat Paine, along with his colleague the architectural historian Alexander Soper, first published their magisterial *The Art and Architecture of Japan* in 1955 (Penguin Books, by permission). It still remains an essential account some forty years later.

Page 83. Making Akahada pottery.

Akahada pottery takes its name from the area in Nara in which it was first produced, in the eighth century. At first these earthenwares were created to meet a demand for temple and aristocratic household furnishings, such as charcoal braziers. As the tea ceremony developed in the late sixteenth century, bowls and tiles also became important items of manufacture. Akahada pottery rose to national prominence in the years 1615–25, thanks to Kobori Enshū, founder of the Enshū school of the tea ceremony, who commissioned a great many pieces. Today, Akahada ware is sought by connoisseurs the world over.

The British novelist Rudyard Kipling (1865–1936), on his visit to Japan in 1889, admired the level of Japanese accomplishment in the field of ceramics and recorded his own observations on the making of pottery prepared for export.

Page 84. The Kasuga-Wakamiya Festival procession.

The Kasuga-Wakamiya Shrine, a subsidiary shrine close to the main Kasuga Shrine buildings, is the site of the colorful Kasuga-Wakamiya Onmatsuri (festival), held from December 15 to December 18 of each year. Perhaps the most spectacular event in the Nara yearly calendar, the festival dates back to the great famine of 1134, and the prayers offered during the course of the festival seek harvest abundance and protection from disaster. The highlight of the festival is the parade that takes place on December 17. The procession of worshippers in traditional costume begins at the Kōfukuji Temple and ends at the shrine. That evening, many kinds of traditional theater are performed, including *kagura*, ritual dances to the gods, *sarugaku*, the precursor of *nō*, *bugaku*, and others. On the final day, *nō* drama and sumo wrestling are offered.

Royall Tyler, an eminent contemporary scholar of Japanese literature, took up the study of the Kasuga Shrine as a means to examine the way in which literature, the arts, and the religious sensibility were combined in medieval Japan. The extract describing the procession is taken from his 1990 *The Miracles of the Kasuga Deity* (Columbia University Press, by permission).

Page 85. Pampas grass at Asachigahara.

The beautiful area of Nara park where these grasses grow, so redolent of an autumn atmosphere, has always been much appreciated by visitors.

Hirotsu Kazuo (1891–1968) was a popular novelist during the interwar and early postwar period who wrote on various social and intellectual problems faced by his generation. The quotation is from an essay he wrote on Nara. (KM)

Page 86. Festival at Kasuga-Wakamiya Shrine.

Another description of the important Kasuga-Wakamiya Festival activities (see page 84) is given by Christopher Dresser (1834–1904), a gifted English designer and author on Japanese aesthetics as they relate to the industrial arts. Dresser was the first Western designer to visit Japan, during the years 1876–77. This excerpt is taken from his detailed account of Japanese art and culture, published in 1872 as *Japan: Its Architecture, Art, and Art Manufactures.*

Page 87. Yakushiji Temple.

Although famous for the magnificent Buddhist statuary within (see page 70) the building complex of the Yakushiji is one of the most visually striking sights in the city.

This evocative description of the temple buildings by Kamei Katsuichirō is found in his *Landscape of Old Temples in Yamato.* (KM)

Page 88. A distant view of Tōdaiji Temple.

For all the beauty of Nara in the spring and fall, the city in snow provides an arresting sense of space and atmosphere.

The writer Ishikawa Tatsuzō (1910–85), who first came to prominence for his unsparing descriptions of Japanese military activities in China in the 1930s, later wrote on a wide variety of subjects, including Nara. This passage, translated from his 1955 *In My Little Nook,* captures evocatively the sense of place and season. (KM)

Page 90. The Third-Month Temple at Tōdaiji.

The name of the so-called Third-Month Temple (Sangatsudō) derives from the fact that an important Buddhist ritual is conducted there in the third month of each year, according to the traditional Japanese calendar. The temple contains a number of sculptures and other works of art designated as National Treasures. Founded in 733, it has remained intact to this day, except for an addition of a chapel in about 1200. The structure is thus the oldest in the entire temple complex.

Watsuji Tetsurō (1889–1960) is one of Japan's most eminent modern philosophers. Early a student of such European thinkers as Kierkegaard and Nietzsche, his 1919 travel account, *Pilgrimages to Ancient Temples*, chronicled his discovery of the beauties and profundities of the ancient culture of his own country. (KM)

Page 91. Head of the Healing Buddha at the Kōfukuji Temple.

This three-foot high bronze head was unearthed in 1937, during the work done on the foundations of the Eastern Golden Hall of the Kōfukuji Temple. It dates from approximately 680 and represents all that remains of the main deity of the Yamada Temple, which was located some twenty miles to the south.

Fosco Maraini (born 1912) the leading Italian scholar of Japan in this century, was also an inveterate traveler. His 1959 volume *Meeting with Japan*, from which this extract is taken, still strikes the reader as full of imagination, vitality, and erudition, even after nearly forty years (Viking Press).

Page 92. Deer in sunlit Nara Park.

Deer, long associated with Shinto, wander freely throughout the park (see page 51).

Nikos Kazantzakis (1883–1957) is probably the best-known Greek author of this century in the English-speaking world. Renowned in his own country as a playwright, novelist, and poet, his works (*Zorba the Greek, The Greek Passion,* and *The Last Temptation of Christ*) often show a metaphysical dimension. Kazantzakis made a trip to China and Japan in 1935, and this citation is taken from his journals, published in English as *Japan, China: A Journal of Two Voyages to the Far East* (Simon and Schuster, by permission).

Page 94, 95. Traditional Nara crafts.

In addition to the making of Akahada pottery (see page 83), many ancient craft traditions are preserved in Nara. Pictured here (top to bottom, left to right) are:

Weaving. The excellence of Nara's woven materials is mentioned in the earliest known written document in Japanese history, the *Kojiki* (Record of Ancient Matters), compiled early in the eighth century. By the beginning of the Edo period, around 1600, Nara's woven hemp textiles were considered the best in the nation. They are often used for the exquisite traditional *nō* and *kyōgen* costumes, as well as for the highest quality of household goods, such as tablecloths and curtains.

Lacquerware making. Lacquerware is one of several Buddhist gifts to Japan, first imported from Korea, then soon followed by a number of craftsmen who left the continent to settle in Japan. Lacquerware quickly became an important medium for Japanese art. The first public exhibition of the treasures of the Shōsōin (see page 79) in 1895 brought international recognition to Nara's preeminence in this traditional craft.

Maskmaking: Among the arts and crafts Buddhism brought to Japan in the early seventh century were masks used in performances of ritual dances such as *bugaku* (see page 21). *Nō* drama and certain varieties of comic *kyōgen* storytelling developed in the eleventh century called for the creation of masks in a more vernacular style. A number of Nara artists still work to produce masks of the highest quality for a variety of theatrical genres.

Making India ink. The eminent monk Kūkai (774–835), sent as an envoy to China, is said to have returned in 806 having learned a technique still much treasured in Japan: the making of brushes and India ink. India ink was first produced at Kōfukuji, which remained one of the major temple organizations in the city. During the Edo period, ink-making became a major industry. Today, Nara produces some ninety per cent of the India ink made in Japan.

Making brushes for calligraphy. After Kūkai returned from China, he presented the Emperor Saga (reigned 809–823) with one of the first brushes made in Japan, in the village of Imai, near Nara. Nara itself soon became the center for production of these implements. In 1977, the Ministry of Trade designated Nara brush-making a Japanese traditional craft, and calligraphers everywhere consider Nara brushes among the most desirable for their artistic efforts.

Making Nara dolls. Still a popular souvenir for tourists today, Nara dolls first appeared at the end of the Heian period, around the beginning of the twelfth century. They began as brightly colored ornaments for the hats worn by theatrical performers in the Kasuga Shrine Festival (see page 84). During the sixteenth century, Nara dolls took on what was to become their distinctive artistic form, portraying characters from the classical *nō* repertory. These dolls are much admired for an exquisite stylistic balance achieved between the roughly chiseled blocks of wood from which the characters are carved and their bright, elaborate coloring.

Yanagi Sōetsu (1889–1961), an important philosopher and critic active in the interwar period, did much through his writings to define and articulate the nature of the beauty inherent in Japanese crafts. The present passage is taken from his *Folk-Crafts in Japan*, first published in English in 1936.

Page 96. Snow falling on lanterns.

Even as the snow falls in Nara in the depths of winter, a sense of renewal is born again.

This theme, often taken up by Japanese poets, is well-expressed in the poem by Ōtomo Yakamochi (?718–759), a noted poet and regarded as the chief compiler of the *Man'yōshū*. His work often shows a new lyric introspection that links him to the development of the *waka*, the 31-syllable form adopted by the court poets for over a thousand years. This translation is from the Nippon Gakujitsu Shinkokai edition of the *Man'yōshū* (Columbia University Press, by permission).

The "weathermark" identifies this book as a production of Weatherhill, Inc., publishers of fine books on Asia and the Pacific. Editorial supervision: Raymond Furse. Typography, book, and cover design: Liz Trovato. Production supervision: Bill Rose. Printed and bound at Oceanic Graphic Printing, Hong Kong. The typeface used is Perpetua.